The •

AMIDON

ELEMENTARY SCHOOL

A Successful Demonstration in Basic Education

Every man who knows how to read has it in his power to magnify himself, to multiply the ways in which he exists, to make his life full, significant and interesting.
—ALDOUS HUXLEY

The ∎

AMIDON
ELEMENTARY SCHOOL

A Successful Demonstration in Basic Education

by ∎

Carl F. Hansen

Superintendent of Schools
District of Columbia

Prentice-Hall, Inc. *Englewood Cliffs, N. J.*

Third printing .... March, 1963

PRINTED IN THE UNITED STATES OF AMERICA

03258—B & P

To Ruth

| beloved wife
| teammate
| classroom teacher

This book is affectionately dedicated.

INTRODUCTION

IT IS MY DUTY, I THINK, TO TELL YOU THAT THIS IS NOT A research paper, of which there is a plethora in the literature of education and to which I have no desire to add. More than anything else this is the story of how a superintendent's ideas about elementary education, accumulated after much experience and thought, were translated into action in the Amidon School.

Amidon was the name of an older school in the same area, which was demolished in 1957 to make way for a Federal Redevelopment Plan for the neighborhood. Unforeseen delays in re-populating the area presented us in 1960 with an all-new 25-room elementary school, with an all-new staff and pupils. This rare opportunity was grasped to initiate the modern, subject-centered curriculum which has become known as the Amidon Plan. This book is the record of the inception, development, and results of that plan; and the last section of the book is the first published record of the results attained, as evaluated by the pupils themselves, and by teachers, parents, and independent outside experts.

Something of the autobiographical will be detected in this volume, a fact I acknowledge without embarrassment or apology. After all, the formulation of the ideas expressed here resulted from extensive observation and analysis as I engaged in the practice of education as a student, teacher, principal, and superintendent. It is, I think, in the personal quality of the judgments and in the demonstration of them in operation in a school that the justification for this volume lies. This factor should be pointed out so that you will not expect a comprehensive discussion of educational thought and practice.

IS IT TREASON TO CRITICIZE?

To some of my associates here and around the country, the announcement of the new Amidon concept amounted to treason against education. This view suggests that a superintendent has a special responsibility to defend existing practices. When he fails to perform this duty he degrades himself and his profession.

The most difficult thing he can do is to become a critic of the way his own schools are functioning. I must acknowledge the discomfort I feel myself whenever I make critical comments concerning practices in the classroom. It is far easier to decry the lack of money, the short-sightedness of those who put dollars ahead of child development, the inertia of a community that wants good schools but can't get things moving, the pressures of special interests for time and attention in the school curriculum, the widening disintegration of the home and the resulting harm to children. There is an infinite variety of targets for a superintendent to attack. While it is proper for him to find fault with things outside his organization, if he raises doubts about teaching practices, curriculum organization, time schedules, and academic standards it seems to some that he is disloyal.

In education there is no end to the search for ways to improve the work we are doing. In this respect we are like the medical profession, which is constantly searching for new answers to old problems; or like industry, which, never satisfied with itself, directs upon its practices the sharpest kind of criticism and moves into new procedures and develops new products with never an apology for being progressive. In common with other fields of human endeavor, when we look for better ways to educate children, we imply that improvement in our line of work is possible just as it is in all human activity.

SHOULD A SUPERINTENDENT BE AN EDUCATOR?

Let me say here that this assessment of the situation is not made in bitterness. Nor am I making any kind of claim for a more sympathetic understanding of the superintendent's position. I am more than a little impatient with self-pitying pronouncements about the misunderstood superintendent, complaints about the pressures exerted upon him, and the resulting complexity of his emotional problems. What the superintendency needs is the kind of person who develops his own ideas about education through independent thinking and then states his views so that everybody can understand them. Although no special courage is needed to say what one believes, leadership in public education is not a pink tea affair. Any superintendent should conduct a no-holds-barred attack against ignorance, prejudice, under-development and professional smugness. He should relentlessly seek to build opportunity for the highest possible level of individual and national self-fulfillment.

Because of my strong convictions about what education ought to be, I refuse to be nothing more than an apologist for the *status quo*. I am willing to battle toe-to-toe with the disparagers of the idea of free and universal education when the motives of their attack seem to be anti-democratic. But I am just as unwilling to be the naive defender of any and all practices in education simply because this is the role expected of a school superintendent. I do not intend to be the mouthpiece for any one simply because this may seem to be the sporting thing to do.

WHAT IS THE EFFECT ON STAFF?

It is not impossible for the superintendent to learn from his staff. In fact much of my own education occurs this way. Sometimes staff officers plan for this, especially if they believe the superintendent may be wandering off the reservation.

I vividly remember an occasion when I was invited to confer with the supervisory staff of our elementary schools, all lovely and intelligent women deeply devoted to their points of view. Thinking of this as an opportunity to expound some of my views about teaching, I was somewhat surprised to find that a well-organized presentation of the department's views began from the moment I sat down at the conference table. From the chairman to staff members in well-planned routine the discourse flowed. I listened, too entranced, I must confess, to do much more than that. The purpose of the meeting was obviously to educate me, to return me to the fold, so to speak, rather than to continue to wander off like a black sheep into unfenced pastures. While I generally prefer a seminar-type discussion where the superintendent may also participate, I valued the indoctrination planned by the supervisor, too, because it revealed earnest convictions, which, even if incorrect, deserve respect for their sincerity.

To show how difficult an intrusive superintendent can be, and how much insight and forebearance are required of his staff, a respected and admired associate, thinking to be kind, said to me, "Well, at least, it is worth something to have a superintendent who has some ideas about education."

It is very likely you may be thinking that I am sensitive and insecure about wanting to employ at least a part of my energy to improve the quality of education. To convey this impression is not my purpose in describing these experiences. Rather, I want to acknowledge the fact that educators look with a cold eye upon innovations which seem critical of existing practices, as, by nature, innovations are.

On many occasions in talks before teachers and parents, I have stated my position on educational doctrines which are, in part, expressed in the Amidon concept. These views include support of systematically and carefully selected content, clear identification of goals, direct instruction by the teacher, maximum use of textbooks, large-group instruction, and concentration upon the basic subjects. They also include sharp disagreement with the child-centered philosophy in education which excludes the adult in its preoccupation with psychological experimentation in child growth and development. I disagree violently with the happiness-oriented doctrine which over-plays self-direction, satisfaction of transient wants, and government by whimsy. I cannot abide the disintegration of personality which occurs when children are pressured into making random, purposeless, and immature choices before they are ready for this level of responsibility.

In defining my personal educational doctrines, I do not yet expect everyone to accept them. Though I favor compliant followership now and then, I also consider the arbitrary imposition of a philosophy upon a school staff to be both degrading and wasteful. I prefer to think of these declarations and even the establishment of the Amidon School itself as a nudge in the direction that American education must take in these times and conditions. Even without the imperatives of our present concerns, stronger teaching is necessary for maximum individual growth.

Though children should not be taxed beyond their capacities, the educational stress point should challenge them to use to the fullest whatever talents they have. The disciplined mind is the best instrumentality for self-realization. Present educational methods fall short of the goal of universal intellectual behavior.

WHAT DO I REALLY THINK ABOUT ELEMENTARY EDUCATION?

From the contents of this book it may be generally assumed that I am disenchanted with elementary education. The ideas applied to the Amidon School will seem to indicate dissatisfaction with what they are intended to replace. While this is impeccable logic, the point should be made that elementary education, though weakened by its indiscriminate adaptation of new educational theories, has the vitality and flexibility to become a most effective instrument for the education of children.

Nothing happens in teaching unless it happens to the learner. This is the key to what is now going on in the modern elementary classroom. In the hands of a good teacher, whether elementary or secondary, this guide to teaching produces good results, because the good teacher does everything she can to see to it that what happens is worthwhile, challenging, and tested.

The *weakness in elementary education* is the studied neglect of substance, logic, and direct instruction. Within recent years in the District school system, I have heard elementary educators deride subject matter as something almost beneath contempt. I have heard a highly placed educator say, "I was never any good in arithmetic. I've not needed it. Why make so much fuss over it?" I have heard teachers described as "subject-matter minded," and hence automatically disqualified for appointment. I have seen phonics tarred, feathered, and ridden out of town on a rail— to return for clandestine use behind closed classroom doors.

At any rate, unbalanced concern for the learner and the corresponding neglect of what is to be learned enervate the value of the emphasis on the characteristics of the learner. It is for this reason that, although I am an ardent admirer of the "living" quality of many elementary classrooms, I feel compelled to do what I can in our school system to put more meaning and order into the work of the classroom.

While this book, then, may speak a great deal of the weaknesses in elementary education, I retain great respect for its

accomplishments and the potentials in its many unique characteristics. As you will see when the details of the Amidon concept
are described in action, learner-oriented instruction is earnestly
protected. Vitality, creativity, enthusiasm for experience, improvement in interpersonal relationship, flexibility in management, and the status of the teacher are strengthened rather than
weakened.

I believe further that the public must be included in discussions
of school problems. Only an informed and unhappy public can
bring about improvement in the quality of school service. Thus,
the public must have the truth, all of it, whether it is good or
bad or mixed, and the responsible superintendent must face forth-
rightly his duty to reveal the facts about his schools. There is no
surer truth in a democracy than that an enlightened populace
will find the way to solve its own problems.

THE REAL CRISIS IN AMERICA

In any book like this, where personal views are related to
national concerns, the sense of urgency will always seem greater
to the author than to the reader. While I am not proposing the
Amidon concept as a cure-all for educational problems, I am
convinced it is a means to better education. Unless we step up
the quality of education in this country our future is likely to
be an unhappy one.

As superintendent of schools in the nation's capital, I have
frequent opportunities to participate in activities at the local and
the national level designed to improve the product of our schools.
In these discussions, whether on such questions as job opportunities for youth or the needs of first grade pupils whose progress
in school is negative, the one persistent question is, "How can
the quality of education be stepped up?"

I have come to the conclusion that the major crisis in our
country is an educational one. I have come to believe that our
failure to anticipate and meet our problems is a mark of past
deficiencies in our educative mechanism: we have failed to educate for the responsibilities of citizenship in the present era.
Hence, we are confronted by many problems which a knowledge-
able citizenry should not have allowed to develop and for the

solution of which we are intellectually unprepared. I am inclined to think that present education is wholly unsuited to the preparation of youth to meet the new, unpredictable, and immensely complex problems which they will face. In other words, in education we have to repair a leaky roof and at the same time rebuild weak foundations. I believe that the new Amidon concept is a demonstrably successful step toward these goals.

Contents ∎

INTRODUCTION

PART I ∎ THE AMIDON BEGINNINGS

PART II ▪ THE AMIDON IN OPERATION

Part
One

THE AMIDON BEGINNINGS

chapter one

BACKGROUND ISSUES

AND PROBLEMS

THE AMIDON CONCEPT IS NOT A RETURN TO ANYTHING. IT IS, I hope, not a free ride on a pendulum sweeping back from an extreme position on the right or left. The Amidon concept does not undertake to establish a middle position between two extreme points of view, because to do so is a questionable compromise to establish an unquiet peace between warring educational factions.

The Amidon concept is the taking of a new position, an advance beyond the present gains in educational techniques toward new ideas drawn from the confluence of many present ideas. It is defined in such a manner as to have meaning of its own, that is, to have a characteristic identity, rather than to be a mixed salad of extremist ideas about the nature of education.

ISSUES IDENTIFIED

When the issues are defined, the pendulum-like character of thought in public education comes into sharp focus. The existence of this condition is partly the result of uncertainty as to purpose, method, and value in American life. The public schools mirror the conditions of the society in which they function. Some of the ineptness and indecision of public education can be ascribed to the matrix which shapes it.

But this is not explanation enough for the extremism in the

3

philosophy and, to a lesser degree, the practice of education. Some of it stemmed from rebellion against earlier inflexible and formalistic methodology and subject matter. Some of it can be laid at the door of the new and developing discipline of psychology, which though unsteady on its feet, is beguiling, like an infant trying to walk.

There needs to be a tempering of ideas into workable and practicable tools. As the issues are defined, they will give more meaning to the Amidon concept.

■ First Issue: Education for Intelligent Behavior or Life Adjustment?

Is it the primary responsibility of the schools to promote intelligent behavior or life adjustment?

In recent years, the chief direction makers in public education (including the Educational Policies Commission of the National Education Association and the United States Office of Education) have rendered reluctant obeisance to a definition of *the purpose of the schools as one of intellectual development*. Usually in such cases this objective is described as coordinate with social, vocational, and physical needs. Or, intellectual competence may be defined as equal to, but not necessarily the product of, the transmission of the cultural heritage. Most leaders in education, and perhaps some in political and literary fields, fail as yet to comprehend *the axiom that without capacity for intellectual behavior the individual is not likely to manage with good judgment his affairs in aesthetics, for example, or the vocational and physical aspects of living.* Knowledge is useless if it does not contribute to rational behavior in all activities.

In the Amidon concept, education is designed to improve the intellectual quality of human behavior. As this is done, the individual's capacity to adjust to or change the conditions under which he lives will be enhanced. Thus, not mere adjustment is desired, but in addition intelligent manipulation of the conditions of living is presupposed as a major objective of human existence.

The world is nothing more than what it means to the individual at any given time. What he does in response to events is a measure of his intellectual acknowledgment of these factors. In other words, for the individual, thinking about something makes it so. Without the act of thinking, the individual experiences nothing, and for him, nothing exists. When he is faced with a problem, the intelligently behaving individual applies *mind* to its solution. If he does not, his response is to a high degree non-intellectual, or irrational, or insignificant. The problem remains, the answer is unavailable, and the effect of this is harmful to the individual and generally to others with whom he associates.

Consider three illustrations:

1. The tenth grade boy, influenced by a desire for status with his crowd, left school to earn money. His first job was working as a laborer on a construction crew. With his first earnings he bought a pair of $30 shoes, a status symbol of great importance to his group. Soon, however, he tired of the work he was doing, became irregular in attendance on the job, and finally was dismissed. When the foreman fired him, the boy's anger flared up, and he assaulted his boss, injuring him painfully.

2. One day a white youth left his high school in great rage because of a bad grade in English. When he approached an entrance to a neighboring high school, he met a Negro boy who was just leaving the school, having been excused early to report for an after-school job. Giving vent to his anger and hostility, and without warning, the white boy struck the Negro on the mouth.

3. While on playground duty one noon, a teacher was forced to break up a fight between a girl and boy, both in the fourth grade. As she kept the straining, hard-breathing children apart by grasping a wrist in each hand, the teacher asked, "Why are you so angry at each other?"

The boy answered, "She said my mother drinks. She doesn't drink any more."

The girl said in tearful anger, "He said my mother drinks. She doesn't either any more. She spends her money for new clothes for me now."

Behavior is usually not either altogether intellectual—that is, built on thought processes—or entirely below the level of consciousness, prompted and guided exclusively by feeling. Thought and feeling are only rough designations of the origins of human behavior, there being something of both in varying proportions whenever the individual acts. The object of education is not to rule out feeling as the source of purpose but to increase the influence and quality of mind as a guide to action.

Intelligence Defined

Intelligence, then, is the name given to a way man may behave when confronted by a problem situation. If his car stops running, a man will be engaged in intelligent behavior if, to solve the problem, he calls upon his experience, seeks new information, evaluates his findings, applies and tests them out.

In concrete terms, he will recall other times the motor has stalled, under what conditions, and what he did about it. He will perhaps try to add to this information by making new checks, such as the amount of gasoline or the condition of the points. He will act in accordance with his findings, the simplest being, for example, to get some gasoline if he is out of gasoline. And then he will test his theory by trying to start the motor. If all these things fail, the intelligently behaving man goes to the nearest telephone and summons help.

In contrast to such behavior, a temper tantrum during which a man may actually engage in violence against the vehicle, or a trial and error attack upon the motor, removing this part and then that in an effort to find out what is wrong, illustrates a nonintellectual approach to the problem.

But, as is frequently the case, feeling enters into and becomes fused with the act of problem solving. To illustrate; during a piano recital being conducted by the music teacher, a five-year-old boy played his little number very well up to a certain phrase on which he became stuck. Three times he started anew and three times he came to a dead stop at the same point. Then he dismounted from the bench, kicked the piano, in an apparently calm and business-like manner, and then without a change in expression returned to his playing. This time he went right through to the end of the piece.

Intellectual Behavior Universal

If we describe intelligence as a problem-solving approach to problem situations, intellectual behavior then is a universal experience. Within this concept, ranges of difference in problems and the individual's ability to work them out are recognized. Thus intellectual behavior is not limited to the few; in varying degrees it is within the experience of all.

Because of the universality of intellectual experience, intellectual education becomes the right of every pupil.

Such education, leading as it must to rational behavior in response to the perplexities of life, quite clearly should be geared to each pupil's level of growth, it should be planned for his use, and it should be required by his needs and those of the society in which he functions as a dynamic being.

School officials, curriculum builders, and teachers must provide learning experiences that are intellectually challenging to every pupil. Thus the traditional belief that intellectual behavior is within reach of only the chosen few must be replaced by the belief that it is a possibility for every human being.

An intellectual aristocracy composed chiefly of persons who pride themselves on their learning has come close to setting a whole populace against scholarship, an attitude manifested in such expressions as "eggdome" and "egghead."

No small share of responsibility for this unfortunate attitude toward scholarship may be laid at the door of the teaching profession. At one time the myths of classical Rome and Greece were read and enjoyed by youngsters the country over—until the hot, dry winds of intellectual analysis swept over them and sapped them of their vitality. A noted critic once said of the study of Caesar: "The conspirators who killed Caesar for me in my youth were many."

Consider if you will, the point of view rather common to teachers of modern foreign languages: Only the able should take courses in French or Spanish or German. A teacher of French, a good friend, thought I was quite unreasonable when I asked him: "Do only the able, the highly intelligent, use French in Paris?"

An example is available to show how a language, if taught the way people learn languages, can make a valuable contribution to the education of pupils not considered to be intellectual:

A girl with a serious behavior problem, who literally kicked and screamed in defiance of classroom discipline at times, was entered in an elementary school ungraded class for over-aged girls. The class, though composed of non-academic pupils, had a gifted and imaginative teacher who taught them conversational French. The new girl, at first sullen and rebellious, soon became enchanted with the French. She developed an excellent pronunciation and re-produced independently things learned in the lessons. In the program at the end of the school term, she sang French songs with another girl and joined in French conversation with the class as a group. By this time her personal adjustments had so improved that the teacher could safely ask her to take over the class any time when she had to be out of the room.

Another: In a four-room school building, a group of children with severe mental handicaps are developing, among other areas of growth, skill in the academic subjects at *their* level and capability. When they enter the school, most of these children are inarticulate. Because they are being taught at their level, most are developing intellectually as measured in speech, in writing and reading, and even in better capacity for rational self-management, although most of them will always need sheltered opportunities for living and working.

On the other end of the scale, the honors classes were recently set up in the District of Columbia schools from the fourth grade through the twelfth grade. While this movement calls for no particular hurrahs, since many school systems have programs of one kind or another for bright pupils, the establishment of the honors program here reflects, as does the program for the retarded child, local emphasis upon intellectual growth commensurate with ability.

Intellectual response to problems is, therefore, multi-level; that is, of different levels of complexity, its character depending upon the individual and his purposes. But it is clear that *education for intelligent behavior* is a common need, and that the best way to achieve the adjustment to, or control of, environment is through preparation for disciplined thought.

The ultimate purpose of education is not an indulged and egocentric individual but a self-disciplined one, capable of intelligent decision making in every aspect of living. He must be mature enough to face with balance the difficulties, frustrations, and satisfactions in his personal and public life, and able with vigor and determination to achieve the difficult and accept the impossible. With emphasis upon intellectual development, the Amidon system seeks to promote for each pupil not only the highest possible level of rational behavior in relation to controllable problems, but also a perspective and a depth of understanding which will enable him to live with conditions beyond his control.

Therefore: The primary purpose of the schools is to educate for intellectual power so that the individual may wisely use and improve his environment.

■ Second Issue: Basic Academic Subjects or Activity Units?

Should the schools stress the basic academic subjects as the best way of educating for intelligent behavior, or should they encourage the construction of a wide variety of activity units as the organizing principle for the presentation of subject matter?

Basic Subjects

We need to know what we are talking about here. In the elementary schools the basic academic subjects are: reading, composition, grammar, spelling, speech, mathematics, science, geography, history, art, and music. These subject fields constitute the primary systems of organization of human knowledge. Variants and specializations are, of course, numerous at higher levels of scholarship, as for example biochemistry, linguistics, or quadratics. Because the mind can know chiefly by the ordering of knowledge into related patterns, man's analysis of his environment has compelled him to organize his findings into comprehensible units in ordered, sequential, and logical forms. It is doubtful that he could otherwise have extended his analysis of nature to its present complexity and it is certain he could not preserve and transmit his discoveries without the discipline of organizing principles.

What are called the basic subjects, therefore, are the product of man's search for knowledge and his time-tested method of putting it together into usable form.

Activity Unit

The activity unit—activity being used here to suggest a physical doing by the student—is fundamentally an attempt by educationists to re-structure human knowledge around new principles of organization, primarily determined by the social nature of man; that is, his presence in an environment consisting in part of other human beings and his need as an organism for the satisfaction of physical and psychological wants.

In an early grade, for example, the home may be the theme. This becomes the organizing principle around which knowledge related to the central theme is clustered. In the home are mother, father, sister, and brother, so the content of the curriculum contains information about these persons, their roles and characteristics, how to get along with them. The subject matter becomes a trite combination of things biological, sociological, psychological and tautological. In some cases the subject contains items that are derived from the fields of mathematics—a grocery bill: geography—locate the grocery store; science—eat carrots for good health; composition—write a paragraph about vegetables. The unit, then, is a method of organizing knowledge around a theme. It is not dissimilar to an expository theme or article, for example, on the operation and use of the internal combustion machine.

When I survey trends in educational practice, sometimes I find them quite the opposite of what is demonstrated in the Amidon concept. For example, a recent curriculum bulletin of a great city school system made this claim for distinction in its elementary program: "There has been a change in methodology—from separate lessons in discrete subjects to the unit method in which planned, coordinated experiences are organized around a central theme or problem." In the same house organ, I found the statement that "the widest single effort to establish a unifying thread in the secondary school curriculum has been involved in the development of the core program."

I consider the core program to be not unlike a delta at the mouth of a great river—wide, undefined, shifting and soft. This is the kind of fuzzy curriculum organization that, in my opinion, should be replaced by organized basic subjects.

I go along with the third teacher who is the subject of the following conversation:

> It seems that one teacher was talking to another about a third teacher.
>
> "Do you know," said the first, "She has never taught a unit?"
>
> "What in the world does she teach?" asked the second.
>
> After a moment of silence, the first teacher said, "I guess she teaches reading."

The main question, in my judgment, is not whether to abandon traditionally organized subject matter or that organized around a central theme. The question is, which should come first; that is, which should have primacy in the school curriculum.

I think the issue is easily resolved in favor of organized subject matter, with many opportunities to use the basic disciplines in problem-solving exercises. Thus, the unit theme returns to its proper role in the school curriculum where it accompanies, follows, and supports the study of organized subject matter. It should be a common practice for teachers to assign problems for study, to encourage independent research, to elicit creative work in the arts and sciences. But these should not overwhelm and push aside order and substance in basic subjects as does the unit-dominated curriculum. It is time for us to awaken to the fact that *the unit method of curriculum organization* has become the Frankenstein's monster of the classroom; experimentation in this direction has gone far enough. At few times in our history has there been so much need for strength in education: for substance, for order and logic, for holding to a straight furrow, for developing the power of critical and independent thinking. We can no longer afford the fluctuations in practice that have resulted from ill-conceived theories of learning, from interesting ideas and innumerable nostrums of varying degrees of plausibility devised by self-seekers and dreamers attached to the fringes of the teaching profession. In the main, our strength has been found in the work of teachers who have kept their feet on the ground, who have taken the new slowly enough to use the best of it. Surely we need to give the best of our teachers the philosophical and practical support they need, and one thing we can do is to assure them that the teaching of the basic subjects is a proper and respectable thing to do.

Therefore: Make organized subject matter primary in the curriculum, but continue to use units as a means of cross-pollination of disciplines.

■ Third Issue: A Preplanned Curriculum or Pupil-Teacher Planned?

As yet unanswered is the question of what to teach. Even assuming that the elementary school day will be scheduled mainly for the basic subjects, their content is not as a result automatically determined. Mathematics, for example, is a body of knowledge by no means presently defined as to what is of paramount importance, or at what grade levels the materials should be placed, or how it should be taught. In the field of grammar, how much should be taught, and at what grade levels, is exceedingly difficult to determine; as a result the subject is often either neglected or over-emphasized. Most confused about what to teach are the specialists in the social studies. Even the social scientists, the geographers, and historians, cannot agree on what to select for the classroom. As a result, textbook writers and curriculum makers are forced to select items to be taught by the rather pitiable method of reviewing curriculum guides from around the country to find out what ought to be identified for teaching, and then to supplement the "science" of this method with personal hunches. The shoddy mixture of specious research, poll taking, and personal guesswork, attractively printed and illustrated to cover up its flaws, becomes the textbook in the happy and complacent American classroom.

Too Much Pupil-Teacher Selection

It is, of course, a fact that out of the vast array of human knowledge a selection of what should be taught in the classroom has to be made. This obviously goes on in every classroom every school day. It is a responsibility generally left to the teacher, with such help as she can get from curriculum guides, which because of their general nature usually find their way into a bottom drawer of her desk, and from textbooks which are so little used that few seem to care if pupils do not have them.

It is hardly surprising that, having confronted the task of curriculum selection unarmed with organized scholarship, theorists and practitioners in education have tacitly agreed to leave this for the pupils and the teacher to do. They have said with disarming plausibility that the curriculum should be limited only by broad outlines, it should be variable, and it must always be creative, in that it should emerge from the interests and imaginations of pupils and teachers as they live together in the classroom. This, they say fervently, is far more dynamic than prescribed and pre-planned curriculums formulated from rigid and bookish scholarship. (In the parlance of the educationist, scholarship is always "rigid" and "bookish.") The assumption is that the choice is between one or the other extreme position: either complete freedom by the teacher or rigid prescription of content by outside authority.

Moreover, the proponents of this impromptu curriculum claim that, since the pupils helped determine what is taught, the unfavorable effect of pressure to learn is avoided. If the curriculum is pre-planned, pupils are under pressure to learn it even though they may not want to, or may be "unready" to meet the requirements in the course of study. If the pupils help to plan the curriculum, their individual needs will be met, because, it is believed by these worshippers of child nature, their choices will be intuitively good for them. The argument proceeds further to the conclusion that determining the curriculum on the needs of pupils will provide continuity because, through some happy force in nature, individuals on their own will select things to do that improve the quality of their experiences. For the children, it is as if they were free to eat anything they want from an unlimited menu because their need for food will lead them to the right choices. Their innate wisdom will lead them to choose oatmeal rather than apple pie for breakfast. For the adults in charge of the classroom, the problem is simply to move with the tide of their pupils' needs as defined by the pupils themselves, a procedure which relieves the teacher of responsibility and makes evaluation of her work impossible.

The final rationalization for this position is that since not even the subject matter specialists can agree on what ought to be selected for teaching, nothing is lost if this is left to the teacher to do. This is like saying that, because no one has discovered a cure for cancer, the patient and the family physician may as well take care of the problem themselves.

Because of the wide acceptance of the theory that curriculum making should take place in the classroom, textbook writing has become chiefly an exercise in trying to guess what the pupils and teachers will be interested in, and putting these estimates together in the lightest and most appealing manner possible. As a result, facts, ideas, and concepts, when they do appear, especially in the social studies texts, are lost in an underbrush of words. To tell a fact directly and boldly in a textbook is not to be thought of by the "good" modern textbook writer.

Scholars and Specialists Should Predetermine Content

How do we move out of this weakening but comfortable atmosphere of letting nature take its course in the classroom? This is a difficult move, because when pre-planning is suggested, the cry always goes up that children's psychological development will be warped by the increased demands made upon them.

Once, in an off-the-record meeting of representatives of the major educational associations, I proposed that scholars be included in national commissions to be set up to define curriculum in the major disciplines. From the violent reaction to the word "scholars," I learned that to professional educators the word is loaded with bad connotations. It clearly caused painful remembrances of the arrogance of academicians in relation to educationists. This is not without cause, if the history of the shameful antagonism between scholars, academicians, subject specialists, and leaders in education, is read correctly. No party to this protracted vendetta has much to be proud of.

As I see it, subject matter must be carefully selected. This is not a job that pupils and teachers can do well in the day-to-day transiency of the classroom. It requires the services of scholars, specialists, and educators, and can be achieved only after intensive study. Moreover, once the items of content are selected for placement in the curriculum, textbooks should be written to supply this content for study in direct, succinct, and clear form. Finally, guided by a pre-planned curriculum the teacher can enhance, adjust, and enliven the content if she will abandon her role as companion and return to that of teacher.

Therefore: Subject matter should first be selected by scholars and specialists, placed in the various levels of instruction by educators, and presented by informed teachers with full respect for individual differences among pupils.

■ Fourth Issue: Grouping by Academic Ability or by Age and Grade?

Everybody knows that in the literal sense homogeneous grouping is an impossibility. The most that ability grouping can do is to cut down the range of academic differences.

Ability Grouping in the District of Columbia Schools

Using intelligence quotients, achievement scores, and teacher judgment for selection, pupils in the District of Columbia public elementary schools are placed in three main groups: *the honors,* at the fourth grade and beyond; *the regular* and *the basic* groups, from the first grade. The basic classes are for the mentally sub-normal pupils, who are identified by such measures as intelligence and achievement tests and teachers' opinions.

Ability grouping for academic instruction now extends in the District of Columbia schools, in different degrees, from the first through the twelfth grade. Beginning in the elementary school, the basic curriculum provides an especially designed pathway for the student whose ability to achieve academic success is limited. The aim is to provide a maximum challenge at his level, with immediate possibility for transfer to more difficult levels when he is ready. The general program from grades one through twelve, the honors from grades four through twelve, and the regular college preparatory programs from the ninth grade, are all designed to reduce ranges of differences within classes in order to establish maximum challenge for every pupil and to facilitate individualized instruction, insofar as possible, for each.

Prior to the adoption of the three-track elementary curriculum, although Washington's elementary classes were heterogeneously organized, special classes such as those for the atypicals (that is, the slow learners, the emotionally disturbed, and the physically handicapped) had long existed. In most school systems special classes are used to reduce the ranges of differences; ability grouping is not really new despite the wide-spread philosophical objection to it.

Many in our community disapproved any extension of ability grouping to apply to the gifted and to those in the middle ranges. To some, ability grouping is a violation of democratic tradition, and to others, a violation of the principle of within-class grouping which has become a sacred cow. For some few of our principals, ability grouping is simply too much work to bother with, especially in schools with high mobility rates.

Some Consider Grouping Undemocratic

The anti-grouping tradition in American public school education persists chiefly because it is associated with an interpretation of the nature and function of the individual in a democratic society which holds that the value of human personality and the contributions of the individual to his social order are one and the same thing. On this false premise, no differences, it is contended, should be drawn between respect for the personality and the value of the product of the individual's effort. It is assumed, therefore, that every pupil has a right to be in classes with every other pupil, because otherwise equal respect for personality is denied him. From this comes the strange declaration of faith, often directly or by implication expressed in the current literature, that our democracy can never rise higher than the level of its average citizen.

Failing to comprehend the fact that democracy is a stern and demanding mistress, leaders of American education tend in the main to reject ability groupings on the grounds that intellectual elitism might be created. In general, responding to thoughtless influences, they have held education on an equalitarian plateau. They seem to define excellence as an average of all possible achievements rather than as achievement related to the task and to the capacity of the individual worker.

A Democratic Society Encourages Differences in Accomplishment

It is extremely fortunate that accomplishments in our society have often risen above the level of the average of our citizens. Because of the accomplishments of top-level men in science, manufacturing, law, literature, and labor, we live more comfortably, with greater stimulation and with improved security in health and body, than if the product of the minds and efforts of all our citizens were averaged down to a mythical mid-point of quality. A false sense of democracy that clutters the minds of some educationists fortunately is not reflected in the workings of the democratic concept.

It is high time, I think, to understand that ability grouping in school is consistent with the ideal of respect for the dignity of every personality. There can be a concurrent encouragement of the efforts of all pupils in ratio to their abilities without any corrosion of the principle of equality. Unless we do this to a greater degree than is now the custom, the growth of our democratic system will continue to be circumscribed by a cocoon of false theories. In support of this position, I need only to call attention to the unfortunate results of "averaging down" cultural activities in magazine writing, television programing, and advertising to the level of an abstract average citizen. Although a great deal of "ability grouping" occurs in the daily affairs of citizenship, much more of it would elevate the tastes and habits of all citizens. In the same way, a fair amount of congenital ability grouping has always taken place in public education, despite protestations to the contrary. The real issue is how to be self-conscious about the process, so that it can be done with good judgment on a less limited scale than presently.

Effect of Grouping by Age and Grade

In place of ability-achievement grouping, a system of setting up classes by age and grade has prevailed. In its widest application, this method of putting pupils into classes has presupposed automatic promotion, which means that the pupil remains with his age group no matter what kind of work he does in this group or grade. Automatic annual promotion produced classes that were unrestrainedly heterogeneous.

What problems this has caused can be readily imagined. In a sixth grade class I observed the inevitable result of grouping by age and grade: an excellent teacher instructing two sixth grade boys from a first grade reader. While I admired the obvious care for individual differences, I was disturbed by the practices which necessitated it. Here was the costly end product of a series of flaws in management and theory:

(1) The automatic promoting to each higher grade of boys whose reading problems should have long before been identified and resolved;

(2) The excessive heterogeneity in the class which required the teacher to divert time from the whole class to these two boys;

(3) The clearly evident failure to do anything constructive for the two boys in their present class setting.

No matter how she tried, that sixth grade teacher was not going to be able to teach these boys to read.

Favorable Placement

We see, then, how futile it is to group by age and grade. Yet, do we wish to group only by achievement and ability? If this is done literally, then the academically retarded pupil would remain in groups far younger than he—indefinitely. In such social settings, his attitude and that of his classmates would be distorted to the extent that little learning would take place. The answer is a procedure for class assignment which places pupils in groups where they will be socially and academically congenial. This is not a capitulation to the practice of automatic promotion, since no child who is capable of doing the work of a class should be allowed to "pass" if he fails to do what is required. But it does mean that favorable placement, determined by the pupil's ability, achievement level, and attitude, the climate of the classroom, and the strengths and weaknesses of the teacher, undergirds the three-level curriculum system of the District of Columbia elementary schools. The plan includes much more than ability grouping; hence the class organizations often overlap on such factors as mental age and reading and arithmetic levels. But the ranges of differences within the class are reduced, so that each pupil has a better chance to learn and the teacher a better chance to teach. The democratic spirit of the school is retained despite the opinions of those who believe that democracy is merely seeing the same.

It is the job of the schools to give every child a maximum educational opportunity. But to be one, an opportunity must be fashioned to fit the pupil. Otherwise, he may be wearing educational garments which he has either outgrown, or which are much too large for him.

Ability grouping for academic instruction based on the favorable placement doctrine provides a reasonable and workable answer. The purpose is to reduce the ranges of difference, not to find students that are cut from the same pattern. Care must be taken to distinguish between ability grouping and homogeneous grouping, which is an unrealistic objective.

I am convinced that education in this country can meet the democratic needs of our society only by developing multi-level groupings for academic instruction. Experience in the District of Columbia with the four-level curriculum in the senior high schools and the three-level curriculum in the elementary schools offers substantial evidence that ability grouping steps up the educational opportunity for most students.

The Amidon system conserves the sytem of ability grouping now in wide practice throughout our school system. In seeking the most favorable placement of each pupil, the Amidon school principal groups pupils to reduce ranges of age, ability, and achievement, as I hope all of our elementary principals do.

Therefore: Assign each pupil to a curriculum level such as honors, regular, or basic, only after careful study of intelligence, achievement, attitude, and age factors, taking into account the characteristics of the class and teacher, so that he may be given placement most favorable for achievement.

■ **Fifth Issue: Teach the Whole Class or Small Groups Within the Class?**

Before long someone is going to charge me with inconsistency because I advocate ability grouping *between* classes but disapprove extensive ability grouping *within* classes. One of the reasons for ability grouping is to make the class more nearly uniform as to achievement and thus able to respond to instruction given the entire class. With this in mind, any superficial conflict between the two systems of grouping disappears.

Why require the teacher to work with the whole class? This, say the supporters of within-class grouping, will be a return to the old way of teaching where no one paid any attention to the learner and gave consideration only to the subjects. "Once again," I have been told, "teachers will be planning lessons weeks in advance, will be teaching textbooks page by page, and will lecture from the front of the room while most of the class dozes, daydreams, or worse. Better restore the birch rod, so the teacher can enforce attention."

My calamity-howling friend has forgotten, if she ever knew, that there have always been good teachers who could make the dullest subject lively and exciting. Teachers like this knew their pupils well and, though perhaps not so loaded down with the accouterments of psychological analysis, understood them as individuals with differences and similarities.

Plausible Reasons for Class Grouping

The practice of dividing the elementary class into sub-sections has a long and tiresome history that is hardly worth pursuing at this point. It is supported by rationalizations that stem from many sources, most of them more reasonable than the conclusion fathered by them. In composite these genetic causes include a wish to submerge the teacher in the child-group, to individualize instruction, to encourage the social growth that allegedly derives from group activities, to do something expedient about the problems generated by automatic promotion, to justify heterogeneous grouping by classes, and to encourage activity, participation, and sharing by the pupils in the smaller groups.

Chief Results

The chief results of within-class grouping are to wear the teacher out with trying to teach eight to a dozen different groups in a day, to proliferate ridiculous group names, to hide from pupils the facts about their placement, to make chair shuffling a part of the curriculum, to require heavy reliance on work-book lessons to keep the untaught children busy, and to fractionate teaching time to the point that each pupil enjoys very little direct instruction in the course of the day.

Chair Shuffling

I clearly remember the expression on a sixth grade teacher's face when I walked into her classroom one morning just as a reading group was breaking up after a lesson at the front of the room. The noise of chair-shuffling obviously pained her, and her disquietude with the awkward migration of chair-burdened pupils to their desks showed clearly in the set of her countenance. With this insight into the deeper processes of teacher thought, my questioning about within-class grouping became sharper.

Frequent eruptions of pupils and furniture in an elementary classroom, I had discovered, seemed not to have the uncomplaining support of teachers that is usually taken for granted.

I have been in enough elementary classrooms to have arrived at the conclusion that a very high proportion of teacher-pupil time is spent in movement to or from small-group instruction. While the ebb and flow of persons and things in the grouped classroom may have value as physical exercise, it is hardly suited to the art of teaching, the employment of which is the main reason for the teacher's presence in the classroom. All too often after spending a half day in elementary classrooms I have come away trying to remember how often and for how long I really saw teachers in the act of teaching. Even counting the listening lessons when a teacher hears a small group read, the proportion of time given to teaching seems pitifully small. One reason for this is the system of setting up numerous small groups within the classroom.

I must say I am more than ready to see a reduction in dependence upon work-books. I want to see less of chair shuffling and more of concentrated teaching. I have long since been disabused of the theory that because learning is an individual process, teaching is therefore at its best when it is a one-to-one tutorial arrangement.

Therefore: Teach the whole class, using small group teaching only when needed for remedial or special developmental instruction.

■ Sixth Issue: Earlier Placement of Content or Emphasis on Readiness?

No doubt the concept of readiness is a major contribution of the longitudinal study of children's growth and development. I am all for the science of observing and recording the changes in bone structure, in muscle tone, in quality of hearing, of eye fusion, in temperament, provided caution is used in deriving conclusions. The practice is to state such conclusions as final although generally they result from averages of extremely few observations. It is most important that such hasty generalizations should not be used as infallible guides to teaching by gullible and insecure educationists.

Readiness Theory an Excuse for Poor Teaching

Among the most misused myths in education is the idea that readiness must always precede teaching, as if it were a discrete attitude of the process rather than integral with it; as if readiness can be easily defined in the concrete situation by instruments such as tests; as if teaching ahead of readiness is the primary cause of emotional disorder, when actually it is likely that the poor quality of teaching is far more responsible; as if a comforting declaration to parents that their child will learn when he is ready is a valid excuse for not teaching him.

I must relate a story that is at the apogee of teacher gullibility in respect to believing that children will learn when they are ready. This is about a young man whose ability to read was so poor that he dropped out of school and entered the armed services. When he returned to civilian life, he sought aid for his reading problem. He prevailed upon a phonics specialist to tutor him in his home after regular school hours. First, there were three lessons a week with a systematic phonics program. Then after several months, only one lesson a week and then came the time when the boy was ready to go back to school. He returned to high school and successfully completed requirements for graduation. Later, one of his teachers, not knowing the boy had been tutored, told the boy's mother, "Your son's reading was much improved. It just goes to prove that a student will read when he is ready."

Neglected Children

I am forced to believe that more neglect has been shown children because of the readiness theory than for any other cause, including deliberate mistreatment by irresponsible parents. If a poll were taken, it is likely that many parents could report having been told by their children's teachers, "Your child is not ready." The tragedy of this unbelievable development in the history of

American education is that the theory is propagated in good faith. But the visible stupidity of reliance upon such an idea— as that a child should not be taught to read until he reaches a mental age of 6½ —is inexcusable. No testing instrument yet exists to measure mental age with this degree of refinement; numbers in such test results are bands rather than specific dots on a line of measurement. The teacher needs to understand much about the growth of children, but she needs to be told that the findings of studies in this field are tentative, often far too specific to be reliable, and may be diversionary, because they are used to distract the teacher from her purpose, which is to teach. They give supervisors false but comforting doctrines against which to measure what the teacher is doing. In the face of all of this I yearn for good old fashioned common sense about children and steady, organized teaching with sensitivity to their behavior while in the teaching situation. A teacher who does not know if her pupils are following her is not worth her salt. A good teacher knows what her teaching is accomplishing at the moment of presentation.

Readiness and Learning Not Separable

As to the doctrine of readiness, I find it impossible to accept the concept as a useful tool in teaching. This puts me on the extremist level, but I believe I can justify my rejection of the readiness concept. The chief reason is that readiness to learn and learning are not literally separable. To teach a child to turn the pages of a book is to teach him a reading skill. Preparation for the next lesson in arithmetic is a part of the teaching process. So examples may be multiplied to show that what we have called readiness is chiefly a phase of teaching. Moreover, the delay feature built into the concept has produced a theory of postponement which is still broadly accepted in education.

Postponement Theory

Not too long ago a teacher told of her disappointment about having to reduce the content of what she was teaching. Her principal told her:

"We follow the curriculum here. We don't go beyond it. We don't push the children."

The teacher asked:

"You mean the sky's not the limit when it comes to teaching?"

"Now you just don't teach too much. Just wait. They'll catch up," was the principal's reply.

Thus is illustrated the postponement theory at work.

The practice of postponing content is in part an outcome of the readiness theory which cautions against giving the pupil too much to do too early. So it has become law that one may not teach reading in the kindergarten. *The Amidon idea repeals this spurious limitation of the teacher's right to teach and the pupil's right to learn.* I began to doubt early the rule of no reading instruction to five-year-olds when I observed some years ago a four-year-old child in a school for the deaf writing words on the blackboard. I have not to this date received a sensible answer to the question, "If a four-year-old handicapped by deafness can do this, why not a normal child?"

Evidence is mounting that children can learn much more at an earlier date than we have been led to believe. A mathematics consultant told me the other day that even kindergartners are able to respond to instruction in simple geometry. It has long been known that many children come to kindergarten already able to read to some extent, having learned from the parent at home. I have seen kindergarten compositions of unusual merit.

In a first-grade class I recently listened to a discussion in which one of the six-year-old boys told about dinosaurs. I wondered if he knew what he was talking about, so I asked him to tell me what a dinosaur was. He defined the dinosaur as a prehistoric animal belonging to the reptile family. Teachers these days must maintain their scholarship if they are to be in possession of facts and concepts which go beyond those held by many of their students, even in the earlier grades.

"Postpone teaching formal grammar until the seventh grade," an English specialist told us recently. On the contrary, our fourth grade classes, Amidon style, are learning that words have grammatical labels just as do the parts of an automobile. They profit from an early, direct look at grammar.

Though there are conflicting trends as to difficulty of curriculum placement the capacity of children to learn should never be underestimated. If teaching is well-planned, learning in depth can be assured at much earlier stages in the child's growth than is now believed.

Therefore: Abandon the readiness terminology in favor of sensitive teaching of more difficult content in the earlier grades.

■ Seventh Issue: Teacher-Centered or Child-Centered?

In various educational documents I have seen the teacher called a friend, guide, leader, counselor, learner, participator, director of learning. She has of late become a functionary with almost every possible kind of responsibility but that of teaching.

Confused Seating Arrangements

To mesh with this non-teaching definition of the teacher's duties, the new technology of classroom management requires the arrangement of desks in squares, circles, ellipses, or in "T" or "H" formations, each designed to discourage the traditional practice of stationing the teacher at the front of a room with her pupils facing her in rows.

While children are seated in groups, face to face, or in squares like the ancient phalanx, the unobtrusive teacher is to weave in and out of groups, sharing, participating, planning but never imposing adult authority upon the children in their special world.

In this ideal state, teacher and pupil learn together, they grow up together, they respect each other as co-equals, they establish rules together, they plan lessons together. Individuality is submerged in a groupness that, however idealized, never seems to attain its objective. As individualists, pupils resent absorption by the group; as do teachers, I think. Let us be grateful that this is the way it is.

It is clear, then, that an obvious indication of the undominant role of a teacher is the way the elementary classroom is arranged. Teachers now seem to have a deep sense of guilt if pupils' desks are set in rows facing the front of the room. If they work this way they are sure to think of themselves as old-fashioned and traditional. In their first year, most of the Amidon teachers held to the modern disorder in classroom seating. It is not easy to shake off the influence of the past, no matter how much it has become discredited.

Neglect of Teacher Preparation in Subject Matter

Another effect of the reduction of the status of the teacher in the elementary classroom has been the neglect of subject-matter preparation in teacher training. When teachers participate as a member of the learning group in a classroom and when they are forced to teach in units built on central themes in accordance with the momentary enthusiasms of pupils, the teacher's need for scholarship in subject fields is cut to a minimum. In fact, when curriculum selection is uncontrolled the sharing of learning becomes necessary. No one person, however brilliant and broad her training, could possibly be prepared for the variety of directions a set of lessons may take when the choice is left to the pupils.

Inherent, then, in the child-centered method is a weakening in teacher scholarship. Preparation for such teaching must therefore include more of the technology of child growth and less of subject matter. This results in a devaluation of the medium of exchange in education: Scholarship loses its buying power because of the inflation of methodology. The sad part of it is that too few educators seem to be made uncomfortable by this, too few seem really to care about the absence of "learning" on the part of the teacher, and there is general contentment with focus upon child-centered methodology even though it hides lack of scholarship in the teacher and her supervisors.

Persuasive Reasons for Shift to Child-Centered Education

There are historic reasons, and quite compelling ones at that, for the shift away from the teacher-dominated classroom to one which in its extreme, became child-dominated and, as a result, a microcosm of anarchy. In the literature of satire can be found caricatures of power-drunk pedagogues; of misfits and sadists seeking exculpation by investing their scholars with their sins; of overseers and petty officials bent on making life for their charges as miserable as possible—up to the point of, and not always excluding, physical violence. At one time, it seems, the quality of education was thought to be directly proportionate to the pupils' distaste for it.

In addition to the fact that the classroom was at times a chamber of horrors and a subject-matter museum, a soporific lecture method backed up by copy-book learning discredited the teacher-dominated classroom and stimulated revolution. As a part of this image of the old-fashioned classroom, add the fact that pupils were admonished to attend unremittingly to their studies, to forego all group activities, and to limit their responses to the expectations of the teacher and of the materials.

In this kind of teacher-dominated classroom the extreme of authoritarian pedagogy is illustrated. While some citizens believe that a return to such a system is the best possible cure for the moral sickness of youth today, few responsible people in or out of education have any taste for this kind of classroom, either to see it return or to maintain it if it exists anywhere.

But the Child Needs Adult Authority

But what about the other point of the pendulum arc? What is the child-centered classroom in its extreme form like? Though most modern elementary classrooms reflect some degree of child-centeredness in their makeup, in extreme form it grants the child a license for tyranny. To this teachers who have worked in child-dominated classrooms can attest.

I recall the story of a good and experienced fourth grade teacher who one year took over a class in March after two other teachers had given up trying to establish order. These were not large overaged children backed up against a dam of repeated failure and breaking through by bullying the teacher, as sometimes happened in earlier days. They were from good families in a favored neighborhood. To illustrate the extent to which order was dissipated in this classroom, consider this episode: One morning one of the boys stuffed writing paper under his shirt to look like female breasts. As he paraded up and down the aisles the girls twittered and the other boys, who at first squirmed with poorly suppressed laughter, soon imitating the leader, raked paper from their desks into their shirts and ran shouting up and down the aisles. This was open, brazen rebellion by ten-year-olds! Try to restore order when not one but nearly all the class joins in lawless acts!

Any experienced teacher knows—*and the new ones ought to be told*—that classroom control is possible only when most of the pupils are accustomed to order, expect it, contribute to it, and ignore the overtures of a dissident child testing to find out if conditions are ripe for a challenge to authority. A condition that produces classroom disorder of this kind, it is certain, involves all the pupils and is the result of extended abdication of adult authority.

No pleasantries in respect to the rights of children, no plausible explanations that their home experiences, not they, are responsible, no maudlin fear about warping their personalities if external discipline is applied can wipe away the ugly spectacle of ten-year-olds defying the authority of a teacher in the classroom.

Is it not clear that too much freedom in the early grades will set the stage for the beginning of bad behavior patterns? Should we not avoid giving children more freedom of choice than they are capable of handling? Must we not ask ourselves at what point the principle of self-expression, which we like to encourage in children, may not lead to a form of social anarchy?

Between the teacher and the pupil as the source of authority in the classroom, I choose the teacher. Even if she must be a petty tyrant to maintain order, I would still put the mace of authority in a conspicuous place on her desk.

Authority to Teach

But there is always the most important aspect of teacher authority to consider. It is her right to teach. This is to say that the teacher is expected to know the subjects she is to teach. She is employed to teach these subjects to pupils who are not informed about them. As the informed and authoritative adult in the classroom, she must be permitted to teach.

How does this principle differ from the child-centered method?

In the latter, the teacher is one of the group. The simplest way to illustrate the methodology is to think of a teacher with an arithmetic group asking, "What shall we learn today?"

I was not surprised to hear a mathematics specialist say that in the child-centered kind of elementary education, teachers are unable to teach mathematical concepts for lack of time and authority. They often are inadequately prepared in the subject because where pupil and teacher learn together ignorance is shielded by the difficulty of placing responsibility.

As she works with chalk in hand a good teacher is more than a lecturer. Step-by-step she tells, questions, and evaluates. There is nothing new, so far as the good teacher is concerned, in the present "new" theory of programing for machine teaching. The good teacher has always organized the lesson into parts small enough for pupils to comprehend. She has invariably reinforced learning by an immediate in-class check of responses in the interaction of pupil and teacher, a factor which, I hasten to add, no machine as yet invented has been able to supply, nor is any ever likely to do so. The child as learner is an active participator and is the object of the teacher's attention when she instructs. Good teaching combines child-centered and subject-matter orientation.

Therefore: As the informed specialist, the elementary teacher instructs pupils as the reactor centers of the learning process.

■ Eighth Issue: Phonics for Beginning Reading or as Supplemental to the Look-Say Method?

A few years ago, the issue would have been stated: Phonics or look-say? Progress has been made from that untenable position. Now most reading experts say conciliatory things about phonics. They say, in effect: "We think it quite helpful to introduce, for example, the study of beginning consonants when the pupils need it." Even this equivocal position is a change for the better, although I have observed that many progressivists who have been obliged to accept phonics as a part of language instruction do so with reservations. The result is that the teacher is often confused about the acceptability of phonics. When she is caught doing phonics work, a teacher is often quite unsure what her supervisors will think. A supervisor's lifted eyebrow can unloose a flood of doubts.

As to the use of a phonics instruction system at the beginning stages of reading, the point of view differs sharply among elementary teachers and supervisors. During an interview for a supervisory promotion, a teacher told me straightforwardly that she could not go along with me in my opinion that phonics should be taught specifically in the first stages of reading. In another case, a principal told a teacher that it was all right if she wanted to enroll in a phonics workshop endorsed by the school system, but if she did, she would be doing so on her own and not as a part of his plan for his school.

I am not using these comments by members of our staff to show how individualistic and independent the members of the teaching profession are, or that the word from the top office is filtered through many minds before it becomes action on the operational level. These cases show the depth of feeling about the place of phonics; partisanship in the controversy is supported more by emotion than by reason. In education we are likely to defend and hold tightly to what we "believe in" rather than, as a noted admiral said of his system of teaching his staff to build and operate nuclear powered vessels, "We have no pride in anything we do. If something doesn't work, we get rid of it." This position is a bit too mature and scientific to be employable as yet in education. When we change practices it is generally in the flush of a new enthusiasm and with the romantic obscuration of facts generally associated with a first wedding. When our practices are challenged, our posture is one of defense. *It is this way with the phonics controversy.*

Since *the early introduction of phonics* is the *keystone* of the Amidon system, the justifications and procedures will be explored in detail later. But as for reaching a position on the issue, the question is primarily one of being realistic and informed about the phonetic characteristics of our native tongue and then teaching children to use it by cooperating with it. To use phonics in the earliest grades and even in the pre-school period is to raise to the level of consciousness what children must sooner or later stumble upon themselves. When we say, use phonics as a teaching method, we are saying, "Let us direct the child's learning rather than leave it to chance insights." To do this in any area of knowledge or skill is the reason for schools.

Therefore: Teach a system of phonics at the earliest stages of reading instruction to help the pupil more quickly and reliably use his native tongue by learning from the first how to use the principles of its operation.

■ Ninth Issue: Teach the Whole Child or Supply All of the Educational Needs of the Child?

This issue defies concrete definition, yet it is one of the most troublesome confronting the school and community today. It is a field for careful soul-searching by educator and layman alike. The answers given to the questions raised determine the quality and scope of education, the character of its services to children, and the relative emphasis given to the several elements of its curriculum.

Limit the Responsibility of the Schools

To do their designated tasks well, the schools must, of course, define the limits of their responsibilities. They cannot, for example, reshape the economy which permits poverty to fester in the midst of plenty, although they can educate for economic literacy. They cannot promote the development of public housing projects for the assistance of low economic groups, although they can educate for making better use of urban redevelopment. They cannot support planned parenthood, but they can educate for personal and family living. They cannot serve as welfare agencies, but they can use a free lunch program to improve the educability of children.

In their major role as educators for intellectual competence, the schools must do everything they can to improve the educability of pupils. Hunger among children reduces their educability. Therefore, food services improve the product of classroom effort. The hostile child is not receptive to learning. Therefore, psychiatric services must be, not an adjunct to teaching, but a foundational service which will contribute to the effectiveness of teaching. The child whose vision is impaired will not learn to read; medical services are therefore needed to point out the handicap and ways must be found to supply glasses if the parents are unable to do so.

"You seem to believe the main job of the schools is to teach the basic subjects," an editorial writer once said to me. "Then how can you favor giving free lunches to needy children? Isn't this a welfare service?"

The answer to questions like this is always the same: If the job doesn't seem to be done elsewhere, and if children are lethargic from undernourishment, instruction in reading does not help to enliven them. But clearly it would be far better for their need for food to be supplied elsewhere than in the school, so that the limited resources of the school may be used primarily for instruction in the basic subjects. How much better, for example, for children to be taught at home to brush their teeth than to expect the schools to take expensive time to do this. Or, when it comes to home control of children's schedules, why should teacher time be taken to instruct children to go to bed at a proper hour rather than to stay up until after midnight watching television? Parents often ask teachers to do this duty for them. One parent said to me, "I can't get my children away from the television set. I wish the schools would do something about this."

Consider another example. A mother called me on the telephone, "Miss ———— can't make my boy behave. She keeps calling me about what he does. It's her job to make him behave."

"Can you make him behave?" I asked.

"No. He won't do anything I say. But the teacher is paid to make him behave."

The issue becomes clear, it seems to me, as we consider the great number of additional duties assigned to teachers upon the insistence of parents, special groups, and even dedicated educators. The fact is, of course, the teacher instructs the whole child. At the time of instruction in a classroom the pupil is the product of all that he has experienced. His educability is determined by these events, and by the meeting or the denial of basic wants. But to supply these wants through school services *only when no other help is available* sets a limit to the responsibility of the school to take over the duties of the home and community. This definition of scope of responsibility is consistent with the point of view that the school should put primary emphasis upon instruction in the basic subjects, the learning of which is not likely to take place anywhere else but in the schools.

Some Say, "Teach Everything"

The opposite point of view is that the schools must sooner or later teach the child everything he needs to know. According to this view, the schools are responsible for the total of the child's education. As the practice in education moves toward the realization of this principle, instruction includes such content as shoe shining (I have seen this included as a part of an activity unit), setting a table for company, whipping up a chocolate pudding (a first grade reading-arithmetic project, justified for its help in objectifying instruction in basic subjects), planning use of leisure time, buying in a grocery store, care of teeth, body cleanliness (some would like showers in schools for children who are neglected at home), and, to end an otherwise endless list, the planning of exercise schedules for children who ride to and from school and sit for hours daily before television sets. These are illustrations of the broadening of the school curriculum that is now occurring. Almost without being aware of what is happening, the community is asking more and more from the schools, the ultimate being the acceptance of total responsibility for the education of children.

Although I have to resist an ambivalence on this issue, particularly where such informal educational institutions as the home, church, the streets, alleys, and parks seem to be less and less dependable, I am convinced that limits need to be set to what is expected of formal education and attention is urgently required to upgrade the informal institutions of learning. This is needed to protect the home against the structural weakness that follows when its primary obligations are absorbed by group agencies. The failure to exercise a function invariably weakens the capacity to perform. An unexercised horse cannot be expected to win a race. *Thus, for the schools to encroach upon home responsibilities contributes to the weakening of the home.*

Another undesirable result of an absorption of total educational responsibility by the schools is the corresponding loss of attention to the fundamental curriculum. A lesson in shoe-shining may crowd out a lesson in arithmetic. The undemanding nature of the "practical" curriculum lures pupil, teacher, and parent from the more prosaic, arduous, and seemingly less immediate and useful study of principles and facts in the basic subjects. Therefore, the utilitarian objectives of a non-academic curriculum eventually restrict the time schedule for the academic subjects, which are widely though incorrectly believed to be impractical.

I believe the schools should try to hold to their first purpose, the teaching of basic subjects, using every possible service to improve the educability of the pupil. They should employ the personnel needed to achieve this objective: counselors, school psychologists, and school social workers where needed, health services and food services. The employment of these services should not, however, impede the reconstruction of the home by absorbing its duties. A major social need is the restoration of home responsibility for meeting the discovered needs of the child.

Therefore: While defining the primary objectives of formal education as education in the basic subjects, the schools should acquire and employ auxiliary services needed to improve the educability of children.

■ **Tenth Issue: Teach the "Impractical" Basic Subjects or the Utilitarian Subjects?**

There is an unhappy yet persistent conflict between those who would limit the curriculum to items which have immediate application and those who would put most of the emphasis upon the basic subjects. The extreme view of the utilitarian is that nothing should be taught until the child has a felt need for it. Teach him, for example, to make change when he buys his first ice cream cone. The utilitarians are the advocates of direct experience as the exclusive way to learning. From this point of view, experience is thought of as real and active, rather than as mentalistic, that is, as taking place in the abstract, as would occur, for example, in *reading about* the event or idea.

Experience Is Mentalistic

Those who contend that direct experience is the only true vehicle for learning deny the value of man's most precious talent, his capacity for abstract thinking, for sharing through symbolical means the experiences of others of his or a preceding time.

> I remember well the excitement in the central office of a rather progressive school system when a sixth grade teacher requisitioned a kangaroo. Most of the top school executives thought she was in need of psychiatric care. She was more sane than we think. She was, I am sure, deriding the idea that children can learn only by direct experience. "If this is so," she was asking, "how can I teach about kangaroos unless the children actually experience one?"

In its reaction against the often meaningless book-centered method of teaching, education moved too far in some instances from organized subject matter. Many theorists and some teachers believed it uesless for children to acquire information not immediately needed. Within this point of view, practice to reproduce information upon demand was considered a sterile exercise. In extreme instances, drill and memorization were dropped and actually considered harmful and the teacher who required them was often obliged to do so behind closed doors. For an organized curriculum, pupil-teacher-planned activity was substituted. This methodology required the organization of large units of experience, with the teaching skills and information to be incidental to the need for them as the study unit was developed.

Clearly, utility needs a broader definition than simply direct personal and physical involvement in something happening at a given moment. It should embrace the pervading characteristic of experience as something in which mind and feeling unite in an event which is real even though not operational; that is, not involving at the moment the material elements of the environment. It is not unreasonable to say that at times man's most significant experiences have been non-material because they have occurred on the level of mind and spirit. Hence, teaching is often most useful when it stimulates experience at this level.

Basic Subjects Have "Practical" Purposes

Some believe that sharp differences exist between the academic and the practical or the vocational in their application to daily experiences.

At first glance it seems unreasonable to assert that vocational preparation starts with the beginnings of academic instruction in the kindergarten and first grade. But I believe it can be shown that in the child's very first days in school *basic education sets the foundation for vocational competence.*

Communication is a necessity in any kind of job. In the simplest task, communication consists of understanding oral directions. In the more complex levels of work it often includes the preparation of reports and plans, or the interpretation of difficult printed matter. Employers themselves often declare that competence in the basic skills along with personal qualifications such as reliability and cooperativeness is what they want most in new employees.

I hope that school people are aware of the importance of reading, writing, speech, spelling, and mathematics in the "practical" world of work. My own education in this direction began early in my career. When I was the principal of a high school, a young man—married and father of two—came to see me about his problem. Although he was a laborer in a meat packing plant, he told me that he was afraid he was going to be fired because he couldn't read. "I've got to keep my job," he said. "Can you help me?"

Another vivid illustration is the case of a painter working on a government project. "I want to learn to read," he told a reading clinic director in our school system some years ago. "I am afraid I will lose my job when my foreman finds out I can't read the labels on the paint cans."

Basic Subjects for the Discipline of Work

In addition to the direct usefulness of the basic subjects in practical situations, they help to build discipline in the performance of difficult tasks. This seems to be saying that I believe in the transfer of mental discipline. This is exactly what I am saying: The basic subjects train in precision. This is about as practical as one can be.

Precision and skill in the performance of any task are indispensable in the successful discharge of vocational responsibilities. Habits of industry, pleasure in painstaking effort, and a sense of responsibility begin to be formed in the early stages of human development. Because this is so, early childhood education must provide experiences which develop these attributes. Well-ordered emphasis upon the basic subjects makes an invaluable contribution to this end, because defined lessons and systematic checks upon the individual pupil's performances contribute to the development of good work habits. Hence an effective system of basic education helps to prepare the child for the world of work.

If the schools teach respect for work, then integrity, industry, and sound attitudes become a part of the personality of the individual. These are, it is generally agreed, universally accepted virtues of great and lasting value, because the individual who performs his work assignments with diligence and responsibility is undergoing an experience which builds moral strength.

Properly defined, the school is a place of work with all that is implied in that term. The preparation of an assignment in arithmetic is work experience. It is not a recreational activity to be engaged in at the choice of the pupil. It is not a job the child is to take or leave, depending upon his feelings at the moment. Nor should this experience be disguised in the form of play to make it palatable.

School Is a Place to Develop Work Habits

I believe the school has a greater responsibility for developing good work habits than it may generally be aware of. When it meets its obligation in this respect, it develops character traits that are of the foremost value both to the individual and to society. Satisfaction in work and pride in the quality of workmanship must be developed early in the growth of the individual. If this does not take place within the elementary school years then it tends never to take place. If the schools do not help to develop these qualities, they may never be adequately established, because an easy-going atmosphere in the school room will overcome the good influence of the home where respect for work is being taught, or it will fail to help build strength of character where the home itself is careless about developing work habits.

Failure to develop these traits is costly and dangerous. Too many students and too many adults have acquired a "get by" attitude toward their work as a result of school experiences. The effect of this is felt in many ways: a second call to the television repairman; a stalled automobile that has just left the garage; a disordered household; litter-strewn streets and yards; an airplane crash; death from improperly prepared drugs; a satellite failure.

I think I could make a fair case for the opinion that many of our social ills have some connection with the failure to develop in youth the feeling about work, its value and its satisfactions, that gives importance and significance to life. To the extent that modern education has chosen to ignore this purpose we have been responsible for a loss in national strength. It is time to restore dependable craftsmanship to a place of respect in our value system, and the primary school is unquestionably one place to begin.

In stating the opinion that basic subjects properly taught have a utility that far outlasts the more specific instruction in the so-called practical subjects, I do not suggest the exclusion of the latter from the school curriculum. However, if a choice must be made between teaching the principles of addition and sending a class to the store to buy groceries for experience in adding a grocery bill, the decision is easily in favor of the former. There are times, however, when the schools must provide education in subjects which offer specific training. If the teaching is good, principles may be drawn from such training, thus increasing its importance by use of the inductive method.

While education of this kind, for example, in the shop and home economics curricula, will take place generally at the secondary school level, in special instances courses like these may be needed at the elementary school level. The so-called slow learner may respond only to the concrete and kinesthetic type of education, and hence will need to be taken slowly into simple manual subjects where a minimum of equipment is supplied. There is a limit to the way slow learners can respond to manual instruction, because often intellectual handicap carries over to all activities. Even among teachers who ought to know better, the opinion is sometimes held that the non-academic child can succeed in manual work. The fact is that most such children can learn the basic skills if they are taught by teachers who understand the necessity for making instruction specific and concrete.

All this leads to the conclusion that the first order of business in the school is the teaching of the principles of the basic subjects, with such teaching to include much use of the concrete example for the mentally handicapped pupil. The training aspects of education such as specific job preparation should be assigned to the secondary level, and employed there only in conjunction with an adequate program in the basic subjects and never as a substitute for them.

Therefore: The most useful instruction is in the basic subjects, with emphasis upon principles which are to be taught with application to concrete situations, a major objective of teaching being the showing of such connections.

SUMMARY

Always limited in arc and in lateral movement, the pendulum is a sterile symbol of progress. In education, movement should be progressive in the direction of improved application of the available knowledge about learning. The issues in education should be resolved by the establishment of new principles, always to be considered tentative and subject to change in the light of new conditions, but at any given time useful guides to action. With this condition as the primary postulate, I am convinced that the foregoing ten principles represent a progressive doctrine which merits the formulation of the new elementary program which has come to be identified as *the Amidon concept.*

ESTABLISHMENT OF THE AMIDON SCHOOL

THE PLAN AND THE PURPOSE

IN A RETROSPECTIVE EXAMINATION OF THE EVENTS LEADING up to the demonstration in basic education in the Amidon school, two factors stand out as particularly significant: (1) a superintendent's ideas about education were persistent in their search of a home, and (2) the imminent completion of a new elementary school where there were no children to use it presented a challenge that could not be ignored.

Events seemed to conspire to produce a joining of a set of ideas about education and the opportunity to test them in a new school in a still unformed community. Out of the pressure of use and forged in the heat of trial has come what is now widely known as *the Amidon concept,* a union of fairly compatible ideas. This chapter relates the story of the establishment of the Amidon school.

A New Building Without Pupils

School superintendents in this country are responsible for directing the spending of millions of dollars a year for new school houses. In the great cities such as New York, Chicago, and Los Angeles, the amount of money spent annually on school construction will reach astronomical figures. Even in the District of

Columbia, which forms the center of a large metropolis, limited in size by constitutionally prescribed boundaries, new schools and additions and improvements to existing schools were authorized over the seven-year period 1955–1961 to the tune of approximately 51 million taxpayer dollars.

A school superintendent has two main worries about school construction. One is the problem of finding the money, or persuading the citizens that the money ought to be found, or giving them enough facts so that they can nudge the responsible fiscal authorities into action. For no responsible school administrator can stand by inactive, complacent, or cowed by anti-school pressures while some children are kept out of classrooms half of every school day because of lack of room. The lack of classroom space seems to be a peculiar attribute of big city school systems because of movement from rural areas and the high birthrate that seems to be correlated with factors producing the congestion often found in urban centers.

The second worry is the possibility of building schools where the expected children fail to appear. In budget hearings I am often asked this question, "Have you over-built? Are you putting the schools where they are needed?"

Generally, a new school house is placed in an area where the number of children already present, or expected to be there by the time the building is complete, justifies new construction. Preceding the planning, financing, and construction, much census taking, checking of new housing in being, in process, or on somebody's drawing board, the application of population formulas to the number of new home units expected takes place in school research offices and budget departments. This is followed by extensive discussion in the Board of Education meetings, and, in the case of the District of Columbia schools, before committees of Congress. Everybody needs to be reassured that new school buildings will be needed. No fear haunts a superintendent so much as the possibility of putting up a new building where there are no children.

But this is exactly what happened in Washington, D. C., in an urban redevelopment area within easy sight of the Capitol dome. Not that such a fortunate juxtaposition offered any real protection against misjudgment or from the consequences thereof. Actually, for those of us who work under its surveillance, the Capitol dome tends to be the symbol of a stern taskmaster ready to offer criticism whenever an error in management occurs.

As the new Amidon building neared completion, the denuded acres surrounding it gave little immediate promise of supplying pupils for the school. A new school was up and ready for use before the children had come into the area, not because the school system had suddenly demonstrated an unusual capacity for getting things done, but because the urban renewal agencies had been unexpectedly delayed in building the new homes in the area.

BRIEF HISTORY OF THE AMIDON SCHOOL

The first Amidon was an eight-room elementary building constructed in 1882 in southwest Washington, a section of the city bounded by South Capitol Street, which runs due south from the Capitol Building to the Anacostia River, and by the Washington Channel and the Mall, a broad band of open park land joining the Capitol and the Lincoln Memorial. In this proud community, occupied many years by families of modest means, from whose streets and homes came many of the city's leading citizens, the old Amidon School served with distinction until 1957 when it was torn down because it was within the lines of an inner loop highway.

The major event in this area was the establishment of the southwest redevelopment project. In 1946, the Congress enacted a law creating the Redevelopment Land Agency which was to a degree inactive until 1951 when planning funds became available and the first steps for the complete redevelopment of the southwest area were taken.

By 1953, redevelopment planning reached the stage when it seemed reasonable for the Board of Education to ask Congress to authorize the use of funds to acquire a site, make plans, and construct and equip a new 25-room elementary school to serve the southwest community when the redevelopment was completed. But this date proved to be too early for the pace of redevelopment, because it was not until 1954 that the Redevelopment Land Agency began to demolish the vacated homes and business structures in the southwest area.

Although in 1955 the Board of Education again requested appropriations to build the new Amidon School, the redevelopment agencies were not ready to start construction of new housing and Congress wisely refused to approve the use of funds for this project.

By 1956 things looked brighter for redevelopment, and in anticipation of new home and apartment construction in the southwest, the Board of Education again asked for authority to use funds for the new school. In the appropriation act of 1957 Congress approved the spending of money for site and plans in the fiscal year ending June 30, 1958. The following year Congress took the next step by authorizing the construction and equipping of the new building. The school was completed and ready for use in the summer of 1960.

The new building contains 25 classrooms (two rooms designed for kindergarten and two rooms for the teaching of slow learners); a large all-purpose room for assemblies, indoor activities, and noon-time use by children who bring their lunches to school; a library, and the usual complement of administrative offices. It is unpretentious and inexpensive in construction.

It has properly been described as not unlike new elementary schools anywhere in the country, undistinguished but functional, and pleasantly open to sun and air and colorful in interior decoration. As this new school was being built, it became clear that construction of redevelopment homes was far behind schedule, and that the 148 elementary pupils living in the nearby public housing development and attending an old elementary school slated for abandonment were the only customers for a school with a capacity of 806.

THE SCHOOL AN ARCHITECT OF A COMMUNITY

It is not very often that a school can be set up ahead of the settlement of its community. In the case of the Amidon there was an unusual opportunity to create a school plan and to apply a philosophy that might influence prospective home owners to come into the neighborhood. A new school building which could not be left unused, a developing community which was still to some extent in the planning stage, and the interest of the redevelopment planners in developing an attractive school program, formed a set of circumstances favorable to the establishment of the Amidon project.

In a series of conversations with representatives of the Redevelopment Land Agency and at least one of the major corporations interested in participating in the building of homes, apartments, and community facilities, the question of how to use the school to help build the community was exhaustively explored. I believed that the school system must join with other public and private enterprises in the building of a stable and representative community to which people with children would be attracted. The school must become an architect of the community, and this requires a program to which parents will bring their children even before they are able to buy or rent homes in a neighborhood of the school.

FORMULATION OF THE AMIDON CONCEPT

At this period too, I was becoming dismayed at the slowness of the response to my request for emphasis upon basic education.

Although I had spoken in many public meetings about the need for greater attention to education in the basic subjects, I could not throw off the impression (perhaps hunch is a better word) that changes in many of our more than 2500 elementary classrooms were slow in coming. I was aware, of course, of an increasing use of phonics in some classrooms, but even this seemed more incidental than fundamental. In classrooms I visited I could see here and there evidence of careful organization of subject matter, but in many cases there continued to be heavy reliance upon social studies units as the core of the curriculum. My visits to classrooms and conferences with teachers, supervisors, and principals convinced me that there was general misunderstanding of what I was talking about and many disturbing indications of wasteful procedures in the classrooms.

I think I must share some impressions gained from observations, if the reasons for the formulation of the Amidon concept are to be fully understood. Though I want to acknowledge the devotion and diligence of most teachers in the elementary classrooms, a number of items from my notes on classroom visits will reveal misgivings that required satisfaction. I can show, I believe, that something like the Amidon demonstration had to be forthcoming at about this time in my work as superintendent. In other words, the project resulted from a kind of historical necessity.

A SECTION ON MISGIVINGS

In the following illustrative comments I think I can quickly show why I have become disenchanted with many features of a child-centered system of teaching, including the delegation to the teacher of the main responsibility for deciding what to teach, and expecting her to teach in depth and for mastery with a methodology that is analogous to the quiz-type guessing games popularized on television.

Second Graders on the Subject of Clothing

The morning recess period had ended about ten minutes before I came into the second grade classroom. At the left of center near the front wall the teacher sat with a semicircle of 12 pupils who were answering questions on clothing. The questions and answers ran in this fashion:

"Where did you get your dress?"
"From the store," said a girl. Boys fidget.
"What store?"
"I don't know." Girls slumped in chairs.
"Have you ever heard of cotton?"
"Uh-huh," in chorus by a part of the class.
"Where do we get cotton?"
"From the store." A few giggles, apparently at the incongruity of hearing the same answer given to two different questions.
"Where does the store get it?"

Silence.

In about this way the teacher continued to ask questions as they came to her mind while the pupils drew answers from shallow wells of experience to which the present lesson added very little. As I watched and listened I became convinced that whatever learning was taking place was on the loss side of the ledger: boredom, guess work, inattention, bad speech habits, "s" shaped spinal columns, aimless shifting of hands and feet.

But even more useless was the crayon work being done by some of the class not in the group with the teacher. "I'm letting them use their work-books while I teach the social studies unit," explained the teacher. Whatever the purpose of the seat work might have been, it didn't come through to me, for the children were careless and listless. In the few minutes I was in the classroom, I saw five pupils jump up from their seats like suddenly released spring-activated toys, each one acting with some sort of purpose, such as getting a new sheet of paper, or looking out the window for reasons only known to the child. I suspect one capable of identifying motives would say they were really so bored with it all they literally (but inoffensively) exploded from their seats.

On the bulletin boards, to give another reason for my unenthusiastic attitude about what I saw, were frayed and shop-worn magazine cut-outs of different kinds of wearing apparel taken out of file and used year after year by the teacher to enliven the clothing unit. There was also some "expressive" art work by pupils—mostly splotches of color roughly in the shape of the human form.

It is difficult for me to fix the total blame on the teacher. She was following the line which is prescribed for her in the experience-centered methodology. It will be said, and I must in part concede this, that the best of this kind of teaching can be stimulating indeed—but so is the best of any kind of teaching. Except for accidental learnings, little of any value was accomplished during my stay in the classroom. This, in my opinion, constitutes unintentioned larceny of public funds, which are used to support an inefficient teaching technique, to furnish carelessly used supplies, and to heat and light the classroom. The most grievous loss, however, is incurred, not by the taxpayer, but by the pupil.

While this kind of ineffectiveness is often chargeable to the quality of the teaching, most of it can be laid properly at the door of a methodology which requires a teacher to do what she is not equipped to do: to improvise content with too little time or background to do this with even marginal success; to clutter the school day with scissor and crayon work; to strain to draw from pupils of limited backgrounds vague guesses in response to poorly planned questions; to rely on work-books to keep children busy while a small group is being taught at the front of the room. When the teacher herself ought to be developing backgrounds of experience by direct instruction, I found pathetically serious children cutting out prepared answers to paste in the squares on lesson sheets.

On Becoming Specialists on the Life of the Oyster

Still another disturbing impression refused to be pushed aside by more pressing business, such as defending budgets and planning reports for Board of Education meetings and Congressional hearings. A case in point is the unit on the Chesapeake Bay region, which is our "here and now" geographic section, selected for study in our fourth grades because the early social studies themes are selected for propinquity to the learner.

In one fourth grade class I saw that most of the content was accidental and unselective. The pupils had prepared exhibits of flora and fauna, had made crude pictures of marine life that inhabited the waters of the Bay, and were having rather a good and exciting time dabbling with impressions about the area. The project had developed a high level of interest. But the trouble is, this was about all the geography these fourth graders were to get during the year. Although they became junior specialists in Chesapeake Bay oysters and crabs, they acquired no organized geographic information about other parts of the country.

If these children could name the states of the union, it was because they had learned them at home, from travel, television, or voluntary reading. If they knew anything about the Mississippi

River, their knowledge was the accidental result of a news report or, perhaps, seeing a movie. While a study of geography should include much information such as was gathered for the Chesapeake Bay unit, it will be inadequate in scope unless it is planned in sequential and predetermined order. I found it difficult to see how allowing fourth grade pupils to study the oyster in great detail, as some were doing in this class, could be justified in place of systematic study of United States geography.

Why Can't They All Learn to Read?

Another specter among the skeletons in our educational closet is the fact that, despite strenuous efforts to improve the reading levels of all our pupils, thousands go through the elementary schools without having attained functional literacy. They read so poorly that they cannot keep up with their school work. Many are barely able to do the reading necessary to negotiate our city's streets. They use the daily newspaper chiefly for the comics section. They leave school as soon as they can because they cannot read well enough to succeed at higher levels of education.

A high incidence of functional illiteracy persists in our school system despite what may be modestly described as a significant improvement in the average level of achievement in reading. Since the desegregation of the District of Columbia public schools, when severe academic retardation was first reported on a city-wide basis, what appear to be significant improvements in reading have occurred. In some grades, the median reading scores improved as much as one full year over a period of six years. A sharp increase in the percentage of Negro pupils in these grades took place over this period of years, attesting to the excellent response of these pupils to the stronger emphasis upon the basic skills. It would be inaccurate, unfair, and, I think, ungrateful to ignore the improvements that have been made in reading skills in recent years, testimony to the competence of many teachers and the relative soundness of their techniques.

But this achievement is still not enough, as long as there are large numbers who are not taught to read well enough to do the minimum reading necessary for purposes of effective citizenship. It is not enough, even with some reading scores ranging to the top levels of the test range, to be satisfied with these achievements until we are certain that the good readers are doing the best they can. Often good pupils are retarded in relation to their capabilities.

Nor can I be satisfied when I learn from parents the extent to which they must supplement the school reading program at home. Too many parents have said to me, "If I hadn't taught my child to read, he would never have learned."

Although excellent relative gains in reading achievement have been recorded for the District of Columbia schools in recent years, our intention here is to see to it that no child fails to achieve this important skill, if direct, persistent, and systematic instruction can furnish him the means of becoming literate. The most important place to do this job is in the early elementary grades.

Home Made Textbooks

In the elementary school, I have observed, hectograph ink has become a badge of the teaching profession. With a decline in the use of the textbook, teachers prepare many of the lesson sheets for distribution to pupils. I have often questioned the quality of the lessons, including the legibility of the printing. Perhaps one of the most startling examples of a teacher's effort to tie-in an arithmetic lesson with a seasonal interest came to my attention one fall during the Halloween season. Included among a list of arithmetic problems was this startling bit of logic: "If you have 7 goblins and 5 witches, how many do you have?"

Time Schedules

Periods for teaching the basic subjects tend to be highly flexible in the elementary classroom, especially where extensive use is made of the unit organization of subject matter. One of the first things I look for when I visit a class is the daily schedule on the blackboard. The amount of time is not generally shown, or even the time of the day for any particular lesson. Thus, it is rarely possible to connect the work of the moment with the schedule on the board. I have often found that the opening period, which includes the saying of the pledge of Allegiance to the Flag, seems to be stretched out thinly to give time to what is called "sharing." At this period the children tell about something that happened at home, describe a recently acquired toy, or tell about a news story. Except for this lack of direction, the exchange of ideas, the saying of something with the purpose of telling others, has considerable value, because speech improvement is possible only by practice in speaking. The trouble is that this vague kind of lesson-holding lacks preparation by the pupil and becomes a listening rather than a teaching period for the teacher.

I once saw perhaps the most striking instance of downgrading the basic subjects in a sixth grade schedule posted on the blackboard. Under the columns headed by the days of the week, social studies, art, music, and physical education were listed in blocks of time that ran through the entire week. On Monday afternoon at two o'clock a reading period was scheduled for the only time during the week. The importance of a time schedule is clear. Even if a fundamental subject like reading is given only scant attention, at least this fact is made known.

When Do You Teach?

Among my most unassuaged misgivings is the impression I get in visiting classes that very little time is spent in teaching.

By teaching I mean, of course, much more than hearing pupils read in a group, or the asking of questions and listening to the responses, or observing a committee of children planning a class program. When I visit a classroom I like to see the teacher engaged in the ancient art of teaching. There is so little of this kind of teaching going on in the modern classroom that I might be willing to concede that herein lies our most serious educational deficiency. I am tempted to ask: *When do you teach?*

Quite clearly, I have acquired certain misgivings about a number of practices in the modern elementary classroom. Naturally, I formed theories of my own, not always unique, but at the least an ordered group of ideas which I was led by circumstance to put into operation at the Amidon school. This I did with an awareness of the risk, for it is one thing to sponsor theories about education, but it is another to take the responsibility of putting them into practice. Theories can be defended with more theories, of which there is an unlimited supply. Practice can be defended only by reference to what happens as a result of it. In this position, there is an obvious hazard, and in the case of the Amidon the first test was whether parents would take the trouble to accept an invitation to bring their children to the school.

THE BOARD OF EDUCATION APPROVES
THE AMIDON PROJECT

After having determined to make the Amidon school, otherwise an empty monument to urban planning that slipped out of gear, a center for the application of a constellation of educational ideas, I recommended on March 16, 1960, that the Board of Education approve the Amidon program.

The report to the Board is as follows:

The following is a plan for the use of the Amidon Elementary School when it is completed and ready for use in September:

1. Children now attending the S. J. Bowen Elementary School will be transferred to the Amidon Elementary School.
2. An educational program centering on basic subjects will be developed for the Amidon School. This includes direct and systematic instruction in reading, writing, grammar, speech, mathematics, science, history and geography.
3. The plan for instruction will include experience units as supplemental to the direct instruction in the fundamental subjects. In this connection, opportunities for art and music experience will be stressed.
4. In the plan to be formulated under the direction of the Assistant Superintendent in charge of Elementary Schools, pupils from outside the Amidon zone will be permitted to enroll under such conditions and rules as may be established for the school. An effort will be made to achieve a balance in academic qualifications.

In other words, this is to be a school with a balanced program in honors, general and basic curriculums to the extent possible to achieve.

As an experimental center, Amidon school will be given special assistance by the reading clinic and the subject fields departments such as mathematics, science, foreign languages, art, music, and physical education.

5. Evaluation of the program will be supervised by the Assistant Superintendent in charge of Pupil Appraisal, Study and Attendance.

The Board of Education unanimously approved the establishment of the Amidon Elementary School as an experimental center for instruction in the fundamental subjects under the principles of operation outlined in the report.

If, more than a year later, it were possible to rewrite the report now, I would eliminate the description of the project as *experimental*. To many, probably correctly, the term suggested scientific testing of the Amidon pupils against a central group, so that some sort of statistically sound data could be developed to prove one system of education better than another.

From the outset, some observers questioned the lack of validity in any comparison with other schools, inasmuch as about 70 percent of the pupils were to be selected from all over the city and only parents with a genuine interest in their children would be expected to take the trouble to arrange transportation for them to the school, and only teachers who were interested in the project would be invited to join the staff.

While to some degree these objections are valid, the school is actually experimental in the sense of finding out whether a system of ideas about education would prove to be workable when applied to an actual situation. It is, therefore, not wholly improper to describe the Amidon as an experiment in education. The project is not unlike putting an automobile together to see if it will run. It need not be compared with another vehicle to determine its workability. However, to avoid misunderstanding as to the meaning of experiment in the usual though far too limited context of education, I now prefer to think of the Amidon as a demonstration of the workability of an idea. In other words, to avoid any possibility of claim to scientific treatment of the project, the Amidon is to be thought of as a demonstration school where a system of ideas is applied and where even these are used in various degrees of adaptation, since the project itself is an evaluation of teachers' acceptance of the new ideas—at least, for most, new to them, if not so in the total history of education.

EXPANDED SUMMARY OF THE AMIDON CONCEPT

Reactions to the announcement of the Amidon plan were both supportive and questioning, in some cases on both sides of the ledger, as the result of a misunderstanding of the ideas encompassed within the concept.

To some, as described in newspaper headlines, it was a return to the three R's and a device for setting back the educational clock to the turn of the century. As one parent approvingly declaimed at a PTA meeting: "This is a return to the schools of forty years ago." A journalist asked this question, "If you haven't been teaching reading, what have you been teaching?"

On the other hand, the Amidon announcement created among many teachers and principals of the local elementary schools an uneasiness and anger because the new plan seemed to indicate that I believed their program was less than satisfactory. Because any innovation is a threat to current practice, it inevitably generates a natural antagonism. The following story is illustrative. A parent went to the principal of her neighborhood school to transfer her child to the Amidon. The principal asked, "Well, what's wrong with this school?"

This, of course, is a natural and typical reaction because a request for a transfer inevitably seemed to be an act of criticism of the program in the local school.

Clearer definitions of what to develop in the Amidon school for the coming fall, that is, following Board of Education approval in March of 1960, were a necessity, too, as guide lines for the newly appointed principal and for the teachers to be assigned to the school. To accomplish this purpose, I prepared the statement which follows:

The Amidon Plan: A Summary of Philosophical and Practical Suggestions for the Organization of the School

COMBINING THE BEST OF THE OLD AND THE NEW IN EDUCATION, THE AMIDON PLAN IS BUILT ON THIS HYPOTHESIS: IF YOU TEACH CHILDREN DIRECTLY AND IN A HIGHLY ORGANIZED WAY, THEY WILL LEARN BETTER AND FASTER THAN IS PRESENTLY POSSIBLE. THEY WILL, IF TEACHING IS CONSISTENT WITH WHAT IS KNOWN ABOUT THE NATURE OF LEARNING, GROW WHOLESOMELY, DEVELOP CONFIDENCE AS THEY ACQUIRE COMPETENCE, AND GAIN IN SELF-RESPECT AS THEY ACCOMPLISH DIFFICULT OBJECTIVES.

PURPOSE: Self-fulfillment of the individual is the common objective of public education in the District of Columbia. In this school as in all the public schools of this city, the best possible opportunity for the development of the useful talents of each pupil will be offered.

The aim is to make it possible for each pupil to use his talents to the full for his own satisfaction and for the protection and improvement of the American way of life.

CURRICULUM: Among the many aspects of human development, the capacity to behave with reason and intelligence is of primary importance.

It follows that the most important job of the schools is to teach for intelligent behavior. This objective applies to all students, the bright, the average, and the slow.

To do this the curriculum in the Amidon will be organized by basic subject fields. It will be selective, because only the most essential skills and knowledges can adequately be taught in the school day. It will be specific, so that teachers, pupils, and citizens will be informed as to what is to be taught. The curriculum, although flexible in level of difficulty in relation to the pupils to be taught, should be demanding at every stage of pupil development. It should stretch the mind, create new interests, and ennoble aspiration.

SUBJECT FIELDS: Intelligent behavior is possible only if the individual acquires surely and systematically the tools which make such behavior possible. These are the language and the number systems, which unlock the knowledge and experience man has acquired and preserved and which make it possible to expand and refine that experience. Without these tools, reasonable and predictable behavior is impossible.

In addition to the tools of rational behavior, man must know, understand, and feel and he must reflect upon these acquisitions of experience in order to deal with the problems of living. In science, history, geography, music and art, he can achieve understanding for the kind of reasoned response which is the goal of education.

The curriculum plan for the Amidon is built on the premise that the main purpose of organized education is to cultivate the basic subjects as the building blocks of intelligent behavior.

Reading—This is to be silent reading for knowledge, ideas, inspiration, and recreation. This is also to be for the kind of oral communication that is achieved by reading aloud to others. It will include the memorization of selected poetry.

Pupils are to study words, their characteristics, and the way they work together to produce meaning as the main instrumentality for learning. A word is not only a word but a means to knowing about something.

Reading instruction will begin with study of the alphabet, phonics, and syllabication. This is to be non-mechanical with meaning as a paramount element in such instruction.

The purpose of instruction in reading is to know the word, and learn how to know new words independently. This method will combine seeing and sounding. Much writing will be done to involve the kinesthetic sense in gaining mastery over words.

The meaning of words will, where necessary, be taught by the teacher. The teacher will demonstrate connections between words as symbols and the objects or events to which they refer. This can be done by inductive or deductive methodology. While reading will begin with word analysis, meaning and need are to be stressed as a part of the instructional pattern.

Instruction in the techniques of reading will include directed teaching in interpretation, discovery of purpose, tone, and convincingness; identification of key words, topic sentences, supportive detail, summarizing sentences; use of paragraph headings, tables of content, summaries; reading practice in maps, charts, tables. Getting meaning from the printed page will be systematically taught at each grade level. It will be taught as needed in every subject field.

Writing—Pupils will be expected to write extensively for a variety of purposes. This will include creative writing as well as the writing of reports, letters, etc. Revision for excellence will be expected. Composition serves purposes far beyond mere facility in putting words together in sentences. It improves and refines thinking, and becomes a means of self-expression, thus contributing to self-realization.

Much written expression will be required from the earliest grades. While accuracy and facility of expression are desired, the main purpose is to train in the logic of thought.

Spelling—This will be scheduled for regular lessons, in addition to instruction incidental to writing.

Penmanship—This skill will be taught in scheduled periods.

Speaking—Pupils will be taught the basic skills of speech in scheduled periods at the appropriate levels.

They will be instructed in speech in all possible situations in the daily program. In other words, both planned and incidental attention will be given to this subject.

Grammar—This will be scheduled formally at the fourth grade. This will include the parts of speech and the various grammatical forms most commonly needed for clarity of thought and accuracy of expression and interpretation.

Formal study of grammar, with simple diagramming, will begin in the fourth grade. The purpose will be to teach that sentences follow recognizable structure patterns to convey meaning. Improvement in usage will be sought in speech and writing in all grades and subjects by means of direct instruction for this purpose. Drills will be used when the center of attention is on grammar and usage. When the objective is to stimulate thoughtful speech or writing, emphasis should then be placed on content rather than form.

Mathematics—Valued as a means of developing mental discipline as well as for its own utility, this subject will be regularly taught and incidentally used as a means of interpreting, evaluating, and describing events. Many concepts in algebra and geometry will be consciously taught in the primary grades.

Science—As a regularly scheduled subject, science will be taught for knowledge about the physical environment and as a way of thinking.

United States History—As a scheduled subject, United States history will be taught in chronological order in the fifth grade, and in relation to special events in other grades. The purpose is to understand in depth the significance of the present and to develop appreciation of the privileges and responsibilities of citizenship in a free society. The purpose is also to develop an historian's capacity to see and evaluate primary sources and events as a way of understanding their influence upon human behavior.

Geography—The study of place geography will be scheduled systematically first at the fourth grade, with the United States as the beginning point. World Geography with political and economic phases will be scheduled for the sixth grade. Incidental instruction will occur throughout the elementary grades, with maps and globes to be available at all times. This study will occur in literature, history, art, music, science, and seasonal activities.

Music—This subject will be taught in a predetermined, controlled schedule. The objective is enjoyment, self-expression, knowledge, and inspiration. It is to be an intellectual as well as an emotional experience. It will include knowledge about music as a body of information, as well as experience in producing and appreciating it.

Art—On a controlled and predetermined schedule, art will be taught as a body of knowledge and a form of expression. Every lesson must have purpose, defined and evaluated. Art is not to be confused with physical education. It is not to be employed as a tranquilizer or stimulant for psychological conditioning. It is of value in and of itself.

Health and Physical Education—On definite schedule, these subjects have special and identifiable values. Free play is neither physical education nor health education. Directed experiences to develop the body should be described and provided.

Planned rest periods should be provided when needed, with special attention to fatigue cases.

WEEKLY SCHEDULE: Each subject field is to be scheduled in a weekly program on a predetermined time allotment plan.

Direct instruction in these fields is to have first priority. Reasonable flexibility is needed, but interruptions and digressions should be kept to a minimum. Large unit organization around centers of interest is to be supplemental, and where used is to be carefully planned as to goals and procedures.

METHOD OF TEACHING:

Basic Cycle—The teacher is to teach what is to be learned.

The pupil is to study, practice, and know what is to be learned.

The pupil is to be tested on what he has learned.

The teacher is to reteach as needed.

Basic Principles—The characteristics and needs of each pupil will be studied carefully by the teacher and principal.

The teacher will direct instruction to the learner, taking into account his characteristics and needs.

Interest and motivation will be used to inspire learning. They will not, however, control the teaching processes. They are as often the product of successful teaching as they are the means of it.

Teaching will be directed for the most part to the whole class. Small groups will be taught chiefly to meet special individual needs. The combining of several classes for certain types of instruction, such as demonstrations in science, music and physical education, is to be encouraged.

Pupils will have study assignments that have meaning. These are to be done in the classroom and home in preparation for the next day's lesson. Quality, creativeness and purposefulness of "home" work are of greater value than quantity.

Impartation of Knowledge—Connections between subject and experience, and subject and subject will be shown by the teacher. For example, the study of a poem may require word analysis, or some elements of history, or science, or geography. Such connections are not to be left to chance discovery by the pupils, but are to be induced by skillful teaching or are to be directly pointed out by the teacher.

It is often said that when the learner finds out for himself he learns best.

This is good up to a point. If all learning is based on the finding-out process, the amount, quality, and efficiency of the product are questionable. Too long over-stressed, the prevailing recapitulation theory of learning has delayed and obstructed the learning process.

The individual must build on what has been learned by others. If he wants to know how many feet there are in a mile he should not be expected to measure the distance for himself.

Direct impartation of needed knowledge, therefore, will be prominent in the Amidon methodology.

Problem Solving—In this school, however, there is an important place for research techniques. Problem solving, under selective teaching, is one of the important skills. But this procedure is to be carefully planned, with measurable product capable of evaluation.

CLASSROOM MANAGEMENT: Seating will be orderly. Movement in the class will be according to predetermined rules. Self-directed pupil activity is not acceptable unless prepared for and under adult control. Loose, disjointed pupil activity is questionable as a part of any school-supervised program in the classroom, corridor, assembly room, lunchroom, or playground. Physical activity as needed, therefore, will be planned and carefully directed.

LIBRARY: This should become the center of extensive reading activity. In it books, pictures, graphs, charts, maps, objective materials to promote interest and meaningfulness in reading should abound.

This center should be supplemented by classroom reading centers.

COMMUNITY RESOURCES: Their use should be carefully and profitably planned. These are open textbooks, but they should be read with diligence.

THE ULTIMATE PURPOSE: The school will use every available resource to see to it that each child is in good health or capable of securing it; has someone who cares about what happens to him in school and out of school; knows the meaning of success and failure, the happiness of strenuous effort applied to difficult but generally manageable tasks, and the respect which he can win for himself by his own effort.

THE DESIRED END PRODUCT IS NOT A SPOON-FED, PROTECTED INDIVIDUAL BUT A SELF-DISCIPLINED PERSONALITY INTERESTED IN CONTINUING HIS EDUCATION, CAPABLE OF INTELLIGENT DECISION MAKING IN EVERY ASPECT OF LIVING, AND, MOST IMPORTANTLY, GOVERNED IN ALL HIS ACTIONS BY THE HIGHEST MORAL PRINCIPLES.

RESPONSE FROM THE COMMUNITY

When the plan for the Amidon School was announced, the response from the community and later from throughout the country was almost entirely in support of the project. The telephone calls were often from parents asking how to enroll their children at the Amidon. One was from a staff member with one of the Senate legislative committees who called to say, "I am glad you are putting some starch in the curriculum."

A candidate for a doctoral degree in Stockholm, Sweden, wrote of his pleasure with the idea of putting more into the elementary program, because, he said, he was a victim of "easy" teaching and it took him several years to catch up his losses.

From around the country, in fact from around the world, came letters of inquiry about the Amidon idea from students, teachers, instructors in teachers colleges, academic instructors, school administrators and members of boards of education. The interest of the educators indicates a very important point: it is not only dissatisfied parents who want an improvement in education. As a matter of fact, parents are not by any means the first to be aware of deficiencies in the classroom. Teachers are the most realistic critics of unprofitable theories, not always because they resist change, but because they know what works and what doesn't.

Nevertheless, there was a degree of timeliness in the establishment of the Amidon plan. It was, I think, fairly innate, even if not cheerfully embraced by everyone on the staff and in the community.

Fifteen years ago the Amidon proposal would have been, in my opinion, the cause of a violent reaction, possibly even rebellion, among a great many of the school staff and some parts of the community. It has a home-grown quality which adds, I think, to its hardiness and is partly responsible for the present limited acceptability of the project. But the road ahead was not an easy one. The most difficult thing about the Amidon plan was that to some it seemed not a logical next step in educational practice but an indictment of everything we had been doing so far. This element was included in the reactions to the plan.

THE NEW CONSERVATISM

Soon after the announcement of the Amidon plan, I discovered that the one-time progressivists in education had quite unconsciously become the traditionalists. They are the new conservatives, providing an interesting example of the axiom that today's liberal is tomorrow's conversative.

Few educators these days like to describe themselves as progressives, because the term, unfortunately now associated with an unpopular political ideology, has become opprobrious.

But when they support multiple within-class groupings; automatic promotions without special provision for below-standard achievers; extensive reliance upon pupil-planning in curriculum selection; heavy emphasis on readiness (whatever that is); and the idea that the pupil and teacher should learn together; a methodology which encourages know-nothingism in the teaching profession—they favor "progressive" methods which, though revolutionary in the 1920's, have now become traditional and at this point *outworn*. To conserve these principles against change is a natural objective of their proponents. But they ought to accept the fact that they are the new conservatives in education and, while it is laudable to want to preserve the good in the past, it is hardly forward-looking to build a wall around any system of ideas to protect them against the influence of new thought.

THE CONSERVATIVES COUNTERATTACK

The new conservatives in education, the new traditionalists, lost no time in mounting an attack against the Amidon idea.

In some cases, otherwise friendly and reasonable educators used invective. According to newspaper stories, in a stormy session of the board of education of a nearby school system the merits of the Amidon plan were apparently heatedly explored. Angered by the threat to his own educational posture, a high-ranking school officer asserted that the plan was simply a sop thrown to the reactionaries. The most ungracious thing I have heard said about the plan is that it was devised *to silence criticism of the school program.* All of this is of a piece with a pervading complacency and smugness among educators which causes us to reject every criticism as either the result of bad intentions or of ignorance about education. Too many of us in education have become provincial in our judgments. We believe that our work has become so specialized that only the *cognoscenti* are qualified to have opinions about it. If someone in the school business dares to say that all is not at the best level then he has sold out, either out of cowardice or for political motives.

Another reaction is illustrated in the reported comment of an elementary principal to a parent who asked her to consider using the Amidon system in her school.

"Do you want your child to be told exactly what to do every minute of the day? Do you want him to be inhibited, to learn by rote, to be straight-jacketed?"

Whether this view is a deliberate distortion of the concepts of the Amidon, or is the result of a mistake in interpretation, it nevertheless is a trigger-happy defense of the *status quo*. It is a bristling reaction to a threat to status.

Many principals, teachers, and parents believe in a child-centered, spontaneously developed curriculum, and in big-muscle, expansive, and intuitive activity, as the essentials of a good school program. The Amidon plan challenges these ideas and is a derogation of the values in them.

In our own school system, many anxieties were expressed by teachers, principals, and even some parents. Speaking for a number of his associates, one of the newer principals in our school system questioned the experimental validity of the Amidon exercise, believing that a selective process applied to pupils and teachers alike and, therefore, that they were better than average. He raised a question as to whether the teachers at the new school were really following the plan, especially as to instruction in phonics.

One principal told me she just could not accept the idea that children in the kindergarten and first grades should be taught phonics before they learned words by sight. An elementary teacher who was an applicant for a supervisory position declared she could not accept my point of view on phonics. Because I believed she was educable, I nevertheless recommended her appointment. In connection with a special language program being conducted in seven downtown schools, another teacher refused to accept an assignment as a reading specialist because she would not teach phonics to first graders. "I am," she said self-righteously, "a creative teacher."

These are people of good will who believe in what they have been taught, and want to conserve their beliefs and practices against change. These sentiments I can fully respect. I can understand the desire to preserve philosophies which have been acquired over many years of experience and conditioning, and the defensive fervor with which they are guarded when the welfare of children seems to be jeopardized.

But I too believe in the importance of childhood, and in the wholesome development of the personality of children. The difference is in methods, for I believe it is better for children to be systematically challenged and held to maximum standards than to let them vacillate in a highly permissive environment long before they are ready to assume the responsibility of self-direction. I believe the progressive thing to do is to modify current practices in elementary education to achieve a greater degree of logic and order in our schools and thus to establish a better union between subject matter and the learner than has heretofore been attained.

THE NEW PROGRESSIVISM

Although much good education took place in the horse and buggy days, the Amidon is not a return to the methods of those days nor literally a rejection of modern techniques. *It is, rather, a new step toward the fusion of two main streams in American educational thought: the bringing together of the best that has been discovered about the learning process and selected logically organized subject matter.*

It tends to cast off certain shibboleths and dogmas which have encumbered education for at least three decades. It sharply divorces itself from mythology in education built around fluctuating psychological doctrines. The lexicon of American education is cluttered with terms that have only vague and fuzzy referents.

To throw aside convictions by which we have lived and worked is nothing new in American education. Philosophically we are among the most migratory of professions. Over the past half-century we have slavishly followed trends, adopted one point of emphasis and then another, and a series of new leaders as if we were not quite sure what our function was and who should be our leader.

We have labored to the mountain top with Dewey, walked in the uncharted wilderness with Kilpatrick, entered the labyrinth of childhood fears with Freud, watched children grow longitudinally with the child growth and development movement, listened to the beguiling words of the utilitarians, who advised us to teach nothing except for immediate use, to the activists who led us to believe that a child could learn more arithmetic with a hammer than with a pencil, to the unifiers who declared that because all knowledge is interrelated we must therefore teach in great integrative units.

It is time, now to return to the sanity of order and logic in curriculum organization and to the wisdom of teaching subject matter to children in direct and effective manner, using with judgment what is known about how we learn. *This is the meaning and intent of the Amidon plan. It is the new progressivism.*

Part

Two

∎

THE AMIDON IN OPERATION

IN THIS PART OF THE BOOK THE WAY IN WHICH THE AMIDON School was organized and set into motion will be told.

To have a school in operation by the September following the announcement of its special features the preceding March required rapid-fire administrative action to assemble the pupils, teachers, curriculum materials, and equipment. The enterprise itself was an act of faith. Plans had to be made in expectation of public acceptance, because no one could be sure that parents would elect to take their children from their neighborhood schools to the Amidon, assuming full responsibility for transportation and accepting the many other inconveniences of having children in a school a considerable distance from their homes. Despite the uncertainties, the school staff went to work at once to select a principal and the teachers, to plan for workshops, particularly in phonics and curricula, and to develop into a working schedule the ideas of the Amidon Plan. The results of the effort will be reported under these headings: *Pupils, Teachers,* and *Subject Matter.*

chapter three

PUPILS AT THE AMIDON

PUPILS IN THE AMIDON SCHOOL CAME FROM WITHIN AND from without the boundaries of the school zone. In the first group, all children living in the area were admitted just as is done in every other elementary school in the city. In the second group, children were admitted by selection from applications voluntarily submitted by parents.

The "Local" Amidon Pupils

Within the boundaries set for the Amidon School is Greenleaf Gardens, a public housing development in which lived 148 elementary age pupils who entered the Amidon in the fall. Prior to this, these pupils attended the S. J. Bowen elementary school, a relic of the old Southwest district, and scheduled to be razed. To be eligible to live in the public housing project, a family must not have an income above $4,950.

Two military reservations, Fort McNair and The Naval Gun Factory, were also geographically a part of the Amidon district. Prior to the opening of the new school, the children in these military communities were permitted to attend schools outside their own districts in accordance with administrative policy. In the District of Columbia the elementary and secondary schools are zoned, and children are enrolled in the schools by residence rather than by choice. An exception is possible where parents are obligated to reside in a reservation, as in the case of certain military establishments, or in embassy quarters, church homes, and even, in one case, the National Training School for delinquent boys.

Because of the proximity of the Amidon building, the availability of space in it, and the increasing enrollment in the schools which the military reservation children were attending, these children were included in the Amidon enrollment by administrative order. As is generally the case when children are forced to transfer from one school to another, some of the parents vigorously objected. In spite of the superintendent's efforts to persuade the parents to accept the new assignment willingly, their reluctance persisted. It was necessary to require the transfers, nevertheless, and when the Amidon opened, 40 children from the two military reservations entered the school.

As children of officers and enlisted men, they, along with the children from public housing, formed a strong, cross-sectional, and naturally selected part of the Amidon enrollment. Together they numbered 188 in a total enrollment of 455 pupils.

Selection of Pupils from Outside the Amidon Zone

Shortly after the Board of Education approved the Amidon Plan in March (1960), parents began to inquire about how to enroll their children in the school. Local newspapers, in stories and editorials, and the television and radio stations, finding the Amidon proposal newsworthy, did much to inform the community about the purpose of the plan and how parents might inquire into it.

Selected headlines and excerpts from the news stories indicate the treatment and slant given the announcement of the project. The emphasis on return to the Three R's in these stories shows through the headline: "3-R School Experiment Proposed by Hansen." "Old Fashioned Experiment: New SW (Southwest) School Will Turn Back the Clock." "Board Approves Using New School as Experiment in Old-Fashioned 3-R's." But the headlines did not reflect with total accuracy the news stories they covered. In one case, for example, the text of the story accurately reported: "The Superintendent insisted the type of instruction to be offered at Amidon would not represent a return to the pre-

Dewey days. . . the instruction will be an adaptation of the best that is known."; and other stories stated the purpose accurately as: to teach the basic subjects in a systematic and rigorous manner.

Within a very short time, the number of applications exceeded the space allocated for the opening year. By predetermination, the Amidon enrollment for that year was set at 455, although the school has a capacity of 806. One reason for doing this was that space was needed for children moving into the Amidon district as new houses and apartments were built. Secondly, because children from throughout the city were to be brought together for the first time, it seemed sensible to keep the number at a workable level to be sure that the necessary orientation of pupils to their new surroundings would occur with a minimum of misunderstanding and friction.

Thus the number to be admitted from outside the school boundaries was to be 267, which added to the local children was expected to bring the total to 455. The actual enrollment, however, at times exceeded 470. By the time school opened with its specified complement of pupils, more than 200 pupils were on the waiting list for admission. By December, 601 applications had been received, but very few new pupils could be admitted because transfers from the school were infrequent.

Method of Selection

After the new principal was assigned to the school, she made up her mind to interview the parents who wanted their children enrolled in the school. She had two reasons for this: (1) She wanted to know the parents and the child before either accepting the child or placing him in a grade, and (2) she wanted to be sure that parents were aware of the kind of school Amidon was to be, so that they would know what to expect and could consider very carefully before making a final decision. During the spring and summer months, the Amidon principal scheduled interviews, carefully and helpfully guiding parents, and assigned their children to classes by achievement level and personality characteristics so that grouping could contribute to their success in school. This process is not unique, since all good elementary school principals try to do the same thing with incoming children. But there is no doubt at all but that the time and care given to this procedure accounted for a most efficient and orderly school opening in September.

When I visited the Amidon at ten minutes after nine on the opening day of school, I saw all the classes already at work, as if the teachers and pupils had been together for a long time. The opening day was a test of the efficiency of management, not of the Amidon idea, as it always is in any school. On this test, the principal and her teachers rated an A+, and, because the school was a natural news source, the newspapers accorded this excellent staff well-deserved accolades.

Analysis of Pupil Membership by Sending Schools

The cosmopolitan character of the pupils who entered the Amidon becomes clear from an analysis of the schools they previously attended. Early in the fall of 1960, a survey showed that the 469 pupils then enrolled in the Amidon School came from 110 different schools. The tabulation of the different sending schools is as follows:

SCHOOLS FROM WHICH AMIDON CHILDREN TRANSFERRED

Nursery schools	8
Private schools in the District of Columbia	9
Parochial (church) schools in the District of Columbia	8
Public schools in the District of Columbia	64
Schools from other parts of the country	16
Schools in foreign countries	5
Total	110

When the enrollment of the same date was analyzed as to source, the varied backgrounds of the pupils who entered the Amidon School are shown.

NUMBER OF PUPILS FROM EACH SOURCE

From home into kindergarten or first grade	71
From private nursery schools	9
From parochial schools in the District of Columbia	18
From private schools in the District of Columbia	10
From public schools in the District of Columbia	334
From schools in other parts of the country	21
From schools in foreign countries	6
Total	469

With the foregoing facts in mind, it is clear that our Amidon students were not homogeneous in backgrounds. The differences in their backgrounds made the school a good laboratory for the pupils, because they could learn much from each other. But this factor cannot be construed as an advantage for teaching: Heterogeneity of backgrounds increases the difficulty of administration and instruction. Time and experience in working together are always needed to develop a class and school unity which improve the conditions for teaching.

An encouraging aspect of the public response to the Amidon offering is the number of pupils transferred from non-public schools. Parents often express dissatisfaction with public education by enrolling their children in such schools. When they do so to obtain a higher quality of education rather than the unique contribution of the private schools—such as, for example, education in religion—the public schools suffer from the loss of support and the stimulation for improvement which the dissatisfied parent will supply. Although I am of the opinion that non-public schools are essential to the public good for their special advantages, one of which is that they often set high standards against which to measure the quality of education in the public schools, they should be used by parents who want and can afford them rather than as a protest against public education. I have in mind as a goal the attainment of standards of service in public education equal to those in most non-public schools, except possibly for the exceptional and very costly private establishment. To paraphrase Dewey on this point, any public school should be as good as the most concerned parent wants and can afford for his child. The fact that a large number of parents placed their children in the Amidon rather than continue them in non-public schools indicates their desire for the strength of a basic education curriculum.

To illustrate the parents' views on this question, I recall a conversation with a mother of an Amidon pupil during a meeting of parents and teachers at the Amidon School. "This school gives us what we wanted when we sent our daughter to a private school last year," she said. "Our child asked us how much tuition we were paying to send her to the Amidon. When we told her we did not have to pay tuition because it is a public school, she said, 'I thought you would have to pay, because this school is better than the one I went to last year.'"

Distribution of Pupils by Race, Occupation of Parents, and Achievement Levels

In October, 1960, more than 70 percent of the Amidon pupils were non-white, and of these all but a few were Negro. The percentage of non-white pupils was only slightly less than the city non-white ratio, which was slightly less than 80 percent in the same month. Because of residential factors, a number of Washington schools are all-Negro and all-white. In other schools the proportions of Negroes or white pupils may run from less than 10 percent to more than 90 percent. The point is that while the total school enrollment is 80 percent Negro, this is by no means the typical distribution. While the Amidon proportion of Negro and white pupils is therefore consistent with the city-wide proportion, this distribution is not actually typical.

The presence of both Negro and white pupils in the school was taken for granted by the parents, who accepted the arrangement as natural and good. They applied for the admission of their children voluntarily, showing that if they had any reservations about integration, these were discounted in their desire to obtain the kind of education the Amidon promised to offer. At the risk of inserting an irrelevant point here, I want to emphasize that parents want above anything else top-notch education for their children. If they are given assurance of this, their anxieties about desegregation will lessen and shortly disappear. With its voluntary membership, the Amidon is a demonstration of this point.

As to occupations of parents, the distribution is as follows:

Professional	77
Public Service	112
Skilled workers	116
Unskilled workers	23
Domestic workers	8
Housewives	157
Unemployed	9

The records the pupils brought with them to the school and parent interviews with the principal served to guide the placement of pupils in classes. In the third grade, for example, one class was composed of pupils who were rather severely retarded in reading as was indicated by the level of the reading materials they could use. Two basic classes were established for about 36 pupils who were indicated in the record to be severely mentally handicapped. As in most school systems, the school enrollment throughout the city includes children who need placement in smaller classes with specially trained teachers. The Amidon was no exception to this rule.

It became clear even without a total program of testing that achievement levels varied so widely that ability grouping was required. In this respect the Amidon pupils were typical of the total school enrollment.

Parent enthusiasm for the education of their children was uniformly high particularly among those who took the trouble to bring their children to the school, often very long distances. From the outset, the support of most of the parents was complete and extremely helpful. But to say that this is unique is to disregard the fact that in many schools, especially in the more stable communities, parents also are intensely interested in the education of their children. In fact, this city is noted for the vitality and spirit of its parent-teacher associations.

GUIDES TO THE CARE AND TREATMENT
OF PUPILS

Here I want to set out some ideas about the management of pupils, not so much from a pedagogical as from a guidance point of view. But don't expect to encounter here the erudition in the guidance field that you would expect from a specialist. What I have come to think about pupils is generally the result of experience, observation, and some objectives or goals which seem to me to be important. These are suggestions I would recommend to the staff of the Amidon and, for that matter, to the staff of any school in the District of Columbia.

An analysis of these recommendations will show that under the Amidon concept the characteristics of the pupil must be understood and taken into account as a part of the teaching-learning process. The use of organized subject matter and direct instruction, including effective testing to measure progress, and a study of the pupil's needs, abilities, and personal background must be integrated into teaching. One without the other is incomplete, just as an automobile would be rather useless if it lacked either a motor or a steering wheel.

1. Information about a pupil should be accurately recorded and sensibly used, but the record should not be considered a substitute for teacher judgment. If you are a teacher who has examined many detailed reports on pupils, you must have been as disgusted as I have been many times with the sententious comments about their personalities and the clutter of dogmatic I.Q. and achievement test scores.

The child's record is not the child. Sometimes the record prejudices the teacher against the child. It is better for the teacher to become acquainted with him as a person than to become confused by recorded details about him. These are never as trustworthy as a compassionate and sensitive respect for him.

The worst possible use of information about a pupil is to consider it as a fixed and reliable determinant of what to teach him and what to expect of him—and the nadir in this respect is to gossip about a child's characteristics in social situations. That these things are sometimes done is illustrated in a letter I received from a prominent local physician. In this communication he reported that he had recently heard teachers at a social gathering openly discussing children's I.Q.'s. He stated that, during what the doctor described as "gossipy" conversation, one of the teachers agreed to look up the I.Q.'s of children of a neighbor. In another case, he overheard a teacher say that she had been impressed by the ability and social adjustment of a new pupil, but after she found out that his I.Q. was only 110 she said, "I cannot grade him as an outstanding student now."

The writer of the letter concluded: "I believe that the purpose of the I.Q. is neither one of entertainment nor a short cut to the classification of the student."

2. The recorded information about a pupil should be carefully screened.

Sometimes teachers make notations on a pupil's record that seem to originate in anger. If this is the case, the whole record is of little value. At any rate, it should be used by the new teacher with a grain of salt. In fact, a good principal always reviews what teachers put on pupil records, and will refuse to accept acrimonious comments.

A good question to ask is: "How accurate does the information about a pupil's characteristics appear to be? Is the information objective, restrained, significant?"

On one pupil's record brought to my attention, a teacher wrote that he was "malicious, brutal, dishonest, a gangster-type, dangerous."

Evaluations of children's behavior as placed on permanent records should be always constructive. The record should never be used to put the child on trial as if he were a wrong-doer before the bar of justice. The needs of the child should be conservatively indicated, but a catalog of his weaknesses may seem to leave little to build on. When examining a pupil's record, a teacher should have an eye out for strengths upon which to build.

3. The principal should provide the teacher with a summary of salient characteristics on every pupil before the opening day of school.

The principal is primarily responsible for placing a pupil in a classroom. To do this with judgment, she needs to know each pupil as well as she can, using the cumulative record and her own personal knowledge of the child to form a conclusion about placement. To know the pupil she should also know his parents.

Bringing the pupil and the right teacher together is the most important responsibility a principal has. Even in large schools where she may have the help of a counselor or assistant principal, she ought to take personal charge of pupil placement.

The summary of the pupil's significant characteristics should include an estimate of his achievement level in the basic subjects, his apparent ability as shown by mental age and teacher opinion, the strong points of personality development and the significant problems in his way of relating to others and in meeting difficult problems, health strengths and weaknesses, such as sight or hearing weaknesses, and the factors in his home situation which help or hinder his education in school.

In such a record, estimates should be understood to be flexible and probable rather than fixed and infallible. When the teacher uses the record to plan her teaching, she should be aware of its tentative nature, and thus feel authorized to substitute her own evaluations as she begins to work with the pupil.

4. *The slow-learning pupil should be identified and favorably placed for instruction before he experiences excessive frustration in standard classes.* The school should provide for the education of the slow learner within the comprehensive elementary or high school. Separation in classes or by subjects is needed. If the teaching is vigorous, basic, and well-planned, the slow learner will achieve academically, and may be able to progress to more difficult levels of instruction. Only in the most exceptional cases should pupils be assigned to separate schools. To do so tends to limit their experiences and reduce their opportunities for transfer to a higher curriculum level. In every case, it must be remembered that these pupils are capable of learning and therefore teaching must be maintained at the level of the greatest challenge.

Failure to plan a strong program in the basic subjects for the slow learner is an all too common occurrence. I am aware of cases where the principal will shunt them into off-center classrooms where they are isolated from the main stream of school activity. They are sometimes given a daily fare of disjointed and undirected experiences in manual work that amounts only to custodial treatment until they are old enough to leave school. On this point a mother wrote a telling but quite illiterate letter in which she pleaded for a more substantial program for her son. She said in effect, "I don't want him to spend all his time cutting things out with scissors. I want him to learn to read."

The slow learner requires a degree of specialized teaching. He will need to learn by application to concrete use. He may not be able to apply the rule that a verb must agree in number to new situations, but he can learn that with "we" the words "are," "were," and "have" will be used. He is likely to have a short attention span, so that lessons must be simple and short. He may be lethargic or stolid in his responses to ideas, but he has the same emotional wants as any other pupil. He can show interest, respond to praise, react to ridicule, be hurt by repeated failure. Possibly unresponsiveness is something learned from repeated rebuffs by parents, playmates, classmates, and teachers. More than in any other case, education for the slow learner becomes a drawing-out from a reserved and walled-in personality the responses that brighten the human spirit. Finally, the slow learner needs the security of knowing what is expected of him. Hence, careful lesson planning with programed learning stages is a necessity. There can be no choice on this: They learn when they are taught in well-defined lessons.

I believe it is extremely important to reconsider our traditional definition of the slow learner. First, I dislike having him labelled as mentally handicapped. This implies a crippling and incomplete mental development. For him as an individual, life must not be pursued as if he were suffering from a deformity. It ought to be a complete and whole life within the range of his intellectual powers.

The common practice is to identify the slow learner as one who is seriously retarded in language, generally in reading, speech, and writing. In identifying the slow learners for special instruction in areas of academic retardation, the schools should not make the mistake of believing it to be an automatic sequel of this condition that they are also retarded in social, physical, and emotional growth.

Labelling, grouping, and administering a special instructional program should be consistent with the identified areas of retardation. It should be said of a student, "He is a slow learner in mathematics or in reading, or both," rather than simply identifying him in a general sense as a slow learner. It is important to keep in mind as well that in the context of the student's total personality, the condition of being a slow learner may be only a temporary one, if the causes are found and can be corrected.

It follows, therefore, that when educators talk about slow learners they refer rather commonly to those who for one reason or another have difficulty learning to read, write, and compute. It does not always follow, however, that these students are retarded as to physical or social or emotional growth. Actually, they may be advanced in other skills, as in physical activities, or in social and leadership competencies. They may be able to exert unusual influence upon others, as in the example of a gang leader who dropped from school because he was not able to do the required work.

The condition of slow learning may prevail in important areas other than the academic, but our traditional preoccupation with this facet of education has prevented the necessary study of such problems. No one, for example, who is average in reading is considered a slow learner if he is excessively retarded in the use of a hammer and saw, although this may be symptomatic of an emotional retardation which may later nullify other skills.

A student may be severely retarded in social attitudes, for example, his skill in getting along with people, and yet be quite successful in academic studies. He may be brilliant in mathematics but irresponsible and even amoral. He may be highly capable in reading but incapable of singing.

The avoidance of categorical thinking about slow learners is highly necessary to assure (1) greater refinement of identification, (2) a more careful assessment of needs, and (3) the development of a program of instruction directed toward those needs. The educational program should also provide for development of gifts other than academic. It should certainly lead to the elimination of retardation in the basic subjects when these are the result of bad teaching or improper motivation.

We need always to be aware of the fact that a student may be a slow learner because this has become a way of life for him. Slow learners are sometimes made, not born. The school program may have contributed to this development. It certainly must work to avoid doing so and give the identified slow learner an improved chance for learning.

5. *The pupil's needs and characteristics are guides to instruction rather than reasons for pessimism about his educability.*

When a pupil enters a class, he brings with him the characteristics which nature (his biological heritage) and nurture (his environmental influences) have produced. The schools sometimes become too deeply involved in tracing the causes of the characteristics of pupils, thus making the classroom a cheap imitation of a laboratory in experimental psychology. Under sensible direction, however, the school can learn about the genesis of behavior, and with this information more readily accept the child as he is when he enters the classroom. From this point, professional and balanced preparation can be made to improve his behavior, a term, by the way, I am using in the broader sense to mean all that an individual does as a human being rather than in the sense of behavior as good or bad in a moralistic sense.

Understanding the basic cause of unusual behavior helps the teacher to accept and work with a pupil who might otherwise be unconsciously rejected. To illustrate:

A third grade boy came to school one Monday morning in a sullen and rebellious mood. Normally difficult, on this particular morning he was unusually hostile, discourteous to the teacher, aggressive and disruptive during most of the morning. When the class was dismissed for the noon recess, the teacher talked to the boy about his attitude. With patience and kindliness, for she never matched anger with anger, the teacher won the boy's confidence. He then told her that on the Sunday before his father had "beat up" his mother, brother, and sister because he was angry at his sister for something wrong that she had done. The violence of the father, the injustice of his actions, even though the boy was not included in the punishment, caused the boy to be antagonistic and hostile in school the next morning. It is sad but true that teachers often say that many children are disturbed on Monday mornings because of family conflicts or overstimulating activities during the weekend. "It takes most of Monday to get a class settled down," one teacher told me.

Another illustration of the importance of accepting children as they are when they come into the classroom and then trying to get an understanding of causes of exceptional behavior is the case of a fourth grade boy who at times almost exploded into erratic, uncontrollable behavior. He did such things as suddenly bounding from his seat, running pell-mell into the hall or the cloak closet, or laughing aloud without apparent reason, or making irrational remarks. The teacher and principal were unable to find an explanation for this behavior from the record or through psychological examinations until the teacher became aware of the boy's unusual preoccupation with foods, especially candy, of which he seemed always to have a supply. She suggested a further physical examination which, because of the information about the boy's desire for sweet foods, included a check on blood sugar level. It was discovered that the boy was the victim of diabetes, thus needing medication and diet for its control.

Teacher attitudes toward pupils must be mature, sensible, and helpful, and never condemnatory, even where the behavior pattern is so bad that the pupil must be assigned to special placement. Upon inquiry, a teacher will find that even when a pupil directs his rebellious behavior toward her, this is not really a personal affront. In the treatment of these cases, the teacher must always conduct herself in a professional manner.

A critical educational problem is the lack of preparation for learning with which many children begin schooling. No one should discredit teachers for this condition, but unless strenuous efforts to obtain needed resources are made by the community under the leadership of the schools, criticism is very much in order. Many of these children will be the problem learners, the dissatisfied, unhappy, frustrated youngsters of later school periods, the early school leavers, and to some extent, the delinquents. It is clear that the problem requires maximum resources at the early elementary stage for the benefit of the community as well as the individual children.

There are two approaches to this persistent educational problem. *The first* is to improve the factors which condition children for school experiences. As has been said, many children enter the schools with severe cultural and emotional handicaps. The alleviation of this problem may not be expected solely from the schools. A total community attack is urgent if the educational disabilities suffered by many children are to be removed.

The second approach to the problem, however, the schools can do much about. They can improve the quality of education by better teaching, better curriculum organization, concentration upon essentials, and the provision of improved services at all levels.

The purpose of education is to improve the quality of human behavior. This objective does not presuppose that when a pupil comes to school he must conform to a common set of standards for behavior. It does mean the transformation of human action steadily and by degrees into something better than it was before. Therefore, growth in good directions is relative to the starting point; that is, improvement is related to preceding behavior.

A fundamental concept in American education is that every pupil should have a place in school where his behavior can be improved. Teachers must accept the pupil with optimism about the improvability of behavior. Principals must plan for a placement in classes which will be most favorable to growth. The school system, including the supporting community, must provide a variety of programs and services to make favorable placement possible. Encouraged by community agencies, parents must reassume their time-tested responsibilities for providing a suitable home environment for their children.

chapter four

THE TEACHER IN THE AMIDON

PROGRAM

NO MATTER HOW SOUND THE METHOD OF TEACHING AND THE
system of curriculum organization, nothing can be accomplished
unless the teacher in the classroom has the right feeling for children.

Shortly after the Amidon plan was announced, a teacher from
a midwestern city called me at home. "I want," she said, "to teach
in the Amidon School. I believe in this way of teaching." The
encouragement implied in this statement almost caused me to invite her to submit an application at once. As she talked further,
however, I lost interest in encouraging her to come to Washington.
The cause of my disinterest in the applicant was the sharpness of
her voice, the harshness toward children reflected in her point
of view, a seeming rigidity and an obvious misinterpretation of
the meaning of the Amidon idea. It seemed to me that she lacked
the feeling for people that is essential to the humane purposes of
a good school program no matter what its principle of organization may be. It is unfortunate that many people think that a well-
defined curriculum, emphasis on basic subjects, and a demanding
system of teaching are to be equated with harshness, the dunce
cap, and the birch rod.

Those who believe that children should be made to learn, or
else, the "else" being physical or mental punishment, have gotten
onto the wrong band wagon if they believe the Amidon concept
is the answer to their demands. On the other hand those who be-

lieve that the school is primarily a mental health facility often seem to take the position that education for basic learning requires the teacher to pour learning into a pupil the way milk is poured into a pitcher, and that the milk is a combination of reading, writing and arithmetic. They also fail to understand the meaning of the Amidon concept.

It is very important, then, to discuss the teacher and the kind of teaching to be associated with the development of the Amidon concept. By this means the juncture of subject matter and teaching appropriate to the characteristics of the child will be further demonstrated, and judgments as to the value of the Amidon concept will be more intelligent.

THE SENSITIVE TEACHER

Sometimes people ask me, "If you were to name the most important attribute of the good teacher, what would it be?"

My answer is always: "Sensitivity. The good teacher is constantly aware of what is happening in her relationship with pupils and in their relationships with others in her class. Awareness of pupil responses, overt or concealed, indicates that a teacher cares about her pupils."

The next question is generally this: "Do you put sensitivity above intellectual capability, scholarship, and industry?"

In this is illustrated, of course, the error of assuming that the possession of one gift somehow seems to exclude all others. The good teacher must possess all these attributes: sensitivity, intellectuality, scholarship, industry, moral values. But unless she has sensitivity, then the other qualities are misplaced in the classroom. They are better used in a research laboratory or in the accounting department of a bank.

We Need Teachers Who Care

An elementary school supervisor had completed a year on her new job. "What is most needed to improve the quality of education in our schools?" I asked her. Without hesitation she replied, "Greater concern for each child on the part of teachers." She expanded her point by adding that while many teachers do care about children, some are unable to feel kindly toward difficult or unbrushed or poorly-mannered children. They neglect them, and without a word being spoken their attitudes convey their feelings to the child, who, she pointed out, has very delicate antennae for picking up such signals. "We need," she summed up, "more teachers who care."

The Indispensable Element in Teacher Qualification

Within a few days following the conversation with the elementary school supervisor, I interviewed 15 teachers who were candidates for elementary principalships in our school system. Each candidate was asked the following question:

Among three characteristics which every teacher should possess, which is the indispensable one?

1. She should have intellectual and cultural competence.
2. She should have concern for others, that is, warmth and sensitivity.
3. She should be industrious and diligent.

Except for one applicant, they decided after careful thought that concern for others is the indispensable characteristic. They reasoned that a good teacher must care about the pupil no matter how unprepossessing that pupil may be, how unattractive his presence, how uninvigorating his mental processes. Unless she does, other qualities that she may possess such as intelligence, integrity, and diligence are useless. "The latter can be acquired," most of the teachers said, "but feeling for children can't be gotten from outside the individual. It is something innate in the personality. If it is lacking, the individual should work at something that doesn't require him to put up with young people and their various idiosyncrasies."

"A good teacher has got to care, really," said one.

Although one of my more sardonic associates said during the interview, "Put the brains in the secondary schools and the heart in the elementary schools," I believe "heart" is the indispensable element in any classroom.

What the Sensitive Teacher Can Do

The sensitive teacher is not a "softie," not a maudlin sentimentalist. The teachers chosen for the Amidon demonstration were the kind that knew what they were about; they saw children as human beings, neither as paragons nor as wicked creatures with a natural disposition toward evil. The importance of the teacher's feeling toward children can be demonstrated from actual experience.

I want for every classroom in our city schools, whether or not of the Amidon type, a sensitive and perceptive teacher.

1. *Like this one:*

She taught fifth grade. One of her boys was consistently tardy. Admonitions, threats, and pleading failed to correct this condition. Then the teacher visited the boy's home to see if she could find the reason that so far had escaped her attention. In the home, obviously in dire economic circumstances, she found an invalid mother. The boy prepared the meals, took care of other household responsibilities in the morning, and attended to all the needs of the mother before he left for school. With the support of the principal, the teacher found help for the boy and the mother, and far better than punishment, this eliminated the tardiness. Besides, she looked upon the boy with a respect she had not had before. In fact, she felt humble in his presence, a condition a teacher will usually find ways to conceal.

2. *Or this one:*

A few years ago a German boy entered a fifth grade class in one of our schools. Painfully shy, unable to speak English, rejected by the other children, he was unhappy and miserable in his new situation. The teacher suggested to the class that perhaps the new boy would be willing to teach them German, which he knew so well, if they asked him to. Enthusiastically the class invited the new boy to teach conversational German while they in exchange taught him English. The transformation in the behavior of the boy was almost immediate. His classmates wanted him to help them. He was no longer a foreigner, a stranger to them. He was a person of importance.

3. *Or this one:*

A fourth grade teacher rejoiced over a paper written by one of her slow fourth grade boys because she felt that her pupil revealed a gift of appreciation usually hidden by his inability to express himself. "Spring" is the title of this composition:

> "I have not seen a robin yet.
> Flowers can be real pretty sometimes.
> The breeze feels good, don't it?
> It's very warm today.
> Boy, that sounds good, don't it?
> Randy is singing good.
> Look at the flower buds.
> The grass is turning green.
> Spring *is* a season."

A sensitive teacher will react to this with enthusiasm. The insensitive one will return it to the boy with complaints about faulty grammar and lack of logical consistency. My choice for any classroom: the teacher who can exult over a paper like this from a "slow" fourth grade pupil. This kind fits into the Amidon plan. In fact, the chances are she will get a great deal more writing from a boy like this because she sees something of value in everything he composes.

4. *Or this one, respect with love:*

One of the Amidon parents told of how her son's teacher had the respect and love of the children. "To combine the two is a great accomplishment," she wrote. "My son expressed it well when he said that his teacher had a good sense of humor *at lunch time*. She could relax with them yet have the necessary control."

The Amidon plan includes this kind of pupil-teacher relationship. It is the kind that assures the control in the classroom which is the beginning of good teaching. This is achieved with the love and affection of the children, who want order with love, who abhor uncontrolled activity in a classroom.

The teachers that pupils remember are always those who held them to high performance but handled them with fairness. Pupils have two great characteristics: they honor and respect strength and they love justice.

5. *Or this one, which tops them all:*

The teacher to whom a fourth grade child wrote at the end of the school year: "I know that I am mean and destructive, but I know that you love me anyhow."

Our objective in the Amidon, as in all of our schools, is the development of an abiding respect for one's fellow man. To accomplish this is highly important: first, because with the increasing interdependence of man, social stability is otherwise impossible; second, because learning cannot take place when a pupil is insecure and fearful; and third, because the ethics of our culture system require respect for the integrity of person as a moral and spiritual duty.

The system of public education which has evolved in our nation as a part of its history is perhaps our most unique and important contribution to the human welfare. Nothing so enhances the spirit of man as the fulfillment of his potential, whether this be high or low, and no single agency except the family has so much responsibility in this regard as the schools of this nation.

If we look closely we will see that most teachers who work with children in the schools believe that theirs is a mission of great moral and spiritual significance. They can do no better than to follow the precept that love is the surest foundation for moral and spiritual growth. Because a good teacher loves even the least promising of her pupils, education is both constructive and redemptive. I must let no opportunity pass to say that this principle must be included in the Amidon concept. It is easily identifiable in the school as it is now in operation. In this you see, we are not only talking theory. We are describing practices to show that the kind of education the Amidon stands for requires sensitivity and concern, and should never be misjudged on this point.

More Than Concern Is Needed

To be sure that no misunderstanding may follow our strong emphasis upon concern as the indispensable characteristic of the teacher, I should say at once that this in itself is not enough. Without it, there is nothing. But it does not follow that with it there is everything. To be uncultivated is to be unprepared for teaching. This idea is not to presuppose artificiality or a lack of genuineness. Cultivation, intellectuality, interest in ideas—these are best expressed in the teacher without showiness, the way one may wear handsome clothes without ostentation.

Something in the public respect for teachers suffers when faults of scholarship are advertised in neon lights, as will sometimes happen. Take as an instance the elementary teacher, who wrote the parent of her sixth grade boy that he needed to improve his spelling. Part of her letter follows:

> "I am distressed at Edward's spelling score, so am enclosing it. I'd suggest a *consentrated* program for spelling homework for a while. Thank you again for your *generousity.*"

Then, consider the mural on the bulletin board of a classroom with this caption in eight-inch letters. "Wheels Helps Us."

Following is an example of the effect upon a pupil of a lack in teacher preparation.

> One of the boys in a class for slow learners in our elementary schools was asked to go to the teacher of another class to take a standardized test which he had missed in his own classroom because of absence.
>
> He objected. He told his own teacher, "I don't want to take a test in that teacher's room. I can't understand his country talk."
>
> When I inquired into the problem, I found that the teacher's diction was so poor that his speech was almost unintelligible to his pupils.

A slip of the tongue with international implications occurred when the officials in charge of two different schools made the same mistake. Two brothers, one in an elementary and the other in a junior high school, were being transferred back to their homes abroad, after their father had completed his mission here. The school transfers read: "To Ceylon, India." "An inexcusable mistake," a college professor wrote me. "The children were embarrassed, their father was more amused than hurt, and their American friends were ashamed." So there it is—the teacher and school officer need to maintain a fairly active intellectual pace just to keep abreast of affairs.

Although no one should try to teach without a good academic background, the community does not now look upon its teachers as scholars. It thinks of teachers chiefly as guides and counselors. The idea of the schoolmaster as a deeply learned man (I use the word in a generic sense) has never become deeply rooted in American public education. The image of the teacher in his own study, with time for learning as well as for the duties of the classroom, can hardly take shape in the public mind when, for example, his pay is not as good as that of a truck driver, and the workload of the teacher continues to be excessive. Permanence in the profession is generally for those who can't do anything else as well or who prefer to teach above all else even if they have to drive a taxi part-time to do it. (In one year 13 teachers in our school system did just this.)

The Amidon concept does not guarantee quality teaching. It will sharpen the quality of the work of those now in the classroom, but it will not produce the professional teacher, the scholar, the intellectual in continuous pursuit of wisdom, the enthusiast for learning, the compassionate guide to better things for every pupil in a classroom, the career teacher whose life is teaching.

Putting ordered, substantial, and stimulating subject matter into the curriculum may attract competent young students into teaching. It may help to hold them, if the *what* of teaching is sustained as significant and if, in the *how to teach* aspect of classroom work, the role of the teacher is given importance. To some degree teaching will attain a more respectable status when the Amidon concept is employed in a school system. But its adoption is not likely to correct the deficiencies in teacher preparation or improve the capabilities of those who elect to teach.

The Motivation of Learning

Because learning cannot take place without motivation, this element is not neglected, although it is not peculiar to the Amidon concept.

Motivation is a complex attitudinal characteristic in the human personality. It underlies everything we do, even though it may be at the unconscious level. The purposes which support behavior, either inner or externally observable, are frequently so indefinable as to be beyond identification. Yet some inner drive or need, even if simply physical, activates all human behavior.

As applied in teaching, motivation is used in a narrower sense. It is generally thought of as a reason for learning, as good in purpose and direction, and as capable of being aroused in a planned direction by the teacher.

It is well known that a pupil's purposes in school are the product of all he has been, including the influences of his natural endowments and his experiences from the womb on. Because purposes are modifiable, however, the school is obligated to shape them into acceptable forms and to stimulate an active search for their realization by the pupils. If the time ever was that education consisted primarily of dishing up a bill of fare and expecting pupils to light into it with gusto, then the record ought to show that the Amidon concept does not include this kind of arbitrary separation between pupil and subject matter. Rather, it demands a clear and effective attention to motivation, and its correlatives which are interest, meaning, and purpose.

Success is the best motivator. The fisherman soon puts his lures away if repeated tries produce no fish. My golf clubs gather dust because of the unpredictable ways golf balls act when I hit them. Unscientific as these examples are, I am convinced in an analagous way that *success in school subjects is the best motivation*. In fact, without it motivation becomes negative and will cause aggressive rejection of school.

As has been said, one of the principal characteristics of the Amidon concept is definiteness in curriculum, so that what is to be learned is, at least in a basic way, spelled out for the pupil. No fuzzy and unrestricted roaming for undefined facts and elusive ideas is to be found when the Amidon system is fully developed. The teachable elements of subject matter are carefully selected, although these are undergoing continuous and searching study. Hence, the student knows what is expected of him, and that he is to be taught with a direction and a certainty which will help him to be successful in doing what is expected of him.

I must interject here my impressions of the Amidon pupils at work, which will be developed in greater detail later as a part of the evaluation of this project.

The visitor will note an unusual calm in the school, in classroom, in corridor, with pupils at all the elementary ages seeming to have an assurance and a quiet efficiency that stem, in part, from the fact that they learn as they go along and are successful in accomplishing their work. There is a freedom from tension, stress, and anxiety that is notable in the frenzy of the activity-centered classroom. The evidence supports the view that if a pupil succeeds at his classwork, whether in phonics, grammar, or science, he becomes self-assured, confident, and motivated to continue to do his lessons and all other things expected of him in the classroom. Good teaching and definite content contribute to pupil success, and are the strongest motivations which the classroom can supply.

Even more than this, the child who may not be normally moved to strong effort by his home background will, if successful in the classroom, grow by this means into a motivated pupil who will rise above his beginnings. This is the essential genius in American education. Our nation has achieved greatness because so many of its youth have obtained in the classroom the good taste of accomplishment which was attainable nowhere else. It is the purpose of the organized direct teaching of the Amidon plan to make this kind of experience available to every pupil, rather than to leave it to the chance that the teacher will on her own initiative substitute order and logic for the confusion of an impromptu curriculum.

A Teacher Can Demotivate

The opposite of motivation, which is a shorthand term for purpose, is demotivation, a process that influences behavior against the acceptable objectives of instruction. This is more than simply a failure to generate enthusiasm for the work of the classroom. It is a cause which generates behavior running counter to the achievement of "good" objectives of classroom management.

Sometimes the indifference of the teacher to the presence of a pupil can destroy the effort to participate and the will to succeed. The ways in which teacher indifference is displayed are myriad. The tone of voice, the inflection in an exchange of speech between teacher and pupil, the faraway look when the pupil is speaking, the lift of an eyebrow at what to the teacher seems to be a stupid statement by the pupil, a quick change in facial expression as the teacher shifts his attention to a pupil whom he obviously respects—these are examples of the innumerable telltale signs of disrespect which may be communicated to the timid, insecure, inadequate youngster whose intuitive sensitivity to those symbols of communication is often far more sharp than is usually believed. The result is a degree of negative influence that is frightening in its total, irreducable, and continuing effect upon the pupil. In such ways even the teacher who does not wish to do so unconsciously demotivates the unsure and hesitant pupil. She not only destroys the wish to achieve, but implants the causes of negative behavior.

I have described so far only what might be called the aspects of teacher behavior which innocently, and without deliberate or cruel intent, create adverse performance by the pupil. These come from an inner feeling of the teacher who, though consciously wanting to do right by every pupil, is innately unable to accept the poor, the unprepossessing, the unattractive, the difficult-to-love child, of whom, nature being what it is, there are many in any school.

But, in addition to the inadvertent expressions of rejection, overt attacks upon the pupil's spirit occur all too frequently in the classroom. There are appalling instances to illustrate that teachers and even principals often fall short of attaining the objective professional attitude toward the errant child that we have come to expect of the minister, the lawyer, or the physician who must administer to the needs of their clients, whose difficulties often arise from erratic and even immoral behavior. For example, the angry child who has insulted a teacher should not be treated in anger by the principal. It may be that the principal will have to "throw the book" at the child, but if so it should be lobbed in his direction with emotional calm.

Allowing for those times when professional patience is driven to the breaking point (even parents who love a child dearly will sometimes reach such points of stress), the staff of the school should work with each pupil in a professional relationship that is governed by the desire to be of help. But when the actions of teachers and other staff personnel are specifically and aggressively destructive, then the school experience destroys the pupil's chance for success.

In an end-of-school-year conversation, a school social worker told me how an assistant principal forced a troubled ninth grade girl into open rebellion. "I had agreed to try to help a girl whom the psychiatrist had told me was worth saving. After she returned from the hospital for the mentally ill, I did everything I could to help her. She began to get good grades and to be proud of herself. Like so many children, she had been taught to hate herself but she was beginning to see herself in a new light. Then, late in the spring, she was called to the assistant principal's office for a minor violation of the rules, and I went with her to talk over her problem. In a loud and raspy voice, the assistant principal shouted at the girl, "I know all about you. I know your record. I know where you have been. You can't get by with anything with me." Slapping the palm of her hand on her desk, the woman repeated shrilly, "You can't get by with anything with me."

As another example of overt demotivation, consider the eighth grade mathematics teacher who told a boy about midway through the second semester: "No matter what you do, you can't possibly pass." He had had a record of poor performance, but his counselor had given him and his parents much excellent help; the boy had begun to improve his work, and the outcome looked promising. But all was lost when, after some backsliding—which may be expected in these cases, the boy one day spoke insolently to the teacher and she in turn "told him off," as she said.

Afterward, taking the teacher at her word—a fairly intelligent thing to do—the boy gave up trying and, as predicted, failed because he had responded to an act of demotivation by the teacher.

No one knows how much of this goes on in the classroom. The chances are there is a great deal more of demotivation in classrooms and in principals' offices throughout the school system here and in the country as a whole than one would normally surmise. Trust must be placed in school personnel. This is the reason I want to know about how a teacher really feels about pupils before I hire her. This is the reason I want to make it clear that the Amidon concept is built on the bedrock of teacher concern and sensitivity.

Creative Teaching

The great imponderable in teaching is the element of relationship between pupil and teacher, and between pupil and pupil. How the members of the group get along with one another has much to do with the outcome of teaching. The relationships among pupils, the multiple interactions going on constantly within a classroom, are nearly as important as the relationship of pupil to teacher.

In a classroom where the highest type of creative teaching is going on, the visitor is likely to be almost intuitively aware of the absence of tensions. In such a classroom, children, when they speak, use moderate tones with voices seeming to be low-pitched. As the teacher talks, too, you will note an ease of manner and a soft-spoken pattern of speech, the quality of voice being not strained. Freedom from tension is further noted in the way the children move about in the room. Action is measured, purposeful, not fretful, uneven, or impulsive.

In all relationships within the classroom there is an air of confidence. Each pupil is confident of having the good opinion of his classmates. There is no evidence of the fear of ridicule or rejection by one child of another. Each child, too, approaches the teacher in confidence. He has learned that the adult in the room is dependable, friendly, interested, sympathetic.

This is the kind of classroom climate which encourages creativeness. The security in which creative expression flourishes is gained by the effect of an implicit though recognizable authority. In the kindergarten, the authority is centered in the personality of the teacher. In a sixth grade, on the other hand, the authority upon which law and order rests is centered not solely upon the teacher, but also upon the class itself which has learned to accept responsibility for self-management. By the weight of its opinion and attitude the class itself discourages erratic behavior on the part of a member of the group.

The reason for discussing the authority element in a classroom is to make clear that creative teaching does not require freedom from control. Rather, it does need the good relationships which develop when there is a substantial undergirding of authority, at first adult-centered and then increasingly more adult-child-centered as the children mature. There is no tyranny more destructive to creative expression than that demonstrated by children who have been given more freedom than they can handle. In such cases, the only thing created is chaos.

Creative teaching, it seems, is possible only where relationships are good, where freedom exists within a framework of authority, and where there is clear-cut evidence of adult planning. With its reference to order and substance, the Amidon concept provides the initial foundation upon which to build creative behavior.

CHECK LIST OF TEACHING PRACTICES

A check list of practices expected of the teacher using the Amidon concept will include items applicable to teaching under any set of circumstances. They are listed here as a summary of the most important things expected of a teacher.

1. She will learn about her pupils even before the opening of school in the fall. If any pupils are far above or below the average achievement levels of her class she will advise the principal so that better programming may be done.

2. Her study of pupil characteristics will be used to help her select materials and to make lesson plans.

3. She will request textbooks for the whole class in spelling (second grade on), reading, language (composition, usage, grammar), science, mathematics and geography or history. If the pupils average below grade in achievement, the textbooks may be a grade below. If they average above grade, the textbooks may be a grade above level.

4. Each pupil will be issued a textbook in the basic subjects (reading, spelling, language, mathematics, science, and history or geography—fourth, fifth and sixth grades.)

5. Instruction in the use and care of textbooks should be given at the start of each year and repeated as needed.

6. Instruction in study techniques appropriate to each lesson should be given at the start of the year and repeated at least at six-week intervals.

7. The teacher knows the subject matter far beyond the textbook and brings into each lesson plan interpretations, insights, and additional facts which illuminate each subject.

8. The teacher balances pressure for accomplishment with periods of creative activity which provide a change in pace.

9. The teacher encourages personal and group competition without creating embarrassment or despair. (She will not permit a class to laugh at a pupil's mistake in reading, but she may permit pupils to correct and praise each other.)

10. The teacher is sensitive to pupil development, so that criticism and correction are geared to the pupil's capacity to absorb it without giving up.

11. The teacher plans for the teaching of the whole class, for observed study of carefully given assignments, for the checking of papers, for homework.

12. The teacher is firm, but fair, holding to high standards but respecting the integrity of the individual child.

13. The teacher builds routines upon which the pupils may depend, but she also encourages spontaneity and flexibility with balance.

14. Creativity is encouraged in association with techniques. Rules and principles promote rather than inhibit imaginative thought.

15. The teacher never forgets that an important part of what the pupil learns comes from being in her presence, responding to her example, being encouraged or discouraged by her attitude.

Preparation for Teaching

The teacher is responsible for the transmission of culture from one generation to the next. In the light of this duty, she should have a rich background of experience in such fields as literature, art, music, language, mathematics and science. If her undergraduate curriculum is top heavy with *know-how* courses, the teacher may suffer from the lack of *know-what*. The teacher should be a master of the best in our culture system.

Courses in education would improve mightily under the pruning knife. Moreover, what is taught at the undergraduate level, particularly, should be highly functional, another way of saying the content should be useful to the teacher in the classroom. With time made available by reducing the number of credits in education courses, those in languages, literature, mathematics and science should be increased. To be an effective enthusiast for learning, the teacher herself must have had a stimulating intellectual experience as a student. She too is what she is in large measure because of the kind of teaching to which she has been subjected. Heavy academic courses are sometimes stimulating, exciting, evocative. But they may also be taught with all the somberness of the tomb. Nothing in a subject in itself guarantees interest, intelligibility, creative scholarship. The key is generally in the kind of teaching, which, whether good or bad, tends to propagate itself in the works of those who have been taught. Teachers are in a large degree what they are because of what and how they have taught. Their total preparation for teaching heavily influences the quality of education in the classrooms under their jurisdiction.

No matter what the philosophy of education, the realization of it is impossible without good teachers. The philosophy will, of course, determine what is meant by good teaching. To make the Amidon concept workable, teachers are needed whose preparation will support its objectives.

TEACHER PREPARATION FOR THE AMIDON CONCEPT

1. *Concern for others*

Select students for teacher-preparation only if they show capacity for concern for others, including the least attractive personalities with whom they are associated.

Because students often develop a wish to become teachers very early in their school life, their teachers should be helpful to them in guiding their aspirations. In doing so, teachers in service should look first for the personal qualities which promise sympathy and empathy.

Admissions to a teacher education program should include an evaluation of the applicant's concern for others. But by all means avoid the use of the so-called personality tests to measure this characteristic. Consider the views of teachers and adult friends, the applicant's extracurricular activities and his summer experiences. Be prepared to judge the issue in a personal interview with the applicant.

Finally, instructors in liberal arts departments at the college level should do far more than they now do to guide their students to good vocational choices. Such teachers (for this is the title of honor even for the full professor) generally limit their personal interest in their students to those who display a particular flair for their specialty. These may receive a pat on the back and a good word about going on, say, with the study of Latin or biology or law. But it is a rare case when the academic specialist looks over the fence with which he surrounds himself to become interested in other disciplines, the one generally least attractive to him being education.

I am afraid that the only time a liberal arts teacher will advise any one to move over into education is when the student is on the verge of failure. The liberal arts departments of colleges and universities, in fact the professional colleges as well, ought sooner or later to look upon preparation for teaching as a useful, in fact, a most important enterprise to which their contribution is sorely needed.

Many intellectually endowed students in liberal arts and professional courses (other than teaching) have personal qualities which fit them admirably for teaching. Many, I venture to say, might be superior in another profession, but, because of the special attributes looked for in the teacher, be happiest and fruitful in a classroom. Is it not useful to expect that college and university teachers in the academic departments will assume responsibility for improving the lives of such students and the quality of education as well by advising them to consider becoming teachers?

2. *Demonstrated intellectual capacity*

Admit students to teacher preparation courses only if they have demonstrated an intellectual capacity capable of handling difficult academic and technical courses.

If the student is transferring into education courses after work in the liberal arts department of college, he should be admitted only if he has made grades that were at average or above in the basic academic courses. Admission to education courses should be as jealously guarded as it is in medicine, law and engineering.

If the student is entering a four-year teachers college, he should be admitted only if he has successfully completed the college preparatory course in high school. He should have at least four high school years of English (including a semester of speech), two years of science (the laboratory courses such as biology, physics, and chemistry), two years of mathematics (algebra and geometry), two years of a foreign language (modern or ancient), and up to two years in the social studies. The grades in these courses should be average or above and should have been earned in classes with other students capable of doing college preparatory work.

3. *Competence in basic subjects*

Require students preparing for general teaching at the elementary level to become fully prepared in at least these basic subjects:

English, including reading and phonics, composition, literature, speech, handwriting and spelling. Each teacher, whether **at the elementary or secondary level, should be required to take**

at least three semester hours in phonics, including structural analysis of words.

Mathematics, with emphasis upon the integration of arithmetic, algebra, and geometry in the elementary program.

Science, with course work that will prepare the teacher to integrate science (biology, physics, chemistry) into a program of instruction from the kindergarten through the sixth grade.

History and Geography, with special attention to United States history but with sufficient course work in ancient, medieval, and modern world history, occidental and oriental, to assure background and depth for the teaching of history and geography and for heightening the significance of current events. Geography, with competent instruction in that of the United States and in world geography.

4. General courses in art, music, physical education and foreign languages

All teaching aspirants required to pursue studies in music, art, foreign languages, and health and physical education for general education purposes. When the foregoing subjects are included in the elementary school curriculum the subjects should be taught by specialists.

5. Include only how-to courses in education subjects

Include in education courses only those which contribute directly to preparation for the duties of teaching. These should include how to organize classes for instruction, how to plan lessons, how to evaluate instruction, how to test and grade, and how to interpret and control pupil behavior.

Theoretical and general courses such as history and philosophy of education and psychology should be taught in liberal arts departments rather than in the education departments of schools and colleges. Experimental education should never be included in undergraduate teacher preparation, and only at the postgraduate level when part of the preparation is in research. The student preparing to teach should not be allowed to participate in experimental projects, nor should his courses in how-to-teach be confused by the theories of amateur educationists. Many teachers college instructors go directly from graduate training into teacher training without intervening experience. (I would not want to put my family into the hands of a physician educated by instructors who had never practiced medicine.)

What the teacher also needs in his pre-practice training is an internship experience of sufficient depth to get him ready to take over a classroom with some promise of knowing what to do. Thus, education courses ought to be primarily on the level of how-to. The theory and background courses should be taught in the academic departments to groups or classes who plan to enter or are already taking courses in education.

6. Preparing specialists in art, music, physical education, and foreign languages

With greater depth of scholarship being required of elementary teachers under the Amidon plan, the more highly specialized subjects ought to be taught by teachers with special preparation assigned to single, or blocks of, elementary schools. The specialist should teach his subject to classes on regular schedule, while the "generalist" is relieved to work with small groups needing remedial help, or to plan her lessons, check papers, and evaluate her own instruction. This does not suggest full departmentalization in the elementary schools. But the concept of the fully self-contained classroom where the one teacher does everything should join its ancestors. It is the dinosaur-concept of modern elementary education—unwieldy, cumbersome, and inefficient. It could work only in a method of teaching which correlated all the disciplines into a single and pervading unit of instruction, where what the teacher knows makes little difference anyhow because the chances are that the interests developed in units of instruction would by-pass the teacher's knowledge. Hence, she can learn along with the rest, and her effectiveness is not particularly weakened by her own lack of scholarship.

But under the Amidon system, with the attention on scheduled subjects and preplanned instruction in them, the teacher must once again become a master of what she teaches. With this now being demanded of the elementary teacher, some limit must be set to what is to be expected of her. Thus, some specialization is essential, and teacher preparation should reflect this change.

I am inclined to add that my observation is that in our school system, art, music, and physical education are the most poorly taught by the regular teachers. Until we increase the number of specialists so that they may teach pupils on regular schedules, work in these fields will continue to be poor. Foreign language instruction, on the other hand, now offered in the third, fourth, fifth, and sixth grades here, is superb because the teachers, who are specialists, instruct their classes in 20-minute periods daily. While they teach, the general teacher observes and may be learning along with the class or she may work at lesson planning or attending to administrative duties. As I observe this excellent program under specialists in a subject field, I come to the view that, especially in the intermediate grades, there should be an increase in the amount of teaching by specialists, including among the subjects already mentioned those in mathematics and science.

Hence, teacher preparation should provide for the generalist and the specialist in elementary education, with both being especially competent in academic fields. The era of the elementary classroom as a friendly family group with the mother-image in charge is passing. The new elementary classroom is to be a place of work in fundamental education under the direction of teachers who know what to expect in scholarship and who believe they show their love for children best when they motivate them to achieve at their best level.

chapter

five

$\blacksquare$

SUBJECTS IN THE AMIDON CONCEPT

WE MUST CONSIDER THE PURPOSE OF FORMAL AND SYSTEM-
atic education. The classrooms, materials, equipment; the centering together of personnel and pupils; the interrelationships of
parents, teachers, and community, and the interchange of ideas—
all these make up the operation we call formal education. I
think the most significant way to define the purpose of all this
activity is to describe it as the preparation of all youth for effective citizenship.

It seems to me that education for citizenship entails two problems: a definition of education as preparation for effective citizenship and adaptation of this function to the different objectives
and abilities of students who with few exceptions should complete 12 years of formal education.

PREPARATION FOR EFFECTIVE CITIZENSHIP

The content of the modern curriculum must be suited to the
levels of students' needs and abilities. It must also be pertinent
to the needs of the times and have the effect of providing the
basic equipment which will make it possible for the student to
meet new problems as he progresses into adulthood in a changing world.

It is important to say that in a changing society, education
must go beyond—although it must include—fact-finding requirements. It must train in problem-solving methods. It must prepare
for independence in the intelligent solution of unexpected prob-

lems. It must use the most valid information and conclusions, techniques and processes as a means to new ways of life rather than as brakes on the wheels of progress.

Because I so firmly believe that the only way man can be taught to use his powers of intelligence is through the exercise of this gift, I am convinced that the school curriculum should consist largely of those disciplines which provide for the acquisition of facts and experience and subsequent skill in their reasoned use.

It follows, therefore, that out of the unbelievable range and variety of human activities and experiences only a limited number of basic ones can be selected for teaching in the classroom. These should be chosen for their help in making man a rational being able to attack unpredictable problems.

Since thinking for problem-solving is a responsibility that confronts every citizen, to teach for intellectual competence is the primary objective of the schools. The subjects that most directly contribute to reasoned behavior must, therefore, be the central part of the school curriculum. The question is, *what are they?*

Language and number must be included as basic contributors to intelligent behavior. Their use has enabled man to acquire an increasing amount of control over his environment. The language and number systems are the liberating tools, the instruments which free the mind of its natural limitations, give it power to recognize, and skill to solve, problems that emerge in the experiences of the individual.

To these tools of intelligent behavior, that is, language and number, should be added organized subjects which provide backgrounds of information against which new problems have meaning. These are literature, history, geography, science, art, and music.

If the primary aim of education is the maximum intellectual growth of the bright, the average, and the slow, then the basic disciplines must form the central elements of the curriculum for all children. When agreement is reached on this point, two things remain to be done. The first is to schedule these subjects by levels for differences in ability. The second is the selection of what to teach in the basic subjects and where to place this material in different school years.

The first responsibility of the schools is to help each student to attain his highest level of proficiency in reading and speech, and in the use of mathematics. In addition he needs to know and understand many things in science, literature, history, geography, art, and music.

This is an acknowledgment of the importance of teaching the basic skills (*language and number*), the first purpose of organized education. These skills make it possible for the mind to make choices rather than to accept the dictation which is always necessary where ignorance exists. But people differ in many ways: in capacity, in interest, in purposes. Therefore what is taught must be related to the way the individual student is prepared to respond. Because every citizen must be equipped with a functional competence in the basic intellectual skills, the most retarded learner and the most advanced must have their opportunity for intellectual development at their levels of ability. It is a simple truth that if the schools fail to develop skill in reading, writing, and using the number system it is not likely to be acquired by the pupil anywhere else.

Some educators mistakenly believe that a program of learning by doing related to children's needs and abilities precludes systematic arrangement of subject matter. In this, it seems to me, we have the heart of present-day educational controversy, and, I would add, the tragic flaw in the thinking of those who did so much to make the classroom vital and dynamic.

In most fields, teachers need to know where the children have been and where they are going, if they are to plan for them. This can be done only if curriculum guidelines are laid down for each level of instruction.

Why is it so often assumed that the basic subjects are dull, dreary, and abstract? Or that activity units centered on themes, interests (presupposed), or common human needs, like food, clothing, and shelter, or how to get along with one's parents, are always rich, interesting, and meaningful? A valid response is— the teacher is the key. A good teacher can put excitement into the study of grammar. A poor teacher will make a chaos out of an activity unit on the marriage theme. But to say it doesn't matter what your system of curriculum organization is if you have a good teacher is deceptively appealing and yet very incorrect. This is the ratiocination by which the progressives have alibied their failures. When things go wrong, it is the teaching that is at fault. The advocates of the subject-matter emphasis have been equally irresponsible in decrying the importance of method. In their self-righteousness about intellectual materials, they have been unwilling to face the fact that what a teacher does with subject matter makes the difference. Even a great oak can be smothered if too much top soil is thrown around its bole.

Although subject matter, therefore, will be defined and scheduled in this chapter, it should never be thought of in its school setting as separated from method. Too much depends upon how it is presented by the teacher to ignore the techniques of instruction. For convenience, however, it is useful to discuss subjects separately.

BASIC AND CONTRIBUTING SUBJECTS

In the Amidon concept, as I have already said, two subject fields are basic because they furnish the skills which make education possible. These are language and number. In addition, music and the arts as modes of communication may be included as the means of acquiring knowledge, though in the scope of their contribution they do not approach in significance the language of words and of number in applicability to general experience.

Although the arts, particularly the dance (or gesticulations that may be called dancing) and graphic representations of experience (prehistoric drawings on the walls of caves, for example) antedated the development of language, the chief and most universally used means of communication is now language. Hence, because times have changed, the dance, graphic arts, and music, while still ways of communicating, are for most individuals used in leisure hours, and are generally thought of as sources of pleasure, understanding, and meaning not conveyable by other means. To some degree, not nearly enough to be sure, they are used for expression, either in reproduction or in the creation of new literature in these fields.

Therefore, while art and music must always be included in any good school offering, they are not at the center of things to the extent that language is.

LANGUAGE: KEYSTONE IN THE CURRICULUM ARCH

I have so far refrained from using the term *language arts*. I think I can continue to do so out of consideration for those who have a serious antipathy to the label because it seems to mean a fusion of the branches of language into a kind of mass where the parts are indistinguishable. The term implies, I suppose, a combination of language elements into one teaching process, for example, teaching spelling only in connection with composition, or speech only in connection with composition and literature. Although I am certain that all aspects of language have an inter-relationship which is difficult to analyze, that is, to separate into strands or cells, it is advantageous to teach some of the language curricula in separate sections.

For teaching purposes, the logical subdivisions of language are phonics, reading, speech, composition, usage, spelling, hand-writing, grammar, and literature. I would still place listening within each of these subjects rather than as a special course, although lessons to check and develop listening skills may be introduced from time to time. In the same manner I would ask teachers to help develop study skills as a part of their instruc-tion in any subject, although these are properly included as items for instruction in the teaching of reading and composition. Fi-nally, because the quality of language depends almost entirely upon the quality of thought, instruction in language should in-clude the improvement of logic. While it is not likely that any-one would want to add a course in logic at the elementary level, I would want improvement in the organization and evaluation of thought to be a conscious objective particularly in the language curriculum.

One of the important reasons, for example, for the study of the grammar of the sentence is to improve the way thinking is done, both in the formulation and expression of thought and in the interpretation of what others have expressed in speech or writing. The teaching of reading is far more than word analysis; it must contribute to logical interpretation of meaning. Surely writing and speaking are more than anything else lessons in logic. No separate subject in logic is needed. What is needed is a curriculum which points out to the teacher what she can do in this matter. This is one purpose in education that has been far too long overlooked. There is little in a teacher's background that is likely to make her attentive to the most essential of all objectives: the improvement in the logic of thought.

METHOD OF CURRICULUM ORGANIZATION

Before describing the specifics and placement of the language curriculum, I must tell you of the two principles which were followed in the preparation of the material. These concepts are not by any means original with us, though the deliberate and studied application in the Amidon curriculum may be somewhat unusual.

The curriculum guide should define the specific items to be taught but should not include methodology.

I have put a lot of time into curriculum building in my day. I have worked with excellent and imaginative people, especially in the language field. As a result of the prevailing enthusiasm, through these years, the curriculum documents turned out to be charming narratives illustrating how good teaching is done. Although there were statements about general content by grade, including a good chart on the placement of grammar in our elementary language bulletin, the structure of the course became involved with methodology to the disadvantage of both.

As a result of much observation of the use, or the non-use, of these documents, I have come to the conclusion that content and method should be separated. A content guide should be simple, definitive, and specific. I believe a teacher will use such a guide if one is available. She wants to know what she is responsible for teaching in her grade. She would like to know what the teachers before and ahead of her are responsible for. She needs to have information about the continuity, the repetition, the flow of content grade by grade. She ought to be able to tell from the curriculum chart where she introduces an item for the first time and where she reteaches it for mastery and for progression to a higher level of difficulty. At this point, she shouldn't need to learn how to teach. If she does need this, then information should be supplied in separate illustrative documents. Or she should be given help by those whose jobs include helping teachers with their problems. These staff members are the principal and the city-wide supervisors.

For the Amidon, therefore, in the especially designed flow-charts in language, the items to be taught were listed in chart form and separated from the intertwining and sometimes overwhelming verbiage dealing with methodology. I am convinced that this separation of content and method, when applied to all our elementary program, will increase the effectiveness of the material and the efficiency of teaching.

I am, as you will have learned by this time, completely sold on the idea that what is needed most is a clear-cut identification of items to be taught. It doesn't help much to say that the objective of a lesson is to help a pupil to get along better with his neighbors, to become more loyal to his country, to meet his vocational responsibilities with success. Generalities have befogged teacher, pupil, and parent, not to exclude supervisors and superintendents, to the point that everyone has become accustomed to the happy obscurity of purposes and destinations and has achieved a reasonable contentment with this otherwise intolerable condition. Learning takes place, of course, but it is nondirectional, indiscriminate, and light in weight.

Not by any means easy to do, a tough assignment on which the most reasonable minds can disagree, the selection of content item-by-item and placement grade-by-grade are the greatest challenges now confronting scholars and educators. Unless this is done and done well, education in this country will continue to be a hit or miss affair.

The most notable effort to do this is being made by program planners in connection with the use of machines in teaching. When material is programmed for teaching, the item to be learned is first selected and then it is analyzed so that the learner encounters in successive order a series of easy questions, the correct answers to which lead to learning of the larger item. In this manner, not only is what is to be learned carefully selected but the steps to learning it are broken down into small, easily digested parts. I predict that this movement will make its major contribution by leading us away from the present fuzziness of most curriculum goals, even though there is a danger that with the extensive amount of programing required for machine teaching we may go to the other extreme of being too highly mechanical, too fractionated as to detail, with heavy doses of analysis and a small measure of synthesis.

Select Curriculum Items to Reach Specific Behavioral Goals

In the Amidon school the development of curriculum flow charts was undertaken at once. Especially in the language curriculum, the specific items of instruction were tentatively set up in a flow chart for use the first year. This has been further refined, and is a specific listing of what is to be taught by the teacher and the flow or progression of each item grade by grade.

At this point, if it has not already happened, someone will say, "They all do it. Now comes the pedagogical jargon you always find in a book like this." Consider this a warning that what I will be talking about next will seem to be gobbledygook. But I shall nevertheless try to make clear an important conviction I have about the reasons we have schools and all that goes along with them.

This conviction is based upon this series of premises:

1. What a man does counts more than anything as a measure of his personality, his life and works.
2. What man does is evident in his behavior as shown by observable actions or by inaction.
3. The quality and value of behavior is improvable.

From these postulates I draw a conclusion which to me has great meaning: *Education is for the purpose of improving human behavior.*

I then come to the corollary that in selecting what to teach in school we should know how it will contribute to an improvement in behavior. This requires showing a connection between a desired improvement in behavior and what is taught. For example, it is considered good behavior to put a period at the end of a declarative sentence. In this case the connection between behavior and the item to teach is easy to see, and the object of teaching can be easily labeled as a behavioral goal.

Comes herewith a definition to which this discussion was leading: *A behavioral goal is a desired change in the way the pupil acts as a result of what he has been taught.*

I believe that it is a good thing to determine behavioral goals as an inseparable part of the process of selecting what to teach. If such a goal is of little value, items which promote the indicated behavior may be excluded from the curriculum. If there are goals of relatively great value, teaching and reteaching for mastery must therefore be provided to assure the desired improvement in behavior. In some fields the selection of behavioral goals is by no means easy for the reason that our society is not agreed on what is good and desirable.

How can it be otherwise, when, for example, one segment of our national community is crying out against a policy of participation in the United Nations and another strives just as insistently for greater international leadership? Or, when the great labor movement that has led to improved economic conditions for producer and consumer is caught in a crisis of mismanagement and exploitation by some of its own leaders? How can the impact of the social change called integration upon the systems of public education in the several southern states be overlooked as evidence of how a changing society almost inevitably disturbs the equilibrium of public education? If what stands before a mirror changes its form, can the mirror be blamed when what it reflects is also changed?

It has become, furthermore, all too easy to say that a changing society necessitates changing schools. The equation of these two processes has led to false thinking. This concept has become a pet shibboleth among some educators; among others, it has become a stimulus—the way guilt is a stimulus—so that if school leadership does not respond to a seeming demand for change, it chides itself for failure to respond. In the Freudian sense, school leaders become uneasy because of their guilt. Who can ask for stronger motivation?

In accepting the one-to-one value rating of change in society as equal to change in schools, a significant fact is ignored. Changes in society may not in themselves result in basic modifications of human needs and characteristics. Interplanetary travel will not change the human need for love, understanding, presence, being wanted, sharing, participating, or acquiring food, shelter, and clothing. These requisites of the human mind and body have been about the same in every time and age, because the human personality seems to remain constant in its primary qualities.

What is significant about changing society is the change in knowledge, in skills and manipulations, in concepts in respect to time and space, and in respect to peoples and their backgrounds. What is required as a result of this expansion in human knowledge is not necessarily new methodology of teaching, or a scrapping of the traditional organization of schools, but an updating and deepening of content. As an art, reading will not change one iota simply because it deals with space travel facts rather than overland travel in a Conestoga wagon. More of it may be required, but the processes remain the same. The man is the same whether he drives a buggy or pilots a space vehicle. What he needs to know and understand are different.

What the man always needs is the ability to think, adapt, and learn, all of which depend in part on how he has been taught to do these things. Loose, spasmodic, erratic, and superficial curriculum choices should not be the response to the fact of a changing world. Our mistake has been to talk and act in educational affairs as if a changing social order and changing schools produce the same sum. Think about it. Do they? Are they really equivalents?

What is to be selected for teaching in school therefore needs examination from the point of view of eternal values and persistent human characteristics. New events may change neither of these, but they will influence the selection of knowledge which needs to be taught. With all of the excitement about new developments in human experience, and the new expectations in human behavior which result, let us keep in mind that some things remain the same because the conditions which create them remain the same.

Finally, and these are last words here about the theory of behavioral goals, I want to add these comments before dropping the subject:

Many a page of writing about education has been given over to a definition of goals. Goals are sometimes thought of as very general, such as the attainment of vocational competence, or as very simple and concrete, such as how to drive a nail through three-quarter-inch soft pine.

Goals also may be divided in time relationships. Some are, obviously, long term in nature, attainable if ever only over a long period of time. In fact, they may be a process more than a finite thing, an illustration being the goal of maximum personality development. Other goals may be immediately realizable. The making of an apron is an example, or the correct spelling of *their* is another. It may be observed, however, that concrete goals often contribute to abstract ones.

Actually the specific and attainable objectives in education create the base for the more profound purposes of organized human activity. They are sometimes defined in accordance with who determines them. If the teacher does, then they may be thought of as objectives, as something to reach for in the execution of the day's lesson plan. If they are set forth by the school system as a whole, they may be described as a statement of philosophy. If they are identified from the point of view of the learner, goals may be thought of as growing out of desires or wants, as having something to do with needs, however vague these may be in the mind of the pupil. If they are selected from the point of view of society, which is always an interested party in educational affairs, then they may differ from those selected by the school system, the teacher, and the pupil.

The responsibility of leadership is to bring about a workable reconciliation of purposes for the guidance of teachers in the classroom, not for the enjoyment of research students or the satisfaction of special interests in the community, but for the benefit of the individual and society. The Amidon concept has required a beginning on this, but the job takes more than the sinews of a single school system.

❋   ❋   ❋

It is time now to move on to a description of the Amidon treatment of subjects. What follows is an unabashed discussion of the way subjects are made the central element in the curriculum of the Amidon school and how, at the same time, the child with his special characteristics becomes the co-element in the teaching activity, neither the over-lord nor the dispossessed.

Reading. It is hardly possible to say too much about the importance of reading in the life of a citizen. Not everything one learns is acquired from the printed page; some great and stimulating things have been done without benefit of the printed word. Homer, perhaps, in his *Iliad* and *Odyssey* is the most respected example. But, though men learn by many experiences not directly requiring the use of the printed page, not much is accomplished these days that does not require skill in reading. In fact, from the increase in the amount of printing, especially in the making of reports, digests, and brochures for commercial purposes, comes a new problem: how to speed-read one's way through mountains of material. The alternatives are extended filing space or larger waste baskets. I favor the latter, but at the same time I believe that modern living requires high-level efficiency in the use of the printed page.

The purpose of reading is to get meaning from printed material. This requires the reader to have sufficient background knowledge to understand what is being read. Everyone has had the experience of trying to read material of which he has no comprehension. In every reading experience is a growing edge of uncertainty as to meaning, and the act of assimilating new facts or ideas into those already held by the reader. The process amounts to a reconstruction of experience, which has been described as the essence of learning. Reading as interpretation is therefore full of variations when different people encounter the same material. This is, in part, because everyone brings his own purposes and experiences into the act of reading, these being of infinite variety, and in part because the written word is always an imperfect representation of the writer's ideas.

Reading, then, can take place only to the extent that the reader brings meaning of his own to the act and has a purpose for undertaking the process.

There is reason to believe that the difference between words, whether spoken or written, and the operations or events they represent, is generally so wide that men are hurt, or led into wrong decisions, or are deluded into complacency or inaction, say against social injustice, by too much reliance upon them as a substitute for life or action. Men may read about poverty, yet have no correct understanding of the effect of it on mind, body, and spirit. They may read about jungle warfare, yet be totally unprepared for heat, the tangle of vines and foliage, the noises of insects, fowl, beasts, the odors of decaying vegetation, the anxieties.

Generally there is a long and usually unnegotiated distance from the words about something and their objective referents. As a result, we often accept the word as the thing or event rather than as only a symbol for it. Man has a way of thinking that he has mastered something if he gives it a name. It is true that naming an object or an idea gives power to use and control it, in fact, to "know" it, even though the knowing is at the most superficial level. Everyone talks about atomic energy, and thus possesses a bit of this process. But the great danger in this gift for verbalizing and hence possessing a thing is the substitution of this for the hard work of knowing, understanding, anticipating, and controlling the thing (event, force, idea) thus named.

What it leads to is this: *Pupils must be taught to read for depth.* They must form the habit of translating the symbols of things into what they refer to. This can be done only with a broadening of knowledge, discovery of meanings by direct and indirect experience, ordered study of subjects to produce background knowledge, and direct instruction in the act of reading.

The following suggestions for improving the quality of reading as interpretation apply to the Amidon concept but are not unique to it.

1. The pupil must gain control of the word as the first unit of expression. A special period for phonics is provided. This requires separate treatment, and will be discussed in the next section.

2. The pupil must acquire and be able to use a growing background of facts and principles. Direct teaching is one of the most efficient ways to get this done in the classroom. Visual aids, excursions, demonstrations, dramatizations, and reading to the class are excellent supplements to be used carefully and with controlled schedules. Parents have a very heavy responsibility for developing backgrounds, having it in their power to do everything a teacher can do and more, to read to, travel with, and provide children with direct

experiences which give meaning backgrounds upon which the child's vocabulary may be built. It is a truism that a new fact learned is a new word learned. The best vocabulary-building exercise is to acquire new information.

3. The pupil must be taught how words work together in sentences to convey meaning. This means they should be taught, not simply wait to pick it up themselves. They should be taught the following characteristics of language: (a) The context is a clue to meaning. (b) Meanings of words may shift from context to context. (c) Words represent different degrees of abstraction, and meaning can be gotten only by reference to the concrete example. (d) Words are often metaphorical, so that interpretation can be accurate only when this is understood. (e) Words often shift from use as nouns, verbs, adjectives, and adverbs, and as they do, variations in meaning occur. (f) Words can be used to obscure meaning, delude, and stir emotions, and may be used for dishonest purposes.

4. The pupil needs to be taught how phrases, clauses, sentences, paragraphs, and compositions express and convey meanings. This means they should be taught the following: (a) Phrases and clauses form units of meaning in relation to parts of the sentence. (b) Paragraph structure provides keys to interpretation-topic sentences, supporting details, transitional words or phrases, summary statements. (c) Longer compositions have structure, unity, coherence, depending upon the purpose and kind of writing, such as expository and narrative. (d) Writing expresses an author's purpose and mood by intangible qualities of style and tone.

5. The pupil should be taught to read for different purposes and therefore at different rates. This includes instruction in the following: (a) Reading for study, with note-taking to sharpen analysis and retention. (b) Reading for research, with efficient use of locational aids: table of contents, index, paragraph headings, chapter summaries, bibliographies, card catalogues. (c) Reading for answers to specific questions. (d) Reading rapidly to judge the value of the material for the reader's purpose. This is scanning prior to reading for a purpose. (e) Reading aloud for the sound of the

words as in poetry. (f) Reading for pleasure and recreation: fiction, non-fiction. Enjoyment of books is communicated by the enthusiasm of the teacher and the class. A main center of interest in a classroom should be a reading shelf; in a school, a library; in the home, books, magazines, and newspapers in abundance and used with enthusiasm by the adults in the household.

Phonics. In the Amidon plan, a daily period for direct instruction in phonics is provided. This is in addition to the period for reading.

A separate period is required to be sure that this important aid to reading will not be lost, crowded out, or overlooked in connection with instruction in other phases of reading. The teaching of phonics is thus not left to chance, as it is now in most reading programs.

The main purpose of teaching phonics is to develop independence in word attack. An important extra dividend comes from knowing about words for the sake of knowing.

Instruction in phonics is scheduled to begin in the kindergarten and continue through the sixth grade. When pupils in the lower grades are taught the fundamentals of phonics, a change in content will be made in the upper grades. The emphasis in the upper grades will change to structural analysis, that is, a study of word structure, the use of suffixes and prefixes to change the meaning and the grammatical and metaphorical characteristics of words, since meanings relate in part to these elements.

Two prospects open up. The first is the need for and practicability of offering a period of phonics instruction in all grades through the twelfth, so that students who missed the study of phonics in their earlier grades will be given a chance to make up this deficiency. The second is that what is now called phonics ought to be broadened to include the study of words, not only as having phonic characteristics, but also as having structure, and metaphorical and grammatical elements which influence their meaning. Such a course is not to be confused with those sometimes labeled as word study or vocabulary subjects. The proposed semantic study is for the purpose of gaining power in the use of words by discovering the principles by which their use is governed. The beginning of the expanded study of the way words work is already incorporated in the Amidon concept, and it is in operation in the school. The changes in the phonics content will be made as soon as the upper grade pupils catch up in the fundamentals.

In using a system of phonics, pupils learn from the first that a word is made up of letters and combinations of letters that represent the sounds of the spoken word. They learn that a word is an object with letters and groups of letters just as a cat is an object with physical characteristics such as legs, eyes, fur, and purring. They learn under the direction of the teacher that our language has a system for the translation of sound into recognizable letter symbols and that an infinite variety of words may be written with a limited number of phonetic symbols. Children are taught this knowledge about language rather than being left to pick it up by inferences accidentally drawn on their own. The chief difference in a program of direct teaching of phonics and the *laissez-faire* system now widely used is that nothing is left to chance. The classroom is used for its intended purpose: to teach with planning what otherwise will be learned, if learned at all, only accidentally in experience. Or, I might add, only if the parents teach the material or hire somebody to do it.

To illustrate:

A mother of good cultural background called to ask, "How can I find a school that will teach my children to read? I have five children, four of them in school. My children can't learn by the sight method. But their teachers say they give them phonics only incidentally. I am spending a hundred dollars a month for a tutor. I can't afford this. Why must I do this?"

I am convinced that she represents many parents who feel keenly the lack of organized instruction in phonics. Improvement in reading can be made only by adding systematic instruction in phonics to a presently incomplete program of instruction. This is not easy to do because so much fear and ignorance stand in the way of this reform that only sheer insistence upon it will make any kind of showing at all.

The problems to overcome are a strong indoctrination in the opinion that the study of phonics will result in a de-emphasis upon reading for meaning, that it will detract from a pupil's interest in reading, and that it will produce a generation of word-callers, those legendary individuals who can utter masses of words without understanding their meaning.

A respected colleague lamented that she saw a teacher over-teaching phonics. Said she, "These second graders can sound out any word, but they don't know what the words mean. *Fabulous*—they could sound out that word," she said, "but would have no idea what it means. Isn't it awful?" she added.

"On the contrary, I think this is good," I replied, a comment that for some reason abruptly ended the conversation.

My point is this: Though the pupil may not at the time know the operational meaning of the word, to be able to sound out a word like *fabulous* is important as a step to getting its meaning.

On a visit to one of our elementary schools, I found a bright sixth grade class doing a science lesson on sedimentary rock. A group of boys had made a sedimentary "rock" from gravel of different sizes and a fine soil held together in layers with cement. I asked the meaning of the word "sediment," and the answers came something like this: "It is something in layers." I asked the pupils if they ever noticed that coffee sometimes will form at the bottom of the cup. They had noticed this. One boy came to the conclusion that "sediment" means something that settles and thus has actually no relationship to layers, although the settling may occur in layers.

It appeared that in this lesson one of the important scientific learnings had been overlooked in the meaning of the word "sediment." It is clear that accuracy in meaning must be sought by the teacher. Then I asked if they could spell "sediment." One of the boys wrote the word on the board correctly. Then I asked someone to tell me how many parts the word had, and most hands went up. The right answer was given, and a student divided it into its three syllables.

I then asked the class how many vowels there were, and apparently most of the class knew that there were three. I asked for the number of consonants. The response was that there were five consonants in this word. "What is a vowel?" I asked. "What makes it different from a consonant?" Here, no one knew. They could name letters as vowels, but they could not tell the difference between a vowel and a consonant as to function. The class apparently had a good foundation in structural analysis, but their knowledge of phonics seemed incomplete, particularly as to the values of vowels and consonants.

In this school phonics are taught, not as a systematic subject, but incidentally in the reading program. Being perceptive, the pupils had acquired a considerable power over words. They could have increased this power under stronger instruction. It is also clear from their confusion about the precise meaning of *sediment* that what is needed for this purpose is direct and precise instruction by the teacher. The presence or absence of instruction in phonics does not assure emphasis on reading for meaning. I am sure, however, that word power, that is, skill in handling a word, increases the efficacy of teaching for meaning.

Another obstacle to acceptance of scheduled instruction in phonics is in part the result of lack of training in this subject among most of the present staff in any school system. Most contemporary educators attended school when phonics were specifically excluded from the curriculum. I have found that what one does not know generally seems of little value. The view is, "I get along all right without it, so why can't others?"

The revolt against phonics was so intense by 1920 that it became almost disreputable to include the study of the subject. Emphasis on meaning reached the exaggerated point of denying to the child any direct instruction in the make-up of the word. In some schools teachers were warned against giving attention to the visual or phonetic elements of a word. Though many teachers taught word analysis skills behind closed doors (the underground is not unknown in education), several generations of students came through school disinterested in reading because they could not read. One educator called them "intelligent illiterates" in need of remedial reading instruction in high school, college, and now in adult life.

Those who resist a planned program in phonics in the beginning stages of reading are still unable to acquit themselves of their basic anti-phonics indoctrination or to recognize that their own lack of training in this field predisposes them against phonics. Where the educator yields a point, he usually does so reluctantly, saying, "We always have used phonics," or as one recently said, "Phonics are hard to use until children know all the vowel sounds," revealing a deep and appalling ignorance about the whole problem. His comment further included the recommendation that children should be able to begin sounding out words by the end of the third year. So much ignorance of what children can do should be overcome at once by *education of the educators* in phonics, including demonstrations that can quickly clear up such unbelievable misconceptions.

Suggestions, in summary, are these: (a) Set up a specific time schedule for phonics instruction, kindergarten through the sixth grade, in addition to the reading period. (b) Select a system of phonics instruction and use it city-wide. (In this school system the Phonovisual Method is used.) (c) Establish phonics workshops for the instruction of teachers, supervisors, and principals. (d) Set up demonstration centers, using the most competent classroom teachers to show others how the work is done with children. (e) Provide supervision and evaluation by acknowledged experts in phonics. Many egregious errors are made daily in the good name of phonics. This is not a field for dilettantes. (f) Continue to teach the art of reading as a complex skill, using word power as one of the tools for reading. In other words, keep phonics instruction in perspective with the larger program in reading.

The Phonovisual Method. The phonics instruction system that has been dramatically effective at the Amidon and in other District of Columbia schools is the Phonovisual Method. Teachers and pupils like it for its simplicity, and the results in speech and reading improvement are sometimes phenomenal.

On the day that school opens in the fall, teachers begin with the sight-reading practices that are in common use, and at another period on the same day, they begin the speech sounds shown on charts. The arrangement of the sounds on the charts is meaningful and very important. The Consonant Chart, which is taught first because most short words begin with consonants and because it is the consonants that make speech intelligible, classifies the sounds both vertically and horizontally. Vertically, the first column presents the whispered, or breath, consonants, beginning with the one placed farthest forward (the sound of p, which is merely a puff of breath blowing open the closed lips) and following the lip-sounds with the lips-teeth, tongue-teeth, and tongue-palate sounds farther and farther back in the mouth.

Horizontally, the second column gives the voiced equivalents of the sounds in the first column. The third column shows the three nasal sounds, which are identical in position (though not in production) with their opposite numbers in the first two columns. The sounds in the fourth column are not identical in formation with their horizontal predecessors, but do bear some points of resemblance. All English consonant sounds are presented except the one we spell with z in azure, s in measure, and g in mirage. It is omitted because the pupils will not find it spelled zh.

On the Phonovisual Vowel Chart also, the sounds are arranged in an orderly and meaningful way. Horizontally, the first row gives the sounds we know as "long" vowels, indicating the pronunciation by the spelling—a dash for the missing consonant sound, followed by the silent e which "makes the vowel say its name" as we know it in the alphabet. The second row shows the so-called "short" vowels—with a dash on each side to indicate that the sound usually occurs between two consonants. The rest of the chart gives spellings which indicate other vowel sounds spelled with the letter at the top of the vertical column.

All English-speaking people are far less consistent in their pronunciation of vowels than of consonants. In fact, regional modifications of certain vowel sounds sometimes make our speech all but unintelligible to people from other sections. The Phonovisual Vowel Chart makes no effort to indicate all possible variations, but merely presents those sounds most needed for reading and spelling English words. On both charts different ways of spelling the same sound are indicated in smaller type under the sounds where more than one spelling is frequent.

Three senses, auditory, visual, and kinesthetic, are trained and sharpened by the repetition and close attention required for deriving full value from the chart work. Observation and critical listening result in unusual accuracy in spelling. Alertness and quick perception are often stimulated to a striking extent in teachers as well as in pupils, and a marked improvement in speech is often noted. The pleasure and confidence of the pupil lead to fluency and joy in reading.

(The Phonovisual Method was devised by Miss Lucille D. Schoolfield and Miss Josephine B. Timberlake of the Primary Day School, Bethesda, Maryland, and associates.)

Grammar. As in the case of phonics, grammar has had an uneasy time of it during the past half century. It lost credit during the 1920's when studies purporting to be scientific concluded that the study of grammar made no contribution to the improvement of usage. Grammar also fell victim to the theory of psychological rather than logical organization of subject. Curriculum builders and teachers were advised to individualize instruction, to teach, for example, a rule of grammar when the pupil needed to know it and was able to understand it. Because of this, the conclusion was reached that formal systematic study of grammar should be offered only at the high school level and there only to the bright students. Even among the professionals in the teaching of English, differences developed as to how much, when, and in what manner to offer systematic instruction in grammar. There is a notable softening process operating in the thinking of the leadership of teachers of English. Postponement of difficult studies, psychological and sociological emphasis in place of structural organization of content, acceptance of colloquial speech levels as the standards against which to teach, and a less than sufficient emphasis upon the practice of writing show that this generally highly disciplined branch of teaching has been marked by the debilitating influence of those who place little value on subject matter. This is a pity, too, for education needs toughminded leaders and groups capable of resisting the well-intentioned but misleading advice of the child-study specialists.

At this point, the question is in order, "What do you do about grammar in the Amidon Plan?"

Beginning with the fourth grade, the study of grammar is scheduled for direct teaching. This includes the diagramming of sentences. Prior to the fourth grade, teachers will introduce grammatical principles as needed to explain correct usage.

The purposes of teaching grammar are to improve the logic of thought, to sharpen interpretation, to develop understanding of the way words work in sentences, and to improve the quality of written and oral expression, both as to usage and content.

I consider the systematic study of grammar to be among the most important subjects in a school curriculum. Surely it is as necessary to know how a subject works in a sentence as to know how a spark plug works in an automobile.

Literature. One of the most important subjects in the curriculum is literatuure, not work-horse prose but the kind that is imaginative, pleasing, elevating, and beautiful. I am not opposed to the reading of books about mailmen and policemen, how to get along with the boy next door, or how to care for pets. These are useful on the pedestrian level. But a wonderful part of childhood is the refreshing gift for rapture. This should be heightened and encouraged in the joyful use of the classical literature of childhood.

There are tales and poems which every child should know. What these are, of course, can be a source of much debate. Even to suggest a list will invite criticism, particularly for omissions. But even with this hazard, a list is included in the District of Columbia Reading Curriculum Bulletin. It is by no means the best list that could be selected, yet, among all the excellent modern tales for children, it includes many which have become classics. And these are to be read or to be heard (children love to hear a teacher read—if she knows how) with one objective in mind: the cultivation of pleasure in the words and ideas of good writing.

Composition. In the activity-centered curriculum, opportunities are frequently created so that pupils write for a purpose. For example, plans are made to visit the zoo. Letters are composed for mailing to the zoo keeper. When the class returns from the zoo, letters are written to thank the zoo keeper. Every possible occasion is used to get the class to write letters. And this is naturally good—and yet it is a strange thing that so many young adults write such poor and uninteresting letters, including even teachers, whose letter writing as to form and content leaves much to be desired, as my files can attest. Ignoring content, structure of sentences, even spelling, one wonders how such carelessness in the use of the simple letter forms can occur in the letters written by teachers. With the delimiting stress upon functional writing in our elementary schools and the paucity of writing in the second-ary schools, pupils are leaving our high schools almost incapable of using written communication.

When I ask for more, vastly more, composition in the elemen-tary schools, I have in mind the kind of writing that comes with having something to say about things that really count. This means getting off the ground of repetitive, trite letter-writing sub-jects into more invigorating, imaginative, and intellectual levels of thought and writing. Please believe me, teaching for this kind of experience is arduous. It takes planning to stimulate the minds and spirits of the pupils, to help them see ideas and then to have something vigorous to say about them, to show them how to savor an experience, reflect upon its elements, consider the in-sights it offers, and find the right words to describe their evalua-tions. But what can be done in this respect is evident in the work of teachers who have the love of writing themselves, who see life keenly, and who can be the windows for pupils avid to join in new ventures of the senses and the mind.

I am also convinced that putting one's thoughts down on paper sharpens thinking. The art of expressing a thought in writing supplies a discipline not felt in simply thinking about something or even in speaking those thoughts. In fact, the young should be encouraged to write for their own satisfaction, not simply to hand in something to a teacher, because voluntary writing is the surest self-teaching device I know of. *Composition in great amounts properly stimulated and made creative improves the quality of thinking, and to do this is perhaps the most important purpose of education.*

The kind of thinking to which we should lead pupils requires the acquisition of facts, the coordination of these facts into logical thought patterns, and the expression of these observations in coherent language. It follows, therefore, that extensive experience in the directed organization of thought in written and spoken language is a useful tool for developing the capacity for critical evaluation of data.

If I could wave a magic wand across the school systems of our country, to change the emphasis as I think it should be changed, I would ask for two things: continuous inquiry by students for information to supply solutions to problems, and then the expression of these thoughts in abundant writing and rewriting with major attention to the content of expression, so that out of this writing for a purpose would come disciplined thinking.

Speech. How people talk, what they have to say, and their willingness to say it bears upon their success in school and in affairs outside the school room. If they are given the chance, most young children will talk volubly. But they must have information, the impact of experiences, a situation in which conversation is a part of the way of life, and attentive ears and adult participants.

The art of conversation is a disappearing one, because the family is beset by the shortness of time its members can be together, the pressures upon each one resulting from compacted living, the indulgence in spectator recreation rather than the creation of home-made entertainment. For many children, the ordinary family situation gives little chance for the exercise of speech. This happens in homes of high level of cultivation as well as in those not so endowed.

Another condition prevents the kind of expression needed for the development of mind. This is lack of cultivation in many homes where education, a term used here to include the learning that takes place where cultural diffusion is widespread, is severely limited. Even in a time like this where the means of communication are at their highest levels so far, many families are isolated by ignorance, inertia, and hopelessness. They are almost perpetually unmoved by the events taking place all around them. The result of this is that many children come to their first year in school with such meager backgrounds and so little practice in speech that they are silent, stolid, and inarticulate. When they do speak, they often do so in a dialect that in itself requires modification by speech training in the classroom. These two anecdotes illustrate. One of the children was Negro, one was white.

A third grade child asked: "Teacha, wheah do you keep the lāeds?"

"Do you mean *leads* for pencils?"

"No, I mean lāeds to put on jars."

In the other case a fourth grade girl asked her teacher at the end of the year, "Is I'm gonna pass?"

A classmate who overheard said, "She won't get a very high grade in language, will she?"

Another problem in speech is the high tension effort and the nervous, almost distraught, manner with which some children speak. These result in high pitched, shrill voice levels which make the emotional overtones so excessive that the thought in what is said is often not communicated. And the fact is, that speech of this kind gives evidence of a hasty trial and error kind of thought.

Speech education, therefore, begins with two conditions to be considered. These are the lack of experience in speech in the child's background and the sometimes bizarre speech mannerisms, including anxiety, strain, and excitability, that show in the pitch and rhythm of children's speech.

To do something about these factors requires giving children something to talk about and a quiet yet directed setting in which to talk.

Education to improve speech must be a planned part of the school program. To leave it to incidental opportunity is to neglect it. Moreover, teachers need help in teaching speech. They need to learn how to help the reserved and sensitive child, and the volatile, compulsive talker. Anyone who has taught speech knows that children must be induced to speak by the classroom setting. They can't be ordered to. For some children, to make a beginning is good. For most, telling them about all their mistakes is overwhelming. The teacher needs to know when to praise and when to censure.

Direct speech instruction ought to take the place of the excessive informality of today's classrooms. In the practice of small group teaching, children are so closely grouped that they often do little more than murmur their answers. Observe, too, that they do all their talking from a seated position, so that body participation in the speaking is incomplete. Pupils should learn to stand when talking and to address their remarks to the whole class rather than to recite in small groups where voices are to be kept low so that the rest of the class may be undisturbed.

Choric speaking should be offered in every class. This speech experience involves large groups at one time, helps the timid to overcome their shyness, trains in interpretation and control. It introduces them to good material, and helps to increase enjoyment of poetry read aloud.

Dramatic expression provides a useful experience in speech. Often a child who is timid in being himself will become expressive in the role of another. Plays, skits, and readings should be short; preparation should not become disproportionate in the assemblage of stage settings. The simpler the external trappings, the more efficient is the use of school time. On this point, great restraint is needed to avoid going overboard on big school-wide productions to impress the parents.

Vocal music, I think, is often overlooked for its excellent value in voice improvement. Everything depends, of course, upon how it is taught. It is possible to hear bad diction and interpretation in school choruses. On the other hand, singing can be a very productive way to get improvement in speech.

Then, there is *poetry* to be memorized and spoken aloud. Choose what the pupil will enjoy and let him know that the sound of words in pleasing arrangement adds to the enjoyment and understanding of what the poet is saying. This work should always be assigned with the interest and capacity of the pupil in mind. To force-feed this study may develop a strong distaste for poetry. If training in memorization is desired, and has to be required under duress, be certain that love of poetry is not the innocent victim. Judgment is needed on this point, because sometimes requiring a child to do a task may result in his mastery of it and his eventual pleasure in it. Therefore, the teacher must know how to direct her work to hold children to their best and yet to retain an interest in the subject.

Spelling. The time spent among educators debating whether to teach spelling in lists or to teach it only when needed in writing would add up to many wasted clock hours, especially if the "research" on this subject is included. This is an issue that can be settled in the statement of one dogma: Teach spelling as a skill as you would teach driving an automobile. Study both the theory and the practice of the skill.

Direct teaching of spelling does these important things:

1. It increases consciousness of the importance of accuracy in spelling.

2. It points up principles by which the letter relationships within words work with fairly high regularity. For example, a student will develop an understanding of how words are affected by a final silent vowel. Then, for example, *tune* becomes *tuning* when an orchestra is doing this, and *run* becomes *running* as when a boy is going after a fly ball.

3. It strengthens the habit of *seeing* and *saying* a word at the same time. Good spelling instruction sharpens visual analysis and forms a standard by which a pupil may judge correctness.

4. It builds spelling accuracy into the muscle system. A good speller always integrates eye, ear, and muscle in the art of spelling. The aim is automatic accuracy with self-consciousness enough to cause the writer to check doubtful spelling in a dictionary.

5. It offers specific and concentrated study of the spelling and meaning of the so-called demon words. These words ought to be taught in the earliest grades. They should be learned correctly from the start. But this is rarely done. The result is that many people spend a lifetime trying to unlearn an incorrect spelling when it ought to have been just as easy to learn the correct form to begin with. It is no harder to learn to spell *does* than *dose*. Correct spelling from the start adds incalculable man-hours to the time for instruction in other subjects during a pupil's school career. What is saved in embarrassment and hesitancy later is hard to estimate.

Teach spelling consciously, directly, with attention to the

hard-to-spell words. But, of course, require correct spelling in every paper a pupil writes. Any pupil can learn to spell if he is required to, and is at the same time taught how words shape up as to letters, syllables, accent, pronunciation, and appearance. By all means add a wholesome amount of plain-old-fashioned practice in writing the words for the purpose of learning how to spell them.

Handwriting. This is a functional skill learned in large part by use. It is not unlike walking or playing the piano. It requires the training of the muscular system in hand, arm, and body, as a whole. Posture and control with relaxation are a part of the process; thus attitude as an emotional factor is important. It includes seeing, hearing in a mentalistic sense, perhaps at times actual vocalization to say the word as it is being written, for handwriting is spelling as well as the legible formation of letters. Growth in this skill is slow, beginning with a large and perhaps gross making of letters, and developing into an unconscious stream of writing which permits the unrestricted flow of thought. Handwriting is primarily a tool for the recording of thought, and while attention must be focused on the process in its developmental stage, the aim is to achieve the kind of proficiency which permits maximum attention to the content.

To achieve this goal, periods of instruction in the specifics of the skill allow for habit formations without conflicting with the purpose of saying something important. In most activities, the individual, if he is successful in what he does, acquires a basic form and structure upon which he builds the expression of thought and interpretation, as in the graphic or musical arts. The pianist, for example, must learn the basic techniques before he can fully achieve the perceptive interpretations which he reads into a musical score. Drill, study under critical supervision, and the integration of techniques with interpretation make up the complex of learning activities necessary to success in this field.

It is for this reason that handwriting should be a separate study at the early stages of a child's education to develop an almost automatic legibility without causing this purpose to dominate written expression. Thus, handwriting instruction should be regularly scheduled. All the work in composition should include improvement in this skill, but not at the expense of the content. A judicious balance of attention is therefore needed in this field of learning as it is in all fields.

Mathematics. There is reason to believe that *our most serious educational deficiency is in mathematics.* The weaknesses are less noticeable than in reading, yet the problem is not wholly obscured. In our own school system, achievement as measured by standardized tests is best in science and English expression and is poorest in mathematics. This has been a long-standing problem which the experts in the field have failed so far to find a way to correct. Despite a great deal of attention to this deficit, progress is very unsatisfactory. The chances are that *this is a national problem.* It shows up in the simple business of adding up a bill in a department store. More critically, it is revealed in the shortage of trained mathematicians, and of personnel in fields such as engineering and science which depend upon competence in mathematics. The shortcomings in the teaching of mathematics touch upon our national security, even without reference to Russian achievements.

It is known that no one can be successful in science without a command of the necessary mathematics. In fact, competence in mathematics is more important for college success in science and engineering than competence in science at the beginning stages of study in that field.

The need for mathematics is not limited to the few who will become specialists in this field. One purpose of teaching mathematics is to discover and develop the talents and interests of the professional mathematician, the scientist, engineer, the many technicians needed to operate and assist in the development of new techniques. But the broader purpose is to supply every citizen with what he needs, as a member of a technological society, simply to do and understand those things required of him. Examples easily come to mind: paying bills, estimating budgets, measuring a room for a rug. Knowing something about mathematics helps the individual to be at home with the vast literature of science and technology, in a world which would otherwise be as frightening with its mysteries as it was to the ancient peoples, who, to be at ease in an otherwise awesome environment, created myths to explain such things as lightning and ocean currents, the dawn and the sunset. To switch on a television set without some understanding of the process behind the appearance of the picture would be like emerging from the stone age into the presence of greater mysteries than man in the natural state has ever had to accept. What I am saying is that because mathematics is a system of communication, a way of thinking, and an ordering of the processes of the physical environment into understandable form, it is almost as essential as language. Mathematics is a manifestation of the human mind applied to the search for knowledge.

One of the problems in American education is the failure to know the importance of mathematics. In the fairly recent past the view was that pupils will learn mathematics when they need it. Some years ago a noted administrator told his teachers in effect, "Don't teach arithmetic until the children reach the fourth or fifth grade. They will learn all they will need then." An elementary teacher told me that when she started teaching twenty years ago, she asked her supervisor to help her with arithmetic. The supervisor said, "Do the best you can with it. Don't worry too much about teaching arithmetic. Children will learn it when they need it."

The problem arises, therefore, from the value accorded mathematics by supervisors, curriculum workers, teachers, and administrators. What the leaders in education are ignorant of (and this is no exaggeration), they do not value. What is not valued is never taught enthusiastically. It is given little time in the schedule. This factor has created a deep infection in our educational system, and can be corrected only by re-educating a generation of teachers and administrators and changing the content of teacher preparation. Even the latter is not easy. In our own teachers college, one semester of college level mathematics has recently been introduced into the curriculum of teacher preparation. This was done over the protests of the educational specialists. Any effort to extend this limited requirement heads into a strong tide of opposition.

Much is being done here to give teachers in service further education in mathematics. The teacher-response to the workshop offerings has been encouraging. But I am not sure that the study in these offerings has the depth, continuity, and duration to bring the teacher up to the point of being at home in and enthusiastic about mathematics, and especially to understand the new content, principles, and operations of the presently developing new mathematics.

I believe the former reluctance to give mathematics the "time of day" in the elementary curriculum is now dissipated. But this is a far cry from providing the solutions needed.

What is now needed are decisions by mathematicians as to what the modern mathematics program should be. These need translation into textbooks, with selection to be determined by the scholars and placement by the educators.

The teachers who are to use these new materials need to be re-educated in depth in this subject field. Superficial exposure to mathematics is not enough to do the job.

Specialists in mathematics should be assigned to teach mathematics in the honors classes in grades four, five, and six, if the regular teacher is not ready to do so.

Mathematics should be scheduled *in prime time* and on a daily basis. In this connection, I favor a morning hour, although I am aware that this is a debatable point.

In the Amidon schedule, mathematics has a place of honor, although I am not sure we are doing as well yet as needs to be done in this subject. The new mathematics curriculum, city-wide in use, conforms to the Amidon concept of specificity, an increase in content by grade, and the placement of more challenging content in earlier grades.

Science. No one these days needs to make a case for teaching science in the elementary school. In the District of Columbia public schools, a good and realistic curriculum has been in use for a number of years. It was planned in detail to be used by classroom teachers who were not especially trained in science. We are fortunate here in having a staff of specialists in elementary school science who serve as helping teachers throughout our elementary school system. Hence, in science the Amidon concept had very little distance to go, because science was already included in the weekly time allotment schedule. It was necessary to include a science period in the daily schedule and to prepare a flow chart of science areas and concepts for special attention at the Amidon.

The curriculum guide prepared by the science specialist assigned to the Amidon described the program this way:

The Amidon science program is:

(a) an organized accumulation of factual information and generalizations based on these facts,

(b) an attitude of appreciation of the environment, of desire to search for answers, of courage to look at self and world honestly, and of humility for acceptance of necessary changes,

(c) a way of thinking that is logical and objective,

(d) and a way of behavior that is positive, rational, and creative,

developed through:

(a) direct development of facts, theories, and generalizations,

(b) experiments, demonstrations, and observations,

(c) measurement and quantitative concepts,

(d) research in reading reference material, and

(e) trips, visual aids, and resource people.

If science is well taught, it leads to knowing how to collect, organize, and evaluate knowledge for problem-solving. Education in science, therefore, leads to an improvement in the ways of thinking, to an unprejudiced attack upon problems, to the making of tentative conclusions pending further inquiry for the truth, and to the testing of conclusions by careful observation. Because science has this value, I am not willing to accept the lines of difference often drawn between science and the humanities. I believe that both disciplines are part of the totality of human experience. They both contribute to the humanizing of the human spirit. Those who touch upon the world of scientific inquiry, if they are in actuality trained in the ways of rational thought, ought to be more effective in personal relationships and in understanding of all the characteristics of human nature. They ought to be more capable of approaching problem situations in the fields of social sciences, for example, than if they had not had a background of experience in scientific training. When this is not the case, then something is wrong with the way science was taught. And I must say that sometimes I have found scientists quite unscientific in their methods of thinking. When this results, however, it indicates an omission in the science education of which such an individual is a product.

Science instruction should have cultural value like that acquired when people learn to appreciate literature, art, or music. It should give new insights into the wonders of nature, including man as a part of it. It has aesthetic and humane values.

This is science for every man, including the scientist himself, and this view justifies direct instruction in science at all levels in our school system in proper proportion to other essential subjects.

Science education, moreover, should offer experience and specialization for those who want to find a vocation in this field. It is well known that many choose careers in science because they have had stimulating opportunities in science education.

In the elementary schools, groups consisting of the more able pupils should be set up beginning with the fourth grade, and specialists in science should be assigned to teach them. In schools where such a program is supported by the presence of capable students, a science room should be provided. This calls for some degree of departmentalization for the gifted students at the fourth, fifth, and sixth grade levels. For other students, science may well continue to be a part of the teaching in the so-called self-contained classroom.

Geography. In the Amidon plan, systematic United States geography replaced the unit-organized fourth grade program. The idea was to put direct emphasis upon place geography of the United States in a regularly scheduled period.

In this change, of course, a shift from the activity unit, already discussed in this volume, to organized subject matter provided a visible contrast between the new and the old. The reasons for introducing an orderly study of United States geography were that (1) it assures coverage of the significant facts about the United States; (2) it tends to focus attention in the course upon the characteristics of geography as a science; (3) it eliminates the wasted time and lost motion as well as the hazards of a pupil-teacher selection of what should be taught; and (4) it defines more clearly the responsibilities of teacher and pupil.

This method puts more into the minds of pupils about the United States as a geographical unit than can be accomplished when the teacher chooses units on the Chesapeake Bay, the Mississippi Valley, or mountainous, desert, delta and hot, dry regions around the world. I am in favor of the dictum that what is to be taught ought to be scheduled in advance. The return to systematic study of United States geography is based upon this simple truth.

In the sixth grade, the effort is to teach world geography in systematic order and with general coverage. This plan superseded the unit method of organization which listed Canada and Latin America as a must, made China, Russia, Great Britain, Western Europe as optional. At least a beginning was made in this field, in a setting notably sparse as to prepared materials to make round-the-world study of geography. The aim was to illustrate, to give the pupils enough facts to see a difference between Austria and Australia and to be able to get fairly close on a world map to such places as the Congo, Laos, Ceylon, and Sierra Leone. I want to see, of course, a study of some regions in depth, particularly in these days, Russia and China. For that reason, a teaching guide on Russia, recently completed by our curriculum department is a stimulating addition to our sixth grade program, and accepted for use throughout the city.

Geography, then, is a separate subject in the fourth and sixth grades of the Amidon School. The selection of textbooks has been difficult, because no available text fits the pattern of this program. Most are wordy narratives in which the facts must be searched out. Most are geared to the unit method of organization in deference to the widespread popularity of this system. Nevertheless, the program in geography was instituted at the Amidon School in its first year, under handicaps, but I believe, with success.

History. The United States history course in the Amidon fifth grade is chronological and complete in scope beginning with the period of discovery. This replaces a former curriculum which included units on transportation, inventions, cereals, and related themes. A textbook is used to assure orderly development of study as well as to provide a degree of selectivity. Pupils are taught to develop a time line, so that they will have a graphic representation of the time of the chief happenings in the history of this country.

Many facts and ideas about history are learned in connection with the holidays and special events in the preceding grades and to some extent in the study of geography. The aim, however, is to teach geography and history separately so that the learnings characteristic of each will not be submerged in a mixture of the two subjects. But, while history and geography are taught separately, they are also in the backgrounds of literature, current events, music, art, and sometimes science and mathematics. The direct study of a subject like history does not mean it is to be sealed off in a separate compartment. Separation for direct study is to make certain that the subject will be fully covered.

The study of United States history has a far more important purpose than conveying facts about the development of our country. History should be the means of bringing to young Americans a knowledge of the origins and meanings of democratic ideals, and skill in making critical evaluations of the meaning of these great principles. The aim is to produce an intelligent devotion to democratic ideals so that nothing can destroy it, not even disillusionment because of the frequent gap between ideal and practice. We need to develop in our youth a love of the elements of justice in American political and economic goals, and a determination to keep the way open for their realization by democratic processes. In a good program of study in United States history, these purposes should be highlighted. No opportunity should ever be overlooked to show the gains in freedom that grew out of many events in our history, and to reveal honestly the weaknesses of men striving to secure for themselves the blessings of liberty.

No pupil should leave his fifth grade United States history course without having attained deep convictions about, and an intelligent devotion to, the purposes of American democracy.

Art. As may be supposed, I believe order and structure is as necessary in the study of art as in any other subject. This point of view is contrary to that generally prevailing in art education.

Art should be regularly scheduled for instruction and practice in expression. The two, I agree, are interrelated. It is not likely that simply telling about how to paint an object (I hope this is not offensive to those who have an abhorrence of representational art) will produce a good painting. But I am, I must confess, very unenthusiastic about what seems to me as an observer to be a total preoccupation with intuitive art expression. This seems to be a method of work which includes a child, a brush, some colors, and paper spread out on the floor and then discovering what will happen. In bold, free strokes, the child then paints a Santa Claus or tree or children going to a zoo. I should like to have a count made some day of the number of Christmas trees and Santa Clauses an average child will paint in the course of his school career.

The first grader, when he puts these unstudied blotches of color on paper, often produces a cute, appealing, supposedly child-like representation of what he sees. But how stupid it is to believe that the six-year-old paints *what he sees. He paints what he can paint*—and generally without guidance or direction from the teacher, whose role becomes primarily that of supervisor and controller of paint bottles, brushes, and pupils in various stages of invigoration ranging from stolid to over-stimulated.

Now, when I see a not dissimilar kind of art work done by sixth graders, then I ask questions which of course reveal my lack of artistic perception. On one occasion after viewing a selected exhibit of children's paintings, kindergarten through sixth, I told the art supervisor that I had great difficulty discovering the real difference between first and sixth grade work. Both looked equally gross rather than showing differences in discrimination of line, color, and detail. "I would expect to see greater maturity, sharper discrimination in choice of subjects, clearer detail, more pleasing use of color in sixth grade than in first grade work," I told the expert. His silence led me to believe that he disagreed with me.

It is, certainly, always dangerous to step out of one's field. But I must confess to a deep feeling that the study of art is something more than a romantic, untutored, therapeutic expression of self. It should have the creativity of uninhibited yet directed effort. The achievement of this combination of seemingly contradictory practices is as necessary in teaching art as in teaching composition or science. This is difficult to attain, but that it is so is no excuse for excluding it from the art program.

Another need in art instruction is the development of insights into the meaning and aesthetic qualities of art forms such as painting, sculpture, and architecture. This is specific content now generally neglected in art courses at the elementary level, generally, I think, because some believe that if one puts his mind to art appreciation, he automatically fails to appreciate. This can and does happen in literature and music, for example, but that it does is hardly a reason for failure to instruct in these fields.

The fact is, most Americans are woefully ignorant in the subject matter of painting, sculpture, and architecture, though most have been subjected to many hours of art courses.

The Amidon idea of art instruction, not likely to be widely supported in our own school system for some time to come, is to put some solid ground under it, to supply teaching that will sharpen expression and increase the amount of knowing about art forms from which, if it comes at all, will come through critical appreciation.

Music. The Amidon schedule provides time for the teaching of vocal and instrumental music. In this respect, the program is similar to that in the city's other elementary schools. The subject is mainly taught by specially trained teachers, who include the Amidon School on their itinerary. We have all too few trained music teachers for the number of children at the elementary school level. But progress is being made, especially in instrumental music which is now giving elementary children an opportunity to sudy such music.

In addition, regular teachers on the Amidon staff teach vocal music when they have the skill to do so. This leaves, of course, too much to the chance competence of the regular teacher, who really should not be expected to possess the training and experience to provide music education.

The good program must be just this: music education rather than a catch-as-catch-can treatment of this very important field. To do an acceptable job, a specialist must be available and a curriculum should be outlined in detail. As in other fields, this too consists of a body of knowledge and techniques, which it is the function of education to transmit to the young. The general acceptance of a we'll-do-what-we-can attitude about music short-changes children whose lives and insights can be greatly enlivened if they know and enjoy music, and can at least sing in the shower without creating a neighborhood nuisance.

It will take effort and time to activate this concept of the place of music in the organized curriculum of the Amidon School, but to do so will increase the value of the music and justify the time now being given to it.

Health and physical education. In the first place the school environment should always be conducive to physical and mental health. The things done by pupils or expected of them should be consistent with good health practices. These range from seating arrangement, ventilation, posture of pupils seated and walking, speech habits, and the relationships between pupils and teachers, and pupil and pupil. In this way, a good school program contributes to health in all its functions. The teacher and principal need to be aware of their responsibility to see that this is done.

In addition to the general contribution to physical and mental health, instruction in health and physical education needs to be scheduled. This is to provide assurance that pupils will understand themselves as physical beings possessing emotional characteristics and that they must learn to respect themselves by following good health practices. The daily schedule should also include a period of physical education either on the playground or in the classroom. The curriculum for this subject should include calesthenics, which are to be practiced in the classroom as well as on the playground.

As in the case of every subject scheduled in the Amidon concept, health and physical education should consist of selected items to be taught. This subject, too, has a body of content which ought to be transmitted to the pupils in an orderly way.

SUMMARY

The place of subjects is clearly defined in the Amidon concept. The choice and sequence of content need to be preplanned with the help of specialists (scholars, if the word does not offend you). This rule applies to all disciplines. It tolerates no exceptions for such subjects as art, music, and physical education. The axiom is *if any subject lacks content, it has no place in a school program.*

The selection and ordering of content is a continuing process. The degree to which this has been done for the Amidon School is still limited. Only the smallest steps have been taken so far. But the advantages of specific scheduling of subjects are evident in the emphasis this places upon the selection of content. It also reveals the flaws in the child-centered, pupil-teacher-planned curriculum, because when subjects are to be taught, the need for preparation for teaching becomes evident. It is no longer possible to sweep ignorance under the rug of a pupil-centered curriculum.

The challenge is to achieve an intelligent selection of content in each subject, and then teach it in such a way as to produce informed and emotionally mature citizens who are able to deal intelligently with the problems of living. This, may I say, is a fairly functional objective.

chapter · six

METHOD IN THE AMIDON CONCEPT

TO THINK OF METHOD AS SOMETHING THAT CAN BE SEPA-
rated from subjects and the teacher is nonsense. The elements
of method are in what is to be taught, who is to be taught, the
purposes of teaching, and the feelings, diligence, and intellectual
preparation of the teacher. I am compelled to begin this chapter
with an apology for writing it, because what has already been
said about pupils, teachers, and subjects to some extent predeter-
mines the methods of instruction.

A definition has a way of subdividing what often cannot be
separated from the whole of which it is a part. It is like defining
style as in the case of a writer or the way a woman wears her
clothes. It is not unlike defining personality, as if it were separate
from the person. Or trying to unweave a tapestry design: as soon
as the threads are separated, the design disappears. I say this
because of my belief that method is, more than anything else,
what evolves from the experience of the teacher dealing with
what she is to teach in relation to the pupils in her class.
Because it is a part of the pattern of teaching, method results
from the design, emphasis, and purpose of teaching. Because of
this, any treatment of method must honestly take into account
the resulting limitations as to completeness and accuracy.

THE MECHANICS OF CLASSROOM MANAGEMENT

One point to be cleared up at once is the fact that the teacher
is a mechanic, a housekeeper, and an administrator. This set of
duties relates to the processes of classroom management.

143

Because children are physical they need to be seated in chairs of proper size in arrangements which make good use of light in properly ventilated and heated rooms. These factors are not unique in the Amidon system, and therefore this aspect of method needs no particular definition here.

In the management of the materials and textbooks of instruction the teacher must always be orderly and efficient. Observation of teachers at work will often reveal a wastage of time in this function, with a higher incidence of inefficiency in the activity unit curriculum than in the subject matter curriculum. But there is really nothing in the teaching of subject matter that automatically assures conservation of time.

The efficient teacher begins each day with management plans carefully laid:

1. Pupils are assigned textbooks for which they are responsible in accordance with predetermined system-wide procedures.

2. Pupils are provided with paper, notebooks, writing equipment in such a manner as to make the daily distribution of materials unnecessary. They are taught to conserve materials and to use them in a manner that conforms to standards as to headings, margins, and the use of ink or pencil, so that routines are established early and then become habitual.

3. Gathering and distributing papers prepared by pupils should be routinized so that this process will use the minimum amount of class time.

4. Seating arrangements should be orderly. Sight and hearing problems should be considered where children have impairments in their senses. The pupil's desk should be his work station where he keeps his books and papers in good order. The desk storage shelf should be orderly. Examination shows that these are catch-all spaces that are often cluttered and disorganized.

5. The teacher's desk, file cases, room interest center (science, reading, for example) bulletin boards, and blackboards should be used in orderly but productive manner. The vigorous use of display always presupposes clarity and sharpness of outline, rather than a confusion resulting from an indefiniteness of objectives and indiscriminate selection of materials.

6. Pupil accounting, including roll taking, should be simple. Most school records, including those in the District of Columbia,

overtax the time and ingenuity of even the most proficient teacher. Data on pupil records should include only what is of permanent value in planning for the child's education. Anecdotes should be carefully selected. Transient, gossipy items are out of place on the records. These reports should not be made out during the teaching day, but at the same time, teachers ought not be required to work all hours of the night to make reports.

7. Teachers should check and return papers at the earliest possible time. Judgment is required as to the amount of paper work which is to be handed in, so that what does come in is the best the pupil can do (self-editing and checking should be a part of the preparation of a paper). Paper checking should reinforce learning. Therefore, the time between response and correction should be as short as possible.

The teacher should always give time to reteaching the needs that show up in written work in a fairly general way in the class. Where pupils need individual help, she should work with them during the school day or before and after school.

8. Pupils who are absent should have definite make-up work to do. Failure to require this makes school attendance seem unimportant and also leads to a slow-up in the education of the pupil who gets behind in his work. In a systematically organized curriculum, failure to do the lessons confuses the pupils about subsequent work. The loss of time to teachers and pupils increases as the work goes on. It is economical of time and effort to help the absent child make up the work he missed as soon as he returns to school. When the lessons are clearly defined as in the Amidon system the make-up problem is not difficult to manage.

9. Assignment making is one of the most important jobs the teacher does. An assignment first must be carefully planned by the teacher. This is the blueprint for teaching. If it is not carefully drafted, the house won't fit the lot or the bridge bear the traffic. Presentation of the assignment to the class should be in such a manner that the pupils know what is expected of them, they can work with the materials and texts with understanding, and they have confidence in the value of the exercise. If an assignment introduces new principles, then teaching of these principles at the time is a necessity. Pupils should not generally be asked to ferret out new concepts for themselves unless the lesson is

intended to develop skill in doing so rather than to convey to the learner the principles to be acquired. If this is so, the purpose ought to be explained to the pupil and the processes for making the discovery should be taught. Explorers have always made plans in advance, putting together all the knowledge available to them before setting out into new country. Every lesson that introduces content new to the pupil makes him an explorer. The teacher should help check the compass.

In the structure of the Amidon operation, the orderly management of all classroom functions from the most routine chores to the planning and presentation of assignments is re-emphasized. While this objective is given lip-service in other systems of curriculum organization, it is played down in pupil-teacher planning, in spur-of-the-moment curriculum choices, and in the uninhibited expressionism of the "creative" classroom. Pre-planning and order are not indigenous to that climate.

TEACHING THE WHOLE CLASS

One of the most controversial elements of the Amidon concept is that for most of the day the teacher should teach the whole class at the same time. This replaces sub-grouping within the class, where the teacher works with perhaps a third of the class seated around her while the rest of the class does seat work or activity assignments such as painting a mural or setting up a science exhibit. The whole class process does not propose total elimination of small group or individual instruction. Under this principle, the need for some of this kind of instruction is acknowledged. It is used, however, only when special help must be given to groups or individual pupils and where special projects are to be undertaken by a group or committee of the class.

Such techniques are secondary to whole class teaching processes, and are used only as needed rather than as the governing principle of organization for teaching.

How Can You Teach the Entire Class in Reading?

This question was put to me by an elementary principal, who added, "This is the one part of the Amidon plan I can't really accept. Even with ability grouping, there will be a range of four or five grades in reading level. If a child in the sixth grade is at home only in a third grade reader and another can work with materials at an eighth grade level, how can they learn from the same textbook and teaching?"

My answer is in two parts: *Reconsider the meaning of teaching, especially of reading, and do not equate reading level with learning level.*

The problem in part is that such a class has a low teachability index. The problem is to improve the administration of pupil assignment so that the range of differences within a class is reduced. Such class grouping indicates unregulated pupil programing.

First, Check Promotion Policy

What to do about this kind of undisciplined scheduling? Don't fire the principal, but take a good look at your principles of operation. After many years of efforts to rationalize the great range of differences in a classroom, particularly on the premise that nature makes us all different, I have long since come to believe that our position in this has been wrong and perhaps as costly as any mistake ever made in education.

The first thing to do is to re-examine the promotion theory. Ask why it is that a fifth grader, so far as reading goes, is in the third grade. Ask who were his second, third, and fourth grade teachers, and why they allowed this pupil to get by without learning to read. Does your school promote automatically without regard to achievement? If your system does not support the idea of automatic promotion, how did the principal fail to catch the pupil's reading difficulty, so that he programed him for the higher grades even though he was severely retarded? Finally, check to find out what is wrong with your reading program, anyhow, if children are exposed year after year to teaching that produces such poor results.

Second, Check Your System of Grouping

It is obviously true that with the best of teaching pupil's achievement levels will sometimes range widely. Instead of going wild about within-class grouping, set up groups between classes.

While this is a subject being given the full treatment elsewhere in this volume, let me say that alphabetical age grouping by classes is about as stupid as ordering 30 pairs of shoes of the same size and expecting, say, a group of twelve-year-olds to wear them all with comfort.

Increase class teachability in reading, then, by grouping by classes for the bright, the average, and the slow, with special treatment groups where hospital or clinical techniques are called for.

Avoid the worst sin against the child—justifying a *laissez-faire* programing on the specious theoretical grounds that this is in accord with the best child development doctrine. Generally, the retarded reader and the very advanced reader in any normally distributed class are its most poorly adjusted members.

Third, Reappraise the Way Reading Is Taught

I have come to a conclusion that will cause hackles to rise in anger, but harsh as it is, I must declare it: *most of what now purports to be the teaching of reading is either only a listening exercise or a question and answer drill.*

From the sight-reading exercises to the round-robin reading of stories in the classroom reading group, the teacher listens, helps, and checks rather than instructs. I am excluding here the teaching of phonics, which, if a system such as the Phonovisual Method is used, requires direct teaching. When the first grade teacher shows the class a picture of a dog with the word *dog* under it, is this really teaching?

Would it be more like teaching if with the whole class taking part she printed the word *dog* on the blackboard, named the letters, talked about the *d* and *g*, asked the class to describe the animal it refers to, to name other words beginning with a sound of *d*, and so on, actually teaching the word *dog* as a lesson?

When, from dictation by the class, the teacher writes an experience chart about a trip to the zoo, is this teaching in the sense of instruction?

I favor this kind of exercise in its place, which of course can involve the whole class. But why not be certain that the teacher teaches new words as they are introduced, that she points out their phonetic characteristics, their meaning values, shows how they roll on the tongue, lets all the class learn, interact, and practice? Add this step, or one like it, and teaching will be taking place and the whole class can learn.

If the small group is reading together, while the teacher listens, is it enough for her to ask what the new words are, what they mean, and then begin the dreary round of oral reading, asking the class, "What is the word?" when Johnny gets stuck? Oral reading is needed, of course, but there ought to be a way to make it a good experience for the whole class, coupled with instruction by the teacher.

Should not the teacher plan lessons to show how words get their meaning, how the same words may work as nouns, or verbs, or adjectives, how the main meaning of a paragraph may be gotten out of the topic sentence, how detail is used to support the paragraph idea, how an author chooses words for strength, for concrete meaning, for persuasion through appeal to the emotions?

This is a long enough list to show what can be planned for direct teaching in reading to the whole class in place of the routine oral reading, recitation method, and rote drills which dominate the reading program as I have seen it in hundreds of classrooms.

Better teaching of reading is imperative, and well-planned lessons in this subject can be presented to the entire class with great profit. In fact, a good teacher with careful preparation in some phases of reading skills could instruct two or three classes at once. The individual or small group lessons, then, could be limited in number and frequency to the special needs of the problem learners.

With the present methods of small group lesson-hearing, the miracle is that so many learn as much as they do. This attests to the fact that many children learn on their own. They become quite well-educated in the process of growing up in the home, neighborhood, and school. But much more can be learned if teaching is planned and directed with the completeness that can be attained only if the teacher can instruct the class as a whole.

SUPPORTING PRINCIPLES OF THE WHOLE-CLASS METHOD

A direct look at the principles which justify teaching the whole class at one time will serve to clear up some misconceptions and to simplify an evaluation of the proposal:

1. As the informed adult in the classroom, the teacher is responsible for teaching what she knows to pupils.

This assigns the teacher to an active role again, after a period of time when she was a passive member of a child-centered society. The informed, forceful, and enthusiastic teacher will open new doors to learning faster, lead pupils into selected experiences, and help them to see the meaning of what they are learning. The teacher gives of her learning to the child, where she is the wise, experienced adult of whom questions may be asked and whose own pleasure in scholarship is communicated to her pupils.

2. She can impart information and stimulate learning most efficiently by direct instruction.

The simple truth is that the teacher is in the classroom to teach. This means she is the person who knows and is there to share her knowledge with the children. She is a person who has enthusiasm for learning and can communicate that enthusiasm to her pupils. She is capable of imparting learning with clarity, vigor, and dynamic interaction with her pupils. She knows her pupils, understands their weaknesses, but does not tolerate less than their maximum performance.

With the recent over-emphasis on the child as the learner, the teacher suffered an interesting and almost diasastrous demotion. She became a group leader, a learner along with the children, a moderator of an endless panel discussion, a passive and subdued adult in a situation where adults were to be seen but not heard. In a recent supervisory report on grouping published by a large school system, I came upon the following description of the teacher. She is, according to the report, "a listener, helper, questioner, resource person, a conditioning provider, a recognition giver, a problem solver, a material gatherer, an arbitrator, and an evaluator."

The teacher, of course, does many things in the classroom. Under the Amidon concept, however, she returns to the front of the room with chalk in hand to explain, discuss, reinforce learning by immediate checks on class responses, to teach what needs teaching, check learning, teach again, and test again. From the wealth of her own scholarship she helps her class to see connections between the known and the unknown, giving meaning to what otherwise may be missed by the pupil and taken for granted by the teacher.

An illustration may be found in the teaching of a poem; for example, the *Brook's Song* by Tennyson. To begin with children love this poem, as do adults, for its brightness, its gaiety, and its choice of words that clearly depict the sight and sound of the brook's short Odyssey as it moves on to lose itself in the river.

"I come from haunts of coot and hern"—let us stop at this point to ask, unless the teacher tells something about the coot and hern, how many will "see" these birds as they are, will sense the far reaches of their nesting places? Or should the teacher, in the midst of teaching, instruct the class to find the words in a dictionary? I think not. The tide is in at this point to tell and explain, to let the barque of the experience with the poem move on to its mission to convey pleasure in beauty and thought which comes with a reading of the poem.

We have long been too much impressed with the myth that for the teacher to tell what is to be learned is a bad thing. We have, I think, given too much attention to a method which assumes that children learn best when they undertake a personal research for answers to even the most incidental question.

I am not talking here about the lecture method of instruction. In teaching any new fact, skill, idea, the wise teacher involves the pupils, lets them draw upon experiences, leads them to clear meanings. Of course, the good lecturer will do this, too, but the difference is he does not entertain interaction, and therefore does not provide for the checking of learning as he goes along and pupils may not fully integrate what is being taught with what they already know.

Of all the experiences in a classroom, the most exciting is when something visibly happens to the thinking of a pupil, when there is a flash of understanding that is reflected in the countenance, in the brilliance of the eye, in the pleasure of the smile. When teachers achieve this, it is as if they were opening curtains to let in the dawn after a dark and dreary night.

The teacher who evokes such responses by means of her own presentation is the star performer in the Amidon plan.

3. Whole class teaching individualizes responsibility.

Some experience in group activity is a good thing. Of course, when a child meets and works with an entire class, he is profiting from an experience which, if correctly directed by the teacher, will improve his skill in working with, understanding, and respecting others.

But when most of the study in a school program consists of working with a group in a project, the development of individual responsibility is slow and, in some cases, neglected. In group activities a let-George-do-it attitude is fostered, a few leaders, the more aggressive members, do most of the work, make reports, and take over responsibility. Anonymity suppresses responsibility, and from this experience carelessness, laziness, and indifference are learned.

Whole class teaching puts each pupil on his own. He is responsible for assignments, responses, reports, even more difficult research studies. Hence, whole class teaching individualizes responsibility.

In our enthusiasm for collective action in the school classroom (and the word collective here has no subversive overtones), we have forgotten that learning is individual and that intellectual growth requires an aloneness during which the individual reflects upon, organizes, and draws conclusions. He needs to learn early that he will be quite alone as he encounters many of the most crucial experiences of life.

4. The whole class method permits greater individualization of instruction.

At the end of the school year, a fourth grade boy approached his teacher with hand extended and a friendly grin on his face.

"I want to tell you goodbye," he said in a matter-of-fact way and with a presence that was a surprise to his teacher. "I don't know whether I am going to pass," he added, "but I enjoyed being in your class."

His teacher told me that the boy was earnest and interested whenever she taught with special care to explain the content of the lesson. Although his reading skill was far below grade level, his ability to understand and use information in literature, history, science and arithmetic, the latter two subjects being of special interest to him, was high. Strong and clear teaching made learning an attainable goal for a boy who otherwise would have been helpless in a wilderness of printed words.

This is not to say that reading is unimportant or that it should be neglected in the school program. But the story illustrates the value of direct teaching, where the instructor communicates her knowledge to her pupils with the clarity that can be achieved only after careful study and planning. Although the fourth grade boy in this story could have learned much more if he were better able to use the printed page, direct teaching provided an otherwise unavailable opportunity to learn.

Because, as the teacher told, me, "He could learn if I told him," the boy's warm and appreciative attitude toward her suggested that his interest in school was good and that further effort to overcome the lag in reading was likely. With reteaching, always difficult in reading problems like this, the boy may be able to develop a reading level commensurate with his comprehension level, the latter having come to light because his teacher had the good sense to teach, and the wisdom to encourage the boy to respond in the classroom work where he had the ability to do so.

While I am using this episode to illustrate how direct teaching individualizes instruction, I am also sure that the story shows how quality teaching begins with quality relationships between the pupil and the teacher. Leave this out of the picture, and no system or method of teaching will work. As a matter of fact, the effect of classroom experience upon pupils will be negative. It would be better for them to stay home and watch television, God forbid, than to attend classes taught by teachers who cannot perceive and respect the innate characteristics of pupils in their classes.

It is altogether logical to say that good teaching bridges the gaps in individual differences within a class. This is so because such teaching gives meaning to facts and ideas that can never be acquired by the pupil alone. It recognizes that many pupils can understand far beyond their independent reading levels. I am sure that many pupils who are required to rely upon the self-help methods of the project system could learn far better under the whole class method. I am sure that under this system more pupils will achieve at levels commensurate with their age and grade and that the wide range in achievement which we see in the intermediate elementary grades is the result of bad teaching practices, particularly the neglect of direct instruction of the class as a whole.

5. *Whole class instruction makes more efficient use of teacher time.*

Very little elaboration of this point is needed. Instead of three groups in reading, the teacher will instruct one class. I have heard of teachers in desperation attempting to work with as many as six groups. In such cases, the principal and the top school administration, maybe even the community, need to be called to account for failures in class placement and the provision of special services. But the obvious point is that multiple within-class grouping splinters teacher time beyond reason, increases the amount of lesson planning and contributes to the neglect of all the children.

I hope the time will come as we work with the concept of whole-class teaching that there may be periods in each day when children may study well-assigned lessons, and the teacher may have time for lesson planning, checking papers, and even, if nothing more, a break in the arduous and demanding task of teaching pupils. Better organization for teaching should make it possible to relieve the elementary teacher at intervals during the day. Only those who have taught as much as five hours a day can begin to understand the arduous nature of this task. The good teacher gives of herself unstintingly, she maintains enthusiasm at a high level, and she is in a constant state of interaction with the personalities of her class, judging their responses, anticipating their moods, directing their energies into constructive outlets. The physical and emotional demands of this work are so great that she often ends the day exhausted.

THE TEXTBOOK IN THE AMIDON CONCEPT

Textbooks in recent years have fallen upon evil days. They reflect the anti-subject matter point of view recently in vogue in American public education. Their content and format, especially in language and social studies, mirror the confusion of purposes and method that accompany the unit principle of content organization which has been dominant in the elementary schools, and is currently insinuating itself into secondary education by way of the core curriculum. This condition is chargeable in part to the abdication of leadership responsibility by textbook publishers; their intention, quite understandable, to publish books that will sell; the neglect of scholarship in textbook writing; and the misuse of textbooks by hack teachers assigning lessons page by page without imagination.

Such misadventures, however, hardly justify discarding the printed page, man's most important invention for the perpetuation and dissemination of knowledge, as a means of educating children.

A more intelligent position to take is to re-examine the function of subject matter in education, to reassert the obvious truth that knowledge must be logically organized, to select out of the vast range of such knowledge the essential elements that must be transmitted to each generation, assemble this material in usable textbooks, and then to put them to work as foundations for teaching.

Textbooks Not Considered Fundamental

A measure of value accorded the textbook was revealed in a survey recently completed in the District of Columbia elementary schools. Because the textbook is a key element in the Amidon concept, we needed to know how many would be required to provide each pupil with textbooks in the basic subjects. This was essential to the application of the Amidon concept to all of our elementary schools.

I must confess the results of the survey were startling to me, because it was easy to take for granted that principals had through the years requisitioned books enough to provide one for each pupil. The presumption was that if there was a deficiency, this would have been made known. Principals and supervisors have a recognized responsibility for making their wants known. But when the tabulations were in it was discovered that 148,163 books would be needed to supply every pupil with the basic texts in reading, spelling, language, mathematics, science, history and geography. In other words, many classrooms were being taught with incomplete sets of texts. In some cases, *only the teacher had a copy.*

Because of adherence to the principle of multiple groupings within the classroom, texts were ordered for about a third of each class, roughly ten, to be rotated from one group to another. In order to supply this deficiency Congress authorized an expenditure of $285,000 in the spring of 1961 for new textbooks. While in part the lack of textbooks may be attributed to insufficient funds, the real explanation is that they were not considered a necessity for teaching. They were an adjunct to the process rather than a central and fundamental necessity.

The rationalization for this point of view is that curriculum selection should be made by pupils and teachers planning together. As has already been said, the child-centered view precluded adherence to a systematic organization of subject matter. No more significant testimony to the hazard in this point is needed than the evidence of the textbook shortage revealed by our survey.

The Problem of Selection

When plans were made for the opening of the Amidon school, the choice of textbooks posed a most difficult problem. This was particularly the case in the social studies field, where history and geography texts of the kind we wanted proved to be hard to come by. They seemed to lack substance, the style of writing was mainly narrative in an obvious effort to sugar-coat the content and, from a literary point of view, trite and childish; the subject matter appeared to be scant and uninvigorating. Reader texts continue to be repetitious and limited, with only a few publishers beginning to set them up as textbooks. In a recent and admittedly cursory examination of readers, I found little to commend them as texts. With perhaps two exceptions, they consisted mainly of vapid and unimaginative stories built around predetermined vocabularies selected to develop sight reading. To get directions for the teaching of reading, teachers have to rely on the manuals, because the reading textbooks provided little or nothing in the way of lesson guides.

In a first grade class I recently saw a small group reading with their teacher. They seemed to be doing well, were interested and responsive. The teaching technique was excellent.

When I asked about independence of word attack, the teacher demonstrated that children could name words that rhymed or that had similar beginning sounds.

The textbook had none of them in it. "I teach this to the children," the teacher explained.

"Why shouldn't the text contain simple lessons on word structure, phonics, comprehension?" I asked her.

"The lesson becomes too cut and dried then," she said.

The textbook is not a teacher, though far too many have used it as if it were. It can, however, aid the teacher, give her clear directions, be useful to the pupil who can see as well as hear, and have information fixed so that he can return to it for review.

Until textbooks become more like textbooks and less like feather-weight literature, the subject matter emphasis of the Amidon plan will be difficult to realize in full.

Characteristics of the "Amidon" Textbook

The textbook needed for the Amidon plan has a number of well-defined characteristics:

1. The substance or subject matter should be determined by the scholars or specialists in each subject field, cut to essentials, and placed in grades for maximum challenge.

2. This material should be directly, concisely, and factually

presented. There should be no doubt in the mind of pupil or teacher as to what is to be learned.

3. The purpose should be to impart facts, to interpret their meaning, to apply them to significant problems, to provide practice in techniques for assimilation and use of facts, information, ideas, and to test the learnings acquired.

4. The style or format ought to be simple, unified, and clear, so that the text may be a self-study device for pupils.

5. Subject matter textbooks should be written in some cases at different levels of difficulty. For instance, a United States history text for bright fourth graders should include difficult concepts and provide deep insights into the forces of history. A textbook for the average pupil will cover the same time span but with less depth in detail and more simplicity of concepts or interrelationships. Finally, a simple text for the slower learning classes covering the high points of history over the same time line should be simply written as to style and involvement of concepts, and yet be complete and meaningful.

The differences in difficulty will not be primarily in the amount of material but in its thought levels.

6. Since the content is selected by professionals, the amount should be reduced to allow adequate coverage during the course of the term, a semester or a year, for which the text is written. In some subjects, notably the social studies, textbooks tend to become compendiums so that they may be pleasing to all buyers by containing something for each. The trimmed-down text will be the basic guide to instruction in the term for which it is designed. This would also cut down costs, as well as to make the texts more manageable by pupils.

A lot of people would be happy to see the weight of textbooks cut down out of sheer concern for children who are expected to tote them to and from school.

Use of the Textbook

For the teacher, the textbook is a foundation for the development of her lesson plan. If the content is intelligently selected, this guides her in the choice of what to teach. If the curriculum guides she uses are similarly well done, she is freed of the unsuitable responsibility of judging for herself what should or should not be taught.

"Of course I believe in the use of textbooks," a teacher told me recently. "But they ought not to be followed slavishly. They are a foundation for lesson-planning, but a good lesson plan has to go beyond the textbook to take in the timely interests of the class, the season, the events in the community or even the world. The textbook, in the way I look at it, is not a substitute for the teacher. It is a tool in the hands of the teacher, the way a sewing machine is when a housewife or anyone uses it."

The good use of a textbook, however, does not relieve the teacher of her responsibility to teach. She should present, explain, illustrate, enhance, and enliven textbook and curriculum content. To a reasonable extent she will supplement or deviate from the text guide. Care needs to be taken, however, to prevent time-wasting excursions into special experiences, interests, or obsessions which teachers may have. I have many recollections of complaints from students about teachers who spend class time in presenting their memoirs when they should be, for example, teaching mathematics. My guess is that most citizens who have attended school for 12 years or more will recall at least one teacher who took great amounts of teaching time in extracurricular discussion. Good use of a text will provide the basis for control of the teaching time.

The worst possible use to make of a textbook is for the teacher to assign lessons page by page and then the next day in class have pupils read aloud from it in round-robin order. The next level of misuse, not quite so bad as the first, is to convert the class period into a study hall for the completion of an assignment in the text. Preparation of textbook assignments is a homework job. Another misuse of the text is a reliance upon it for questions and answers. Although this process is a part of a lesson, the teacher should not downgrade her status as teacher by simply becoming a quiz master. Interpretations, insights, relationships of what is to be learned to what is known should be developed with the class. Here the teacher, guided by the text, invigorates the learning process.

Finally, the textbook provides the pupil with the opportunity to study, review, and relearn what the teacher has been teaching. Reliance for learning chiefly on oral presentation by the teacher neglects relearning as an essential part of mastery. Teaching by means of activity units adds to the indefiniteness of treatment, and the accidental selection of content introduces a weakening transiency of contact with knowledge. The textbook, on the other hand, enables the pupil to restudy what has once been studied.

This is the purpose of printing. It provides permanence for the record of man's knowledge. It produced the civilization we now have. What distorted concept of the purpose of teaching has led us to hold the printed word suspect as a means of knowledge? Unless teaching uses the printed word it will be transient and undependable.

The Testimony of a Teacher

In a circular issued in July, 1960, I invited teachers of fifth grade United States history to switch over from the unit method to the use of a textbook. The following is selected and paraphrased from a report received from a fifth grade teacher in one of our elementary schools where students from the District of Columbia Teachers College are trained:

> He selected a book, wrote the teacher, that developed a time concept, emphasized the struggle to gain and preserve our liberties, and provided good review and enrichment exercises. As they studied the text, the class organized projects dealing with elections, school problems, and current events in relation to their historical backgrounds. Thus the use of the text contributed to the developing of study units that enlivened the class work and developed appreciation of ideals, values, and practices in American democracy.

The teacher's summary of the advantages of teaching from a textbook shows that he favored the method for reasons he listed as follows:

1. The program provided definite guide lines for the children and teacher alike.
2. It provided definite and ready instructional material.
3. It provided for sequential development and evaluation of the study skills of the pupils.
4. It helped improve and enrich study habits, as children, through taking books home, reviewed the work of the day or pursued other meaningful assignments given by the teacher.
5. It gave depth and breadth to teaching as children were able to follow the sequence of units as set up by textbook authorities in the field of American history.
6. It provided better opportunities for the evaluation by the teacher of the subject matter learned.

Homework

It should be remembered that schools were organized in the first place because the home became unable to perform all of the educational functions it had managed to do very early in the history of society. The home continues to be an important educational agency and the school is mainly an extension of the home in respect to the education of children. Because of the close tie-in between home and school, the involvement of the parents in the education of the children needs to be given central attention. Homework is therefore a means of enlisting their support of the schools' objectives and in turn provides for strengthening the home as an educational center.

The school attitude toward homework has sometimes led to short-sighted policies. Recently a parent told me that when his son was in the sixth grade a number of years ago, his teacher would not let him take home his books. "We teach differently from parents," she told him. Incidentally, this intelligent father has long remembered, in a rather unkindly way, the teacher's statement. It amounted to a supercilious rejection of the home.

Although homework has a value far beyond that of good public relations, this aspect should not be ignored.

Another hard problem in handling the homework issue is to decide what we are talking about. I find that many educators who say they favor homework are really talking mostly about what parents and children do together rather than about lessons which children are to prepare at home for the class next day. This is not the kind of homework we have in mind in the Amidon plan.

Homework as defined here means the preparation of an assigned lesson at home. This will often require the pupil to take the textbook home, especially when the lesson is encompassed in it. The homework may consist of practice in spelling, the preparation of a written report, the doing of a drill in arithmetic, or review for an examination. Within this view of homework, the home is therefore a study center where textbooks are used and parents may help the pupil.

Because homework has great importance in the acceleration of learning expected under the Amidon concept, guide lines should be useful.

1. Teachers should expect children from the second grade on to do some of their study at home.

2. Parents should be advised that this is expected and that they should make arrangements for this in the daily schedule, including providing a place for children to study and encouraging them to do so.

3. Homework assignments should be specific and clear, so that the pupil knows what is expected of him. He should be prepared by good teaching to do what is expected of him.

4. The amount of homework should be reasonable, probably not to exceed an hour in grades two and three, and two hours through grade six.

5. Homework should be planned with pupils so that they will take the necessary textbook home.

6. Homework should be permitted in any subject, including reading. It is nonsense to believe that if a pupil uses his reader at home before he has the same material in class he will lose interest in the reading lesson, that is, if reading is being *taught* during the lesson.

7. Homework should be used in the classroom. It should never be only "busy" work. It should have meaning, which comes from checking and discussing the lessons in class.

8. Finally, homework is possible for most children, even if the home conditions are limited, if the parents will assist in a sensible way. Working with parents on how they can help their children is one of the most important advantages of a good homework program.

Time Schedule in the Amidon Concept

To find the time to teach the subjects included in the Amidon plan is no easy task. The plan has no meaning, however, unless this is done.

The time schedule which has been prescribed for use in schools adopting the program provides for specified periods of instruction in the basic subjects. This assures direct attention to the content and is designed to place subjects in order of importance, so that the more essential ones are given the more favorable times of the instructional day.

While the daily schedule is to be respected by the teachers, flexibility is recommended when carefully justified by circumstances, including special activities or significant all-school programs. These changes in schedule, however, are to be infrequent.

Where teaching of several groups at once is useful, this is not only authorized but encouraged. It is believed that an increasing amount of such instruction, team planned and masterfully handled, will occur as experience with the Amidon program grows.

Part Three

EVALUATIONS OF THE AMIDON PLAN

TO AVOID ANY MISTAKE AS TO THE NATURE OF EVALUATION of the Amidon Plan in action, I want to say again that *the project does not purport to be scientific.*

In the first place, scientific methods for the measurement of techniques in education have been difficult to apply. Research studies that depend upon precise comparisons of control and experimental groups generally produce unreliable results despite the involved statistical computations which seem to make the findings respectable. Even with the closest scrutiny of pupil characteristics to set up comparable groups, reaching an exact equation is impossible. The most carefully selected groups may seem alike, but in fact are not because the many incomprehensible and relatively non-objective personality characteristics defy identification and weighing. Even the variations in experiences while the pupils are undergoing instruction, including the influence of the teachers who are never identical, are factors that cannot be defined. The variability of many hidden factors reduces the reliability of a comparison of the results of teaching control and experimental groups no matter how precisely such groups have been equated. Hence, because I believe such research in education is of little value, I am making no claim for scientific accuracy in the evaluation of the Amidon demonstration.

I must say also that complete objectivity in evaluation of the Amidon program is hardly attainable, considering my own enthusiasm for the Amidon concept. While what I report from teachers, pupils, and parents reflects an extraordinary unanimity as to their support for the program, it may be that their enthusiasm is engendered at least in part by such things as newness, excitement resulting from widespread interest by others, and the challenge felt by the staff to make the project successful at all costs. Candor forces me to say, then, that this section on evaluation needs to be read sternly, because while I do not intend to hide adverse comment or data about results, I personally came through the demonstration period at the Amidon School surer than ever that the ideas are right and when applied do greatly improve the quality of education. Thus, I ask you to be aware of my personal prejudices in favor of the Amidon experience as you read this section of the book. Yet as you do take a look at the "results" of the year's work with the Amidon concept, keep in mind that what I have seen and learned over this period of time has enhanced my enthusiasm for the project. My prejudice has increased. I am convinced that the Amidon year was only the beginning stage of an educational development which will become more effective as conditions for its use improve with experience.

chapter seven

DISTRICT OF COLUMBIA SCHOOL

SYSTEM

TO TALK ABOUT THE AMIDON SCHOOL, OR THE CONCEPT which is associated with it, as if it were entirely unrelated to the school system of which it is a part, would be something like describing a house without reference to the terrain on which it is placed. The meaning of the Amidon demonstration will be clearer if it is analyzed against a comprehensive backdrop. Besides, this offers an excellent opportunity to say something about the public schools which, because they are in the nation's capital, belong in a way to the entire country. The District of Columbia schools have come in for considerable national attention because of desegregation, particularly, and they need balanced evaluation to counteract the more limited and sometimes distorted reports about them.

SIZE AND SCOPE

This is a fairly large school system, with an enrollment in 1961 of more than 128,000 pupils with an increase predicted for the next five years. But size is not by any means a unique or praiseworthy quality in a school system. In school organization, size is only an increase in the number of schools, each with its own characteristic; and in the number of pupils, each with his unique qualities. The statistics that come across my desk are fairly large: 195 schools, nearly 5,200 teachers, more than 128,000 pupils. But the school system is really one pupil, one teacher, one classroom, one school, standing single file down the long corridor to the sum of them all. I like to keep my eye on the units of measure, rather than the total figures, which are only a computer-system product far removed from reality.

Some of my articulate, perhaps I should say more outspoken, associates remind me now and then that my office is an ivory tower and hence I do not really know what is going on in the classroom. But I like to maintain the illusion that I can pierce the statistical curtain between me and persons in the classrooms, and at occasional intervals know the Johnny or Mary in any school as a living, reacting, and dynamic personality. If you will accept the effort, if not the effect, I will be sustained in my opinion that *bigness* in a school system is only a multiplication of units, and that the essence of the school organization is the individual who occupies a seat in a given classroom at a specified time.

But large numbers of such individuals increase the incidence if not the range of differences among them.

In the larger school system, many pupils with serious physical handicaps will be found, and therefore a special school for the orthopedically handicapped can be set up. In our school system, a model new school has recently been built, and here children who could not get along in regular school groups are taught subjects from the kindergarten to the twelfth grade level. In coordination with the District Department of Public Health, the school supplies physical and occupational therapy and careful nursing care. On the morning of a school day it is both a saddening and an inspirational experience to watch children leave the school busses, some in the arms of attendants, some rolling their own wheelchairs from specially designed vehicles, and some ambulatory. One will observe on their countenances a radiance reflecting inner enthusiasm as they enter the colorful corridors of the building and wheel or walk toward their classrooms. Bigness in numbers makes such a school possible—but bigness of heart in those who through many years planned and fought for this special program is always much more important.

When a school system is large, flexibility exists that sometimes more than counter-balances the impersonal and anonymous treatment often required. It makes possible a greater amount of ability grouping:

> For example, in a school with three first grades, a distribution by evident ability makes it possible to set up an honors class. Of such a class, a teacher said, "I didn't know first graders could learn so fast and so eagerly."
>
> In a jocular vein, an assistant superintendent said, "Then you didn't have to work hard this year."
>
> "Work hard?" replied the teacher, smiling, "I worked harder than I ever have in my life."

It will be said that, if a school system has 340 first grade classes, of course it can do a great deal of ability grouping. It can organize special classes for the immature like the junior primaries of which 103 in 1960–61 provided a year of further education between the kindergarten and first grade, so that the slow-growers don't have to "fail" in the first grade and so the first grade teacher can get at once to the business of teaching what is generally assigned to that age level.

Bigness, though, is sometimes over-stressed as an advantage seemingly not available to smaller school systems. Someone said, "Of course you can have a four-track curriculum in your high schools, because you have so many large schools." Actually, a principal of a three-year high school of 500 can organize the academic classes along ability lines if he desires. Bigness is not the *sina qua non*, although it does give a chance for a greater number and variety of subject offerings. In our 11 high schools, with an enrollment in 1961–1962 of 13,000, a fairly wide range of foreign languages (German, French, Spanish, Latin, and Russian) can be offered—some would add Chinese, Hindustani, Arabic. The mathematics curriculum can provide college level trigonometry and analytical calculus.

Consider the vocational education offerings in five different schools (we wanted to put these under one big roof, but Congress said "No" to the proposal on the premise that the District of Columbia is too poor to afford the eleven million dollars that this would cost). But, bigness does help to justify the establishment of separate vocational schools, the expenditure of fairly large sums for equipment, and a per capita cost of $607 per pupil. And be sure to understand that the vocational schools are not havens for the non-academic student or the trouble-maker. They are our most selective schools: Pupils must pass a screening examination to get into them. Still some of our less astute counselors, unable to shake off their obsolete ideas about vocational education, advise pupils to enroll in the vocational schools only as a last resort.

A Teachers College, fully accredited, an Americanization School for youth and adults from abroad, internationally known for the excellence of its work, a Capitol Page School, headquartered in the Library of Congress, for young men employed as pages in the Congress and the Supreme Court add to the list of special offerings included within the scope of the District of Columbia school system.

In the District of Columbia, no other enterprise touches the lives of so many of its citizens as does its system of public education. Remember that not only the pupils and those employed by the Board of Education are directly affected, but also the parents, relatives, and friends of pupils, businessmen, including suppliers, and many government employees from policemen to Congressmen.

The Amidon School, obviously, is a small unit in a large enterprise. The concept associated with it, however, has proved to have an influence far beyond its locale. It is not unusual for an idea to escape the physical limitations of its original conception.

WHO RUNS THE SCHOOLS?

You do, of course. As voters you send your representatives to Congress and you decide who the President of the United States will be. It may shock you to discover that you are responsible for the school system in the nation's capital, especially if there are things going on here that you don't like. But next time you cast a ballot for a member of your national government, make a note of the fact that your representative will help to decide what the District of Columbia schools ought to be like.

Here is the way you come into the picture as one of millions of enfranchised citizens.

The District Government is headed by a board of three commissioners nominated by the President subject to the approval of the Senate. One of these is a career officer from the Army Engineer Corps assigned to duty on the Board of Commissioners to supervise construction and maintenance of public works. As a member of the Commission, however, he has voting rights equal to those of the two political appointees. The Board of Commissioners runs the city under authority delegated to it by the United States Congress. For changes or additions to that authority, the Commissioners must obtain the necessary legislation from Congress.

In turn, as a part of its Committee system, the House and Senate have set up Committees on the District of Columbia. The majority party designates the chairmen of the House and Senate District Committees, and the majority party has a majority of membership on the two committees. All proposed changes in legislation dealing with the District of Columbia are referred by the parent legislative bodies to their respective District Committees. Proposals for changes in legislation may originate in the Board of Education, for example, to be referred to the Board of Commissioners, who after study and concurrence, will forward the legislative proposals through the Bureau of the Budget to the Speaker of the House and the President of the Senate, where the bills will be assigned to the District Committees. Bills may originate with lobby groups for introduction by request by friends in Congress. They may be proposed, of course, on the initiative of members of Congress.

To illustrate how the Board of Education may initiate legislation: After long study and at least one objective research survey, the District of Columbia Board of Education decided to set up a junior college program as a part of its present four-year Teachers College offering. After the proposal was first approved on May 20, 1959, by the Board of Education, it was referred to the Board of Commissioners, who, after due deliberation and extended staff study, approved the proposal and forwarded the legislative language and a report justifying it to the Bureau of the Budget. This is an agency of the Executive Branch of the Federal Government responsible for examining all legislative proposals submitted by Executive departments, of which the local Board of Commissioners is one. Since the Budget Bureau found no objection to the Junior College Bill it went to the Speaker of the House. After being thrown into the legislative hopper of the House of Representatives, it was referred to the House District Committee.

Having been introduced into the House, the Bill was scheduled for a hearing by a subcommittee of the House District Committee. In this hearing, the superintendent carried the major burden of justification. As is the general custom, the representative of the Commissioners limited his testimony to the favorable policy position of his principal, and the Board of Education members who testified generally also stated the supportive position of their body in respect to the proposed legislation.

In the case of the Junior College Bill, the Senate District Committee also held hearings, following which it approved the legislation, made a favorable report to the Senate in due course, and in this instance the Senate approved the Bill. But the Bill did not become law because the House District Committee failed to report it, and hence the Bill died with the end of the session of the 86th Congress in 1960. It is thus, as you can see, that your representatives control the local school system through legislation which sets the limits of authority given to the Board of Education.

Congress, of course, has previously conferred broad authority upon the Board of Education to operate the schools, appoint a superintendent and staff, and determine curriculum. The statute establishing the District of Columbia Board of Education subordinated that body to the Commissioners in fiscal affairs, thus establishing fiscal dependency upon a Commission appointed by the President, for whom you as a voter are also responsible.

In money matters, the Board of Education can spend only those sums authorized by appropriation bills enacted by Congress and signed by the President.

This is the procedure:

1. Appropriation requests originate from the different school departments in midwinter of a given school year.
2. They are screened by the administrative staff and set up in budget form with justifications by the schools' budget officer.
3. In late spring the staff budget is presented to the Board of Education Finance Committee for analysis. review, ap-

proval with or without changes, and reported to the Board itself, which acts on the proposed budget.

4. After approval by the Board of Education, the budget estimates go to the Board of Commissioners, who refer them to their Budget Department for review and inclusion in the District Budget Proposals.

5. The District of Columbia budget officials extract, subtract, and detract, all without the use of Novocain, generally cutting the proposals on the grounds of insufficient funds and sometimes on the premise that they know better what is good for the schools than does the school staff.

Of course, the budget officers have to be hatchet men, because every district department fights for a position of advantage in respect to the revenue dollar, which is never big enough to satisfy all the demands for service.

Impatience is hard to suppress when one finds himself trying to understand why it is more important to build sewers than school houses, or why the care and nurture of zoo animals supersedes the education of children. It is not cricket, perhaps, to argue that schools ought to have more money at the expense of other departments. But if priorities have to be set up, somebody has to make a case for the education of children.

Essential services, like bread and butter, ought to be supplied in all departments by increased taxation and borrowing if necessary. Providing essential services is self-liquidating—in that they pay for themselves by preventing losses, say from crime or disease, and increasing productivity by the increase of health, vigor, safety, and education.

After the budget officials have made their incisions upon the body of the budget, cutting here and there as they think necessary, they thoughtfully invite the superintendent to be heard by them on the cuts they have made. With an appeal, by turns obsequious, rational, florid and belligerent, the superintendent attempts to get a restoration of deleted budget items. He tends to become especially impatient when a staff member sententiously announces that his investigation leads him to believe that elementary school librarians or counselors are of questionable value. He would be much happier if the budget boys would simply say, "Look, Old Man, we just can't afford them right now."

6. Past experience has shown that after the superintendent's appeal to the budget staff, a few *centimes* are restored to the budget. The next stage is the occasion on which the Commissioners themselves hear the appeal of the Board of Education and its executive staff on the mayhem inflicted upon their budget by the employees of the District of Columbia Government.

7. If you are bored up to this point, or even long before, what apology can I offer? I can think of none. This is not really even the half-way station, so far as the ultimate budget journey is concerned. It is, however, the crucial stage, because unless the Commissioners say "yes" to a budget request, the item is generally dead. If the Commissioners approve an item, it still has to make the grade with the appropriations committees on the House and Senate sides. These are subcommittees of the major committees on appropriations. They are separate, distinct, and quite unrelated to the House and Senate District Committees.

There follows, then, in due course after the January opening of Congress and anywhere up to midsummer, the hearings on the budget before the House Subcommittee on Appropriations for the District of Columbia. While at these hearings the District Commissioners are the advocates of the Budget, which is now a part of the President's budget, each department head is himself the chief defender of his own section of the total District Budget. Interrogation by the members of the committee, who rely chiefly on their clerk for questions, may sometimes last two full days on the school part of the budget. In the course of this analysis, any aspect of school operation may be explored, including how teaching is done, how many phonograph records were bought the preceding year, why Italian is not taught in the high schools, how much is spent on travel.

Rather than moan about this kind of probing questioning, and despite the fact that I think some of it unfair, especially when I am caught short on the answers, I must say I think there is real safety in this process. Deep, revelatory, intelligent, the questioning opens up to light and air what, without it, might become pretty musty, bureaucratic, maybe even of questionable public morality. This is the check-system at work, a ruthless quest for malfunctioning and even malfeasance, and, rather than have less of it, I can see value in some of it throughout the structure of public service at the local as well as national level. School executives are generally above reproach in a moral sense, in the aspect of trust with public funds, but none of us is above needing the stimulus of a thorough evaluation by a responsible outside authority.

Who runs the school system in the nation's capital? In the end you do, in the quality of the people you send to Congress and put in the White House. Within the delegation of authority established by Congress through legislation, the District of Columbia Board of Education (nine members appointed by the judges of the United States District Court for the District of Columbia) constitutes a board of directors who, through their executive staff, operate the schools.

Hence, the Board of Education was able, within the authority delegated to it, to authorize the Amidon program. Interestingly enough, however, when additional money was needed for textbooks to make the program city-wide, it was the appropriations subcommittee that authorized the use of unexpended appropriations for this purpose. Thus, more directly than you think, you as voting citizens have had a hand in the Amidon project.

WHO PAYS?

It is not uncommon for people to assume that because the public schools are in the nation's capital they are supported by the Federal Government. Sometimes it is thought that local school administrators have a pipe line to the United States Treasury. The fact is that most school funds are raised by taxes paid by the residents of the District of Columbia.

In this city taxpayers, like those in other municipalities throughout the country, support local services chiefly through the payment of property, sales, and District income taxes.

Of an appropriation of approximately $268,000,000 for the District Government in the fiscal year which ends June 30, 1962, the Congress of the United States, appropriated $30,000,000 from Federal funds as a donation in lieu of taxes for lands occupied for Federal establishments and for services rendered, such as water supply, police and fire protection.

Another important fact is that to levy all taxes except the property tax the local government must get authorizing legislation from Congress. To raise the sales tax, for instance, the House District Committee must say "yes" to proposed legislation, the Bill must be approved by the House of Representatives, the Senate District Committee must agree and then the Senate itself must approve. Differences in legislation must be adjusted by a Conference Committee of House and Senate members, and if agreement is reached, the Bill must be approved by the President of the United States.

If it happens that in any case, for example, a sales tax bill, a member of Congress objects on principle and if he is a powerful member of a key committee and a tenacious foe of what he disapproves on principle, the local citizens cannot, even if they want to, decide for themselves how much taxes they want to dig up for schools or other services. Political scientists are, I am sure, thoroughly intrigued by the strange twist of events which prevents a city from taxing itself for better schools.

PROBLEMS

The District of Columbia School System has most of the problems of the typical urban center, and perhaps some that are unique. No one takes much pleasure in being in the same leaky boat with others, despite the claim that misery loves company. School superintendents like, however, to mention the commonness of their problems for security reasons—their own security.

But, though I hope not to be ready to consider everything to be for the best, problems demand attention and thus have value. In a way, I suppose, being generally a source of discomfort, problems have been through the ages stimuli for most human progress. Having made it clear now that we are not dismayed by our school problems, a brief run-down on their nature will perhaps enhance the significance of the Amidon concept.

Immigration. Every year many children come into our school system from other states. During the first semester of the school year 1960–1961, 5,600 new pupils entered our schools from outside the District of Columbia. In the same period 2,319 moved from the District to the suburbs or elsewhere.

In these days, too many parents give little thought to keeping their children in school until the year is out. Of course, some do, a small number, but the strong antagonism parents used to have about school disruptions, or a break in the school year, or the importance of regularity of school attendance has diminished. I'm sure some of this irresponsibility is unavoidable because of the way things work out for the family. Much of it, though, comes from the current opinion among adults and children in most schools that not too much will be missed if the pupil is absent. Because this is the way it looks to me now, I was especially thrilled when a fifth grade Amidon girl wrote a note to her principal telling her she hated to miss history, but she was glad the class took off time to watch her performance on a television program. This hints at the possibility of a return to the old-fashioned virtues of work in school, regularity in attendance, and the development of responsibility.

Much of the movement into Washington is from depressed rural areas where economically and culturally deprived Negroes and whites are forced to try their luck in the city. For them, the new frontier is the wilderness of city streets. Many have multiple handicaps to overcome, and their main source of hope is the public school. Hope, which is always a problem in disguise, needs the sustenance of a good system of schools.

Though the schools here suffer many deficiencies and dismaying failures, greater substance and structure in curriculum with increased flexibility for individual differences make them the means to progress for children otherwise tyrannized by their heritage.

I would make no point of the fact that most immigrant families are Negroes, except that others will if I don't. In October of 1961 the ratio of Negro to white pupils in our schools was more than four to one, the enrollment being nearly 81.5 percent Negro. In September of 1954, a white elementary school principal told her newly integrated assembly of children, "You are not Negro or white to us. You are children coming to school to learn." This simple but profound enunciation of a great truth has been our guide in working to meet the problems not of integration but of education. Because schools are established to educate children, attention should be directed to ways by which the quality of education can be stepped up. Among other changes in this school system, the Amidon is a product of this emphasis.

Mobility. In addition to the high rate of migration into and out of the District of Columbia schools, the movement from one section to another within the city during the course of a school year creates many difficult administrative and educational problems. The extent of such movement is shown in a sampling of mobility in 16 schools with a total enrollment of 12,552. In these schools 2,403 new pupils entered during the school year 1960–61 and 1,692 were transferred out, mostly from school to school within the area. The causes of this transiency are multiple: poor and insufficient housing, inability to pay rents, dislocation by change in use of buildings, and, to a limited extent, urban redevelopment. The loss in education is appalling, considering the adjustments required of both pupils and teachers. For every pupil transfer out of or into a school 10 items of paper must be handled by the teachers and principals.

Mobility is a persistent characteristic of big city living. It makes necessary a high degree of standardization in curriculum and teaching practices so that pupils may move into new classrooms where the subject matter and the textbooks are similar to those in the schools from which they transferred.

The Amidon concept, while not originated specifically to meet the mobility problem, will result in a higher level of standardization than is currently practiced. My opinion is that because high mobility is national in scope, an increase in standardization of school practices throughout the country is imperative.

Low Effort Quotient. Any teacher will remember having capable pupils in her classes who, no matter how hard she tried, refused to work. The memory of one such boy has haunted my mind since my high school teaching days. In this case, the young man, whose I. Q. was close to 140, refused to respond to instruction in English, at least some parts of it. "My father says 'ain't' and he is doing all right. He makes a good living," he told me and his tenth grade classmates.

In a broad way this story illustrates how, because motivation is related to the home environment of the pupil, the values held by a teacher in a classroom may be rejected by members of her class. Not that this is always bad, I hasten to say, because the values, the level of cultural attainment, and the quality of mind of the teachers are sometimes surprisingly low. Hence, for some pupils such teachers can offer no positive influence upon motivation. But in any case, the school cannot afford to gear its program to the cultural level or objectives of the deprived home. How to get pupils to accept school content which often seems bookish and remote from their daily experiences poses a problem of great importance in our school system. Failure to accomplish acceptance of school purposes by pupils discourages motivation for school success, at least the intrinsic self-propelled kind. Many pupils, wanting to be admired, will do what they think the teacher wants them to do. They may also be extrinsically motivated by the social mores of their school class. But even this reason for effort falls short of the kind that comes from inner, self-identified purposes.

In the District of Columbia schools, motivation of effort toward approved goals is lacking in many pupils because of the cultural and economic limitations of their families. This is a persistent problem in most school systems, but it is one of very high incidence in urban centers with their high density of impoverished population in the blighted residential areas.

More stultifying than anything else to national growth is the absence in the attitude of many school children of a desire to learn, to achieve, to "amount to something." In contrast I find visitors from all parts of the world to be possessed by an avid, irresistible, almost electric desire to learn, to achieve personal and national goals, and to improve their lot through independent study.

In the past we have put too much emphasis upon spoon-feeding children in the schools, inviting them to choose what they will learn, and in fact, to decide whether or not to learn, fastening blame upon the teacher if they do not learn, when the responsibility for self-improvement must be generated within the pupil. In our zeal to make things easy for children we may begin to make dependents out of them at a very early age. Motivation is not being self-generated today. The characteristic of self-determination in the people who in our earlier history built this great nation is being dissipated by the widespread belief that we have *arrived* and therefore everything is all right with us. In our classrooms we see far too much of the "easy street" attitude among children including those whose families are recipients of public assistance.

In the District of Columbia schools, the direction of effort is toward regenerating the fading, sometimes totally lost, spirit of independence, of a drive to do everything possible for oneself, of ambition to achieve above the present levels of effort. While not the complete means to the end, the Amidon philosophy sets a high expectancy level for the individual pupil, and aims to develop independence of effort, an attribute desperately needed in the nation's capital.

Drop Outs. Despite the many efforts of this school system to develop a curriculum which will increase the holding power of the schools, the incidence of school leaving continues to be high.

"Why is this a school problem?" a citizen asked not long ago. "If a pupil doesn't want to learn, then let him leave school. That is his decision. When he leaves, the school has no further responsibility for him."

A widely held opinion is that if a pupil doesn't want to study, let him go to work.

In the District of Columbia school system, the point of view, not fully supported by every teacher, every principal, or every citizen, is that each child ought to stay in school as long as he can profit from doing so. The responsibility of school planners is to provide the kind of education from which every pupil can profit. Moreover, the economic facts of life are such that job opportunities for the untrained, the irresponsible, and the incompetent have practically dried up. In a tight labor market, few employables are left standing in line. But the number of unskilled jobs is becoming limited to the point that many hundreds of young men and women leave school in our city to roam the streets, generally in anger, in quest of action, in search of satisfactions they are unable to get by socially acceptable means.

It is my belief that a part of the drop-out problem starts in the first grade when reading failures begin. Every encounter with background information about drop outs show that the great majority are academic failures—*chiefly because they can't read.*

Reading is the crucial skill for school success, for satisfaction in school participation, for self-respect in relation to others in a classroom. Would you not leave the team if you were permanently committed to the side lines? If every time you came to bat you ignominiously struck out, how long would it be before you lost interest in the game?

Therefore, the Amidon system, with its stress upon reading instruction, is expected to help reduce the drop-out problem. Any improvement in the teaching of basic subjects will upgrade human behavior.

Academic Retardation. If you could examine the scores on standardized achievement tests in your schools, I predict you would be appalled to discover that many pupils are severely retarded in such basic subjects as reading and arithmetic. Without wanting to make you uncomfortable—although I think we all ought to be about such a condition—I will predict further that in any given regular sixth grade some pupils will be found who cannot read at all. That is, they stumble and fumble with second and third grade material, a level of skill which for all practical purposes is not much beyond the crawling stage.

In our school system, we have been aware of this state of affairs for quite a while. Even conceding the fact that many children come to school almost wholly unprepared to learn, mostly because of the lack of culture-building experiences, the continuing extent of educational retardation points up the need for an objective look at our instructional program, and the raising of some soul-searching questions about it.

In reports of our own city-wide tests we find every year that many of our students read so far below grade level that they are unable to function in the regular classroom in other subjects. In some cases, they are non-readers. In others they can only limp along in the reading materials required of them in such subjects as mathematics, science, history, and geography. The teachers of these subjects often have to try to teach reading skills that ought to have been learned as early as second and third grades. Or they try to do so, and fail miserably, because they cannot really teach the fundamentals of reading while trying to explain, for example, the intricacies of mathematics. It is hard enough to teach the latter as a separate subject.

Measured by tests, which are not the final evaluation—the real test is what a pupil can do with a printed page—great numbers of pupils are either untaught or not taught well. To illustrate, in the sixth grade in 1960–61 there were 1,306 pupils, nearly 14 percent of the total, who were reading below the fourth grade level as measured by a standardized survey test given in March of that school term.

I have given a great deal of time to public explanations that standardized testing inevitably produces statistics which by their nature are distributed over a wide range, with a central point called the median, a process which in itself puts half the scores below and the other half above it. Yet despite every plausible theoretical explanation about the low scores, the fact remains that the children who make them are not statistical units but persons unable to read with a useful degree of skill. I can no longer live comfortably with a theoretical and satisfying explanation of retardation as I think of the hundreds of pupils in our school system who, despite statistical pleasantries, are crippled readers.

Though I must speak of this dissatisfaction, I am happy with the demonstrable fact that since desegregation in 1954 our standard test medians have significantly improved. A limited confidence in the effect of stepped-up teaching of the basic subjects during this period is amply justified. While I take my hat off to the teachers who have accomplished this minor miracle, I will not stand bareheaded for long, while we are doing less than we can with so many who would respond to greater advantage to the methodology and content of a strict, ordered, directly taught school program. The installation of the Amidon concept, therefore, is an answer in action to the patent shortcomings and weaknesses of the prevailing methodology.

Every day that we dawdle in lack-luster inertia we produce human problems that should stir our minds and hearts with remorse. There is a sense of urgency in our need for educational reform that can tolerate no further delay.

YESTERDAY'S AND TODAY'S SCHOOLS
NOT GOOD ENOUGH

In colonial days a blunderbuss might do for bringing home the game needed for sustenance. The woods and streams abounded in live targets, and a clumsy weapon was sure to find a target now and then. In those days, too, formal education could be a hit-or-miss affair without threatening survival. There was always the new frontier to absorb the mistakes. But neither the blunderbuss nor the school room of yesteryear will do the job required for today and tomorrow. Nothing in the District of Columbia school plans, including the Amidon concept, suggest that anything like the simple trial and error teaching of many early classrooms will do today. The Amidon is not an expression of anyone's unconscious yearning for a return to the good old days. The skills and techniques needed in the modern school for today and tomorrow must be superior, I think, to anything so far developed in education. I say this because the District of Columbia school people and most of the community are aware that improvement must be made in the way the schools function, and this can be achieved only by evolving new procedures, by combining the soundest of all the practices in any day or time and carefully judging new ideas before applying them on a wide scale.

chapter eight

PUPILS AND PARENTS EVALUATE

AMIDON

I. WHAT PUPILS SAY ABOUT THE AMIDON

IT HAS BEEN MY OBSERVATION THAT PUPILS WANT ORDER and substance in the school program. They may not often say so openly because they must maintain a fiction among themselves that they abhor school responsibilities. In extreme cases, where the teacher is clearly a malingering time-waster, the older pupils will take open action against the condition. They will join together in appeals to school authorities like principals and superintendents. They will write letters—I have a good file of these. They will appeal for assignment to another teacher, or they will drop the subject if they have a choice, thus preferring to sacrifice an interest rather than undergo the horrors of bad teaching.

Younger pupils also desire order in the school day. They may not consciously acknowledge this wish or even be aware of it. They may seem to enjoy freedom from routine and responsibility. Their free-wheeling behavior in a very permissive classroom may seem to be very much to their liking. But they want and need discipline, control, and substance, for these provide security and challenge. On the other hand, they resent disorder and softness, especially if it seems that the teacher is trying to please them by yielding to their whims. Many first-year teachers make the mistake of trying to get pupils to like them by being indulgent and weak. Most of us who have been through this experience have found that pupils may outwardly seem happy in an undemanding situation but inwardly dislike it and hold the teacher in contempt.

I was not surprised, then, at the enthusiasm expressed by the Amidon pupils for their teachers, who combined concern with discipline, and for the demanding Amidon curriculum which made a virtue of work and challenge. The pupils' comments as reported by the teachers at the end of the first year show how much value they place upon effort and accomplishment.

Pupils' Attitude Toward Work

When the Amidon plan was first announced, many educators and some parents were fearful that the pupils would be overwhelmed by the pressure of work. Nightmarish images of children chained to desks and enslaved by textbooks were obviously conjured up, this being no doubt an expression of a philosophy that because work is a necessary evil, childhood should be free of it.

The children themselves make the best answer to the misguided "don't push me" point of view. Their comments almost unanimously reveal an enthusiasm for hard work under friendly but demanding teachers:

"Amidon," wrote a sixth grader, "is some swell school! We have to work hard, but I like it. You know, I never liked school before."

Another in the same grade told his teacher, "We played a lot last year. It was fun, but we didn't learn much. Now, we hardly ever play, but we're having fun just the same."

In grade five, a girl wrote that she would like some day to be a principal of a school like Amidon. "At my school there would be harder work than at other schools."

From the fourth grade: "My teacher keeps us busy. I am glad I came to Amidon."

Homework

One of the things most pupils seemed to like about the Amidon school is homework. This also supports the conclusion that children want to work if they know what they are to do and if they can be successful in it. Homework also seems to make the parents happy:

"I wish my teacher had given us homework last year," wrote a sixth grader. "My mother always wondered why we didn't get home assignments. She's happy now and I'm learning more—so everybody's happy."

Even fairly late hours for home study were reported. Wrote one boy, "I never go to bed before ten o'clock. I am up working on my homework assignment. It is fun to have homework to do." Maybe this is the kind of competition that television needs.

A first grader who will soon learn better told her teacher, "I like homework. When can we have more?"

Just to be sure that things are not abnormal on the homework front, I must quote a sixth grade teacher on pupils' unhappy comment: "Do we have to do so much homework tonight?"

"Are We Happy Here?"

The doleful spirits who predicted that children would be unhappy at Amidon will be reassured as they read what some of the pupils said about their first year at Amidon.

Much of their joy seems to come from their confidence in themselves, and their satisfaction with what they are learning.

A first grade pupil told her teacher: "My baby sister can hardly wait to come to this school. She says that this must be the best school in the whole world. She says that because I can read stories to her and I am teaching her to say words correctly."

Another first grade pupil said, "I help my brother sound out words. He does not know about Phonovisual." Another exulted (at this age with some appropriateness): "Now I can read the funny paper, not just look at the pictures."

Another in the same first grade told her teacher: "I go to the library and take a book out with my card. Then I go either to my friend's house or my grandmother's house and read and read to them."

The study of phonics seems to have a happy influence in the affairs of children outside of school. Still from the first grade these pupil comments were reported by the teacher:

"Phonovisual is the best part of Amidon. My friends at other schools don't know about it." Another told her teacher, "My father said my speech is much better since I came to Amidon School in the first grade."

Even on the teaching of history and geography, pupils seemed to have definite opinions:

"History," wrote a fifth grader, "makes more sense to me than the social studies I had last year." Another wrote, "I can understand history now because it is taught in order." "History," wrote a fifth grader, "is my favorite subject now. It is interesting presented in order."

Pupils also seemed to like having geography taught in regular order.

When world geography was taught, a sixth grader wrote:

"Because of what I've studied in geography this year, when President Kennedy talks about world affairs, I understand him better."

Pupils did not seem to mind the speed-up. One wrote, "We went faster in arithmetic and language but I learned much more this year."

When pupils learn, they are happy. The sixth grade teacher told this story as her favorite for the year: "In arithmetic class a boy who had never been by any stretch of the imagination a good arithmetic student gave a correct answer.

Then he suddenly said, 'Hey! I figured that out in my head. How did that happen?' "

The same teacher reported that when she returned the work folders in June, several pupils almost simultaneously exclaimed, "You don't need dates on these papers to tell which came first. Gee, did I ever do work like that?"

Grouping within classes has an adverse effect on pupil response which I had not been aware of before.

"I don't mind saying I don't know, now that I am not afraid of being put in the last group," a sixth grade pupil wrote. "The children who need help can always be taught over again." Fear of being "demoted" may actually cause pupils to try to cover up their needs.

No evidence came up to indicate that the more demanding program was harmful to the pupils. Their comments showed an extraordinary enthusiasm, often reflecting a change in point of view about school.

"I hated school last year," wrote a sixth grader. "I've almost always hated school. But here things are different. I know a lot now and I'll bet I'll really be a whiz in junior high school."

The gist of pupils' comments is, "We like Amidon. We are happy there." This happiness, it seems, comes from the quality of education in the school. When evaluated from the pupils' point of view, the Amidon plan seems to have earned a passing grade.

II. WHAT PARENTS SAY ABOUT THE AMIDON

In education, the theory is widely held that parents should not tell the professionals how to do their work. An analogy between teaching and surgery is sometimes drawn: "You wouldn't tell your surgeon how to remove an appendix. Why should you tell your teacher how to teach reading?" Although the analogy is not by any means complete, since parents are teachers whether they want to be or not, it is generally a good thing to leave the formal aspects of education to the professionals.

But to do this does not deny the parents the right to be critics of education. Just as they may properly evaluate a painting, a play, a political platform, even, for that matter, the results of an appendectomy, so they may evaluate the work of the schools. The principle of freedom to judge the works of public servants and other who offer their "wares" for public use is deep in English common law. Applied as it should be to the product of teachers and administrators, the rule upholds, and in fact encourages, parents and other citizens in the formation of judgments about education.

In turn, such views may be rejected by educators, or used with good sense where they promise improvement. If he believes in what he is doing, the educator should not be intimidated by adverse criticism. At the same time, he should not heap imprecations upon the heads of those who find fault with what he is doing.

THE OFFICIAL PTA POSITION ON THE AMIDON

To illustrate the fact that differences in views between educators and parents are tolerable, and that the possibility should not intimidate school leadership, I will report at the outset that the Board of Managers of the District of Columbia Congress of Parents and Teachers refused in the spring of 1961 to approve a resolution to support the Amidon plan submitted by a member of the Board. When the Amidon plan was voted down, the explanation was given me that the group did not know enough about it. "We are not really against it," said the PTA leadership. "We need more time to study it."

There was an element of equivocation in this position, because the PTA Board of Managers had it in their power to study the Amidon concept. It had been before the community for at least a year. It had been fully presented to the elementary school officers who have the responsibility of informing their parents of school proposals. Finally, the Board of Managers could easily have asked for an explanation of the plan by someone from the central office.

Later in the spring I was invited to explain the Amidon plan to the delegates attending the annual city-wide Parent-Teacher Association Conference. After doing so in the allotted 15 minutes, I then observed the development of an unexpected political maneuver. A friend of the Amidon plan introduced a resolution of endorsement which immediately created an embarrassing situation because no one wanted a direct vote on the question at this time and besides the resolution was technically out of order. The leadership group stated from the floor that they did not know enough about the plan to vote on it, a somewhat unflattering observation to make right after I had described its chief characteristics. Finally, after an inconclusive vote had been taken and when I saw that confusion was more likely to increase than decrease, I asked the maker of the motion to consider withdrawing it, saying that I believed it to be unwise to handle educational questions like this by popular vote. Then the motion was made and adopted to defer action until greater consideration could be given to the issue.

A realistic appraisal of the situation is that the parents and principals who formed the more articulate leadership element in the PTA Congress did not at the time of this episode favor the Amidon idea. The resistance to this change can be laid to a fear that if the plan is adopted children will be too rigidly controlled, creative teaching will be stifled, and excessive demands will be placed upon pupils. I must say that if I entertained such fears about any scheme, I would also be very unwilling to endorse it. I certainly can support those in the parent-teacher organization who oppose extension of the Amidon plan if they do so for such reasons.

Another explanation for the adverse position on the issue comes from the well-known fact that PTA leaders generally reflect the influence of their principals. In saying this, I am describing a condition that is just and right. For what does a lay PTAer know about education except as she learns from her principal? What, furthermore, can be more troubling to the head of a school than to have lay leadership dabbling in education? It is not for nothing that parents are almost totally preoccupied with raising funds for radios and projectors, encyclopedias and work books. Two good motives, one hidden and one exposed, doubly bless PTA fundraising activities.

It is not fair, however, to attribute parental caution in respect to the tougher more highly organized Amidon system wholly to the influence of unconvinced principals. Among the leadership element in parent-teacher organizations is often found a deep conditioning against disciplined child rearing and schooling. Parents have been swayed by the fears and anxieties of writers on child development and the widely distributed admonitions against expecting too much of the child. I think, too, that PTA leadership at the national and local levels has been led to believe that the path to learning must be strewn with educational lollipops.

But I predict a change in point of view when they discover that the order and logic of the Amidon approach is not a form of tyranny in disguise. In proposing the extension of the plan to all District schools, the voluntary nature of the invitation was emphasized. No doubt, the proposal seemed to contain an implied mandate, as perhaps it did; in the light of experience with the Amidon I can see no justification for interminable "transition" to the new education.

This report of the official PTA attitude is important to know about as a balance to the enthusiasm of the Amidon parents for their program.

WHAT THE AMIDON PARENTS SAY

I suppose it would be fair to say that the parents in the best position to judge the Amidon idea are those whose children attended the school. Their views may help to settle the dust on the issue of what the experience does to the personalities of children.

Effect on Attitudes

The comments of parents convey the impression that the Amidon school program had a healthful influence upon the emotional development of their children:

> After describing the program as excellent, the parent of a kindergartner wrote, "My child's mental and emotional attitude toward school is excellent." Another parent wrote: "My child has been helped tremendously both in development and attitude."

Learning many things has not been harmful to the first grader whose mother wrote, "She has been stimulated to ask many questions which pleases us very much. It is my hope that schools in India (my homeland) will adopt the Amidon plan."

Another parent of a first grader testified that children love to learn, and are not harmed by it if they are successful. "My son loves school. He has never had a challenge before coming to Amidon, which presented a problem. Now my problem is getting my son to go to bed. He reads and prints every spare moment."

Amidon seemed not to be harmful to the first grader whose mother wrote, "Ellen can't wait to come to school each day and her conversation at home is all about school. We all feel so lucky to have a school such as Amidon where the children delight in homework, writing their own poems and stories." A parent pointed out that school helped to bring out the best in their daughter "in both social and academic development." She was aware, apparently, that both are necessary, but she did not know that success in scholarship creates confidence, as one parent reported, which enables a pupil to do his school work better and to be happy at the same time.

"I believe my daughter's year at Amidon," wrote a mother of a fifth grader, "has been her most challenging. She seems eager to go to school every day and is beginning to talk of becoming a history teacher."

In the parents' comments, happiness in school seems to be tied in with their children's success and progress in the curriculum of the school:

Wrote one parent, "The difference in the attitudes of my children toward school this year as compared to previous years is dramatic. Their progress, especially in reading, has made the long trip to and from school worthwhile." Another comment which joins progress in school to interest in work:

"Our children have progressed surprisingly well and they have taken quite an interest in their work."

To close this section on attitude with a note of "wild" enthusiasm by a parent may not remove all doubts about the effect of the Amidon concept upon the emotional development of children, but it will show that it has not been harmful to parents:

"We are wildly enthusiastic," this Amidon mother wrote. "We have been aware of the extremely happy effect the school has had upon our child and we can but rejoice."

Content and Method

Many parents wisely saw the connection between good teaching and the content to be taught. In many cases they were high in their praise of the teachers and principal, but at the same time obviously valued the substantial organization of curriculum, the step-by-step order by which it was presented, the whole-class method, and an increase in grammar, composition, and the correction of papers.

In describing the year at Amidon as the "finest school experience" of the young lives of his four children—"and they have had many," a parent wrote that the "success of the Amidon—and this has been considerable—is the result of the dedication and conscientious effort of the principal and teachers. Supervision can and does set the tone, defines the objectives, but without the initiative, cooperation, and the ability of the teachers the finest plans are meaningless."

This perceptive recognition of the key importance of the teacher in any plan voices the opinion of most of the Amidon parents, and certainly makes clear that the Amidon achievement would have been impossible without the great and tireless effort of its staff.

In a single statement a mother tells of the influence of Amidon upon her two children and, I believe, describes what every parent would want for his children.

"I have noticed many favorable changes," the mother wrote. "Among these are an obvious overall intellectual growth, the desire to acquire accurate knowledge, the importance of retaining such knowledge, the personal responsibility to seek facts, and the establishment of good study habits." She added that homework time, welcome or not, has become a part of the evening routine.

Another parent wrote that there "is evidence that the Amidon plan has contributed to better discipline of the mind as well as of the body." His fifth grade daughter, he wrote, "seems to have acquired a stronger desire for knowledge through study and hard work."

Another parent said that the organization of teaching material helped the child to realize his goals. "Our daughter," this mother wrote, "has been stimulated to seek additional information not required. This fact makes the plan noteworthy."

This report based on what the parent had observed is one of many which testifies that teaching for substance stimulates intellectual inquiry on an independent level. The parents' point of view on this ought to relieve the disquietude of those who are afraid that the Amidon system will limit intellectual curiosity.

Parents like to know what is expected of their childen. "I am able to notice an 'educational growth' in my children since the beginning of the present school year. It is easy to see where they are, and I can tell where they are headed in subject matter accomplishment."

"I feel that my daughter is learning work and study habits that will help her to improve steadily in the future," a parent wrote. "She is developing responsibility as a working member of her class. She has developed an appreciation for reading and has attacked her home library with ardor."

"The program follows a logical sequence," a parent wrote, "so that the child is not confused and we as parents know where the class is. The program is demanding, but our daughter has lost none of her spontaneity and love of school as predicted by several persons when the Amidon opened."

After praising the manner in which her children's homework habits have been improved, a parent wrote that "children who know that the teacher is in charge of the classroom and is there to teach, guide, and stimulate are willing and anxious to learn." Add to this the statement of another parent who endorses a work atmosphere in the classroom:

"I believe the serious down-to-work atmosphere is conducive to learning and lessens disciplinary problems. The sound educational principle of teachers teaching and the child learning from textbooks has helped my child immeasurably."

Phonics

Some educators are so fearful of phonics that while they grudgingly speak of the importance of the subject they often vigorously oppose direct study, particularly at the early reading stages. Like a pattern that seemed to be predetermined but actually wasn't, enthusiastic support for the teaching of phonics ran through the written comments from the parents at the end of the school term. What they say about the good results as they observed them at home indicates that direct teaching of phonics beginning with the kindergarten is very useful and without any harmful side effects.

This from a kindergarten mother:

"It is amazing the number of things my daughter has learned this year, most of all, the way she is learning to read." From another mother of a kindergarten child: "I feel that my daughter's pronunciation and English have improved, as a result of starting phonics in the kindergarten." Another pleased mother wrote, "With the phonovisual method, my little one, even at the kindergarten stage, sometimes corrects her Mommy and Daddy in their sounding of words."

First grade parents also expressed great enthusiasm for phonics because of the power to read evident in the actions of their children. "My daughter," wrote a first grade mother, "reads everything. It is hard to believe that she has learned so much and reads so well in such a short period of time. She loves phonovisual." "My daughter loves to read and print," said another mother of a first grader. "She sounds out her words. It is wonderful!" Another comment: "Phonovisual is discussed by my daughter during dinner. We are learning so much from her." One parent voiced the kind of "mixed" joy many expressed with the early introduction of phonics: "Having two older children who were not taught to read phonetically, I can see the tremendous advantage of the system."

Discipline

Although a few parents raised questions about the strict supervision of the playground and the "regimentation" of group passing in the halls, others spoke favorably of the discipline in the school. One wrote:

"I am especially pleased that the children are showing a new respect for school, education, and authority. This year I have not heard once such remarks as, 'I don't have to because the teacher can't make me' or 'the teacher can't do anything to you because its against the law' or 'the teacher must be crazy.' I like the 'no nonsense, you are here to learn' attitude. I feel that children can learn early that they have a responsibility to do their best in school.

"I have but one regret, that the teaching methods of the Amidon were not available sooner. In my children's first four years in school they were led to believe that life is merely a big game to be played or not as the children felt. This year they have worked hard and learned because they had to, and much to their surprise they found it could be fun."

Parents with children already past the elementary level often sadly contrast the difference in their preparation and discipline with that obtained by their younger children at Amidon the first year. One parent wrote that she was "grateful that her girls are being taught a proper respect for education and authority, something sadly lacking in public schools and especially noticeable by me in my two older children now in a junior and senior high school."

Discipline is apparently acceptable to children, too, as reported by this parent who wrote:

> "It is particularly inspiring to my husband and me to see the emphasis on fundamentals and inculcating order and discipline in class routines. Our daughter has shown steady progress, has an attitude of responsibility in homework assignments, and works hard. She is happy at Amidon because of the challenge."

So far as I can tell from parent and pupil surveys, greater discipline and better order in teaching are approved. The dictum is again proved: children like a disciplined and challenging classroom if justice is a part of it.

Is Amidon Different?

Apparently many Amidon parents have been told by other principals and teachers and friends that Amidon is really no different from other elementary schools.

> On this point, one parent wrote, "I am so pleased with our daughter's improvement. The difference in her spelling and handwriting since she started is unbelievable. When my neighbors say to me that Amidon is no different from any other public school, I say, 'Oh, yes it is. There is a big difference and my daughter is proof of it.'"

The extent of misunderstanding of the Amidon concept by other principals, my failure not theirs, really, is again illustrated in this statement by a parent:

> "I have been told by people connected with other schools in the District that they already offer 9 out of 10 parts of the

Amidon plan. Even if the statement is true and I'm far from convinced that it is, it's the eleventh and twelfth parts that count: The child is challenged to do his best and teachers are convinced of the idea and capable of carrying it out. As far as our child is concerned, the Amidon is working admirably in all aspects."

Many schools will approach to the Amidon concept in some of its aspects. Variations up to full similarity may be expected. I am certain, however, that many school officials and teachers who believe they have been doing the Amidon plan right along do not really understand it and are perhaps quite naturally somewhat defensive on the issue.

When most of the comments of parents note improvement in their children's work, the benchmark is the work of previous years. Some parents are more direct, less cautious in their comments:

"Decided improvement in attitude toward school. Now, when asked, my son can at least tell me something he did at school other than games he played." Another wrote, typical of many comments, "We are firmly convinced that the Amidon has far surpassed the teaching programs of other schools our children have attended." Another comment, "They seem to be learning much more in this school than ever before." Still another: "Thoroughly approve. Regret that my son did not have a similar background in the two previous grades."

"Compared with neighborhood schools, the plan is far superior," a parent wrote. "We find that a first grade pupil at Amidon is exposed to as much as or more than some third grade pupils."

A parent of a first grader where reading was being taught with the phonics method went to Detroit for a few days. The mother wrote: "She spent some time in school there, too. The teachers there were amazed at her accomplishments in all areas."

A parent of a fourth grader saw a real difference, too, between the work of previous years and the one at Amidon:

"Our son simply glows these days—with interest in his subjects, pride in work, and respect and affection for his teacher. It's the response we've been hoping for since he started school.

"I recently found a paper he turned in to class last year. I asked my son, 'How could you have turned in work looking like this?' His answer was, 'I guess they didn't expect very much from us.'"

A letter from a parent who didn't enter her child in the Amidon also testifies to a difference. The girl was transferred from a private school into the fifth grade of a very good local public school—one of those that will become much better when it is ready to use the Amidon concept. The child entered with achievements up to three years above grade standard and an I.Q. listed at 130. During the two years in the public schools, these retrograded, the mother wrote: "I was not quite content during the two years because the emphasis, for her, seemed to have shifted from basic skills to creative things. I approve of the cultural aspects, but not at the cost of basic skills. I considered asking for her to be placed in the Amidon School for the sixth grade, but thought possibly another year would take care of itself."

There may be good reasons to explain retrogression in achievement, but when this incident is contrasted with the favorable reports from the Amidon parents, the difference seems to lie in the emphasis upon the basic skills.

I am convinced that Amidon is unique in its application of a total concept, and that care needs to be taken to avoid the complacent brush off likely to be given it by other schools whose directors say, "After all, we've been doing all this for years." This is a trap for parents and school authorities that should be carefully checked if they are to avoid walking into it.

NUMBER OF PUPILS TO CONTINUE AT AMIDON

Parental support of the Amidon plan was effectively measured when the question of continuance of enrollment for the following year was raised with them in late March of the first Amidon term.

At that time, the principal sent a short questionnaire to each Amidon parent. In it she asked if the parents desided to continue the enrollment of their child at Amidon and would continue to assume responsibility for transportation and the noon lunch. This questionnaire also included a space for parent comments about the school program and their suggestions for the next school term.

The principal reported that all the children expected to return except eleven, eight of whom expected to move from the District. Of the total eligible group, about 40 percent were from within the Amidon zone and of course were assigned to the school. From among the parents who brought their children into the school from outside the school boundaries, only three actually decided not to do so the next year.

The Amidon parents backed up their good words about the school with the time and trouble to bring their children to the school. The need to go the distance to Amidon will disappear as other schools in the District adopt the plan. In the meantime, the school opened in September of 1961 with five additional classes and an enrollment of 594, up over the limit of 455 set for 1960.

Perhaps two short comments by parents will end this testimonial chapter on a dramatic note. (1) "Can't you add the 7th and 8th grades to Amidon?" and (2) "Resist any attempt to change your methods."

chapter nine

WHAT THE TEACHERS AND THE
PRINCIPAL SAY ABOUT AMIDON

AT THE END OF THE FIRST YEAR, THE AMIDON PRINCIPAL AND teachers were asked to tell what they thought of the Amidon project. They were invited to describe the strengths and weaknesses with complete ardor.

Before summarizing their comments, I want to report how the 16 teachers were selected for the project. The chief responsibility for this fell to the assistant superintendent in charge of elementary schools. She in turn consulted with her director of supervision. I took a hand myself in the choice of the principal whose work I had been aware of for a number of years, dating back to her kindergarten teaching and her selection by an honorary educational sorority for a scholarship which contributed to her attainment of a doctorate in education. I wasn't sure of her willingness to accept the Amidon philosophy, but I was confident that if she could conscientiously do so she had the vigor, enthusiasm, organizational ability, and a zest for working with people, that a new program like this especially needed. She also possessed the important but unobtrusive characteristics of strength and courage which she used sensitively and without arrogance. The new principal accepted the challenge and the risk with vigor and eagerness.

Wanting to be candid yet not morbid about the venture, I pointed out to her the professional risk in the undertaking. The plan could fall flat on its face. The parents might refuse to go to the trouble of bringing their children to the school. They might, after a tryout, decide to transfer them to their home schools. Other principals and teachers would resent the implied criticism of their programs in the Amidon set up. There would be misunderstandings and perhaps even cruelties which might cause her to be hurt. If the idea did not prove out she would, as the working head, be professionally embarrassed for her participation in an unsuccessful demonstration. With the fanfare of publicity attending the project, failure would attract as much attention as success.

Parents, teachers, and pupils all agree that the success of the school depended primarily upon the leadership of the principal, who in turn had the unreserved support of her assistant superintendent and the heads of the curriculum and supervisory departments and her new teachers, whose unstinting loyalty become a notable factor in the operation of the demonstration. Parents and children responded so well to the kindly and dynamic leadership of the principal and the enthusiasm of the teachers that it is difficult to determine how much the Amidon idea contributed to the success of the project.

The Amidon teachers, who quickly demonstrated their capacity to establish parental confidence in themselves and the Amidon idea, came from within and outside the school system. Their average length of teaching service was 13.8 years. Most were permanent teachers, 13 altogether, and only 3 were temporary teachers. It was a bi-racial faculty, eight of the teachers and the principal being white and the remaining eight teachers colored. When they were invited to join the Amidon faculty in the spring of 1960, they had no special preparation for the Amidon-type program. In-service meetings were immediately organized, including a full week on curriculum following the close of school in June, and a workshop in the use of phonics that lasted a full week, all of this on the teachers' own time without any additional compensation. Although the teachers were not selected as demonstration teachers, from the opening day of school they were required to demonstrate for guests from around the world as well as within the system. They met this challenge with great success.

These are the people, well qualified by experience, whose judgments about the strengths and weaknesses of the Amidon idea are to be reported in this chapter. Along with a high degree of support for the main ideas of the Amidon concept, the teachers defined a number of administrative problems which need to be taken care of.

Teaching the Whole Class

To start with, the teachers of the two basic classes agree that teaching the whole class such subjects as phonics, reading and arithmetic is a good thing even for slow learners. It sets up good class *rapport*, said one, and reduces the need for individual teaching, said the other.

The chief strengths of the whole-class method were pointed out by the teachers of the regular grades. "Economizes on time" and "uncovers remedial needs," wrote one. Another declared, "Whole-class instruction makes a real meeting of minds concerning a given subject more possible than small group instruction." "In teaching arithmetic, language, and history, mass teaching saved time for reteaching and remedial work," wrote another.

A fifth grade teacher said that more children are reached effectively through direct teaching of the whole class. Duplication is virtually eliminated, thus giving more time for development and fastening of subject matter. Groups can be organized when individual attention is needed. Another wrote, "Presentation of most subjects to the whole class is an asset. I can give more instruction to more pupils more often. It should be re-enforced with small group instruction when needed." A first grade teacher wrote, "Mass instruction allows for thorough teaching. The teacher can quickly note the pupils who need help, which can be given immediately."

A very articulate sixth grade teacher made a case for whole-class teaching this way:

> Direct teaching stimulates growth and development. It provides for pupil-teacher interaction. It provides for participation in mental activities and the satisfactions of real and vicarious experience in a whole-class situation.

The only *exception* to whole-class teaching taken by the teachers is in reading. The point is made that children must read from books suitable to them. Therefore in any class reading textbooks must be at different levels. I continue to question, however, the validity of the assumption that a class should be sub-divided for reading because the members are at different reading levels. I want to report what I think is the heart of the problem: In reading class the time is now spent primarily in listening to children read rather than in teaching them how to read. Just as the phonovisual system can be taught to the whole class, many reading skills can be taught to large groups with individual differences.

*Teaching Systematic, Sequential Subject
Matter on a Daily Schedule*

Teachers in the Amidon significantly favored direct teaching of subject matter on schedule. A teacher of a class for slow learners wrote that it is important for such pupils to be taught the necessary basic skills. "They are of more value than a pre-vocational type of program," she said. A structured daily schedule is excellent for the slow learners, according to another teacher, "because consistency meets their needs. It provides security and helps them develop good work habits."

Our sixth grade teacher wrote, "Organized, systematic presentation of subject matter provides for maximum learning. A planned program of teaching, testing, and re-teaching eliminates guess work. It insures each pupil a maximum growth." Thus the fear that pre-planned curriculum organization will deny the existence of individual differences is discounted.

"The use of basic texts in series by the whole school adds order and sequence," she wrote. "Setting up a time schedule," she wisely pointed out, "reduces interruptions and school activities are arranged so that they do not interfere with classroom instruction."

Significant is the acclaim given to consecutive and ordered teaching of history and geography in grades four, five, and six.

"It establishes proper sequence in history," wrote one teacher. Another said that after she presented history chronologically more children listed history as a favorite subject than any other subject. She also testified that the textbook is useful to assure logical and proper presentation of material.

"With daily teaching of basic subjects," she wrote, "sugar-coating and camouflaging of materials are eliminated, but interest is sustained by the teacher and children." Her view was that a definite daily schedule provides assurance that all subjects will be taught. "A certain rigidity establishes security in the children, but flexibility is available on special occasions," she declared.

Without exception the Amidon teachers liked sequence and order in curriculum structure backed by the use of textbooks. They also favored a specific scheduling of subjects. They reported that pupils seemed to respond to this methodology with sustained interest. This view by teachers on the ground level should reassure those who are fearful of imposed classroom order.

Phonics

To summarize the teacher point-of-view on the direct teaching of phonics, there was universal and enthusiastic support for scheduled phonics instruction from the kindergarten through the sixth grade, including the classes for slow learners. One teacher of slow learners advised intensive use of the phonovisual system for the non-readers as a speech improvement device and for reading as well. "Phonics gave a real boost to reading," she reported. "The 'too hard' and 'I don't know' attitude disappeared. The phonics program helps with spelling and written English, which were previously hated by my pupils."

One reason she was vitally interested in phonics, wrote a teacher, "was that I recognized a lack in my own education." Children learn to listen through a word, and this is not only an aid to spelling but also to reading and speech.

"Moreover," she wrote, "children enjoy the work. When it rains and they choose an inside grame, they often choose one of our exciting phonics games."

A sixth grade teacher wrote: "The phonovisual method of instruction equips readers with power of word attack. It is an aid to vocabulary building and spelling."

A final selection of teacher comments on phonics will adequately point up the teacher point-of-view. "Used by every class, the phonovisual system should prove even more rewarding in subsequent years. It will establish a standard for every grade. It is also one of the most efficient ways to teach spelling. As a result, most of my pupils thought the words in the third grade spelling book too easy."

Composition, Usage, Grammar

A teacher put both skills and creativity into first priority. "Development of correct English usage is something we owe each child. Creative expression should be respected for what it is, but technical skills should not be sacrificed for it. I believe we serve the child best by insisting that whatever he writes be well-written and correctly written, as we do at Amidon."

Another teacher agreed that pupils should have worthwhile experiences in school but that they need the skills with which to communicate and interpret these experiences. Daily instruction in these skills is needed, she said.

Kindergarten

The kindergarten teacher was one of the most apt learners among pupils and teachers at the Amidon. She wrote, "I was elated by what has been accomplished by the kindergarten at Amidon. During the fourteen years that I have taught kindergarten, never once did I think that kindergarten children could read."

She wrote of her challenge and amazement when she was able to teach 36 out of 67 children to read without difficulty. Others learned such skills as reading from left to right and that a story is made up of sentences. Her children mastered the 26 consonant sounds included in the phonovisual method.

The image of the kindergarten as simply a growing-up place is about to change drastically in the District of Columbia school system.

Areas to Be Improved

In the very tight daily schedule of the Amidon plan, recess or a supervised play period is replaced by directed instruction in physical education. This takes place outdoors when the weather permits. Indoor activity is required when the weather is inclement. The result is that teachers have no break period for attending to their personal needs or for a moment of relaxation.

Teaching without a break during a full morning and afternoon session creates a severe morale problem among elementary teachers. With a clearly defined time schedule, the Amidon plan sharpens the problem. Planning to relieve the unbroken day is needed—for Amidon and other schools, too.

A second repeated request for improvement is in the social studies curriculum of the primary grades. The Amidon teachers want the same kind of defined curriculum for grades one, two, and three that is available for grades four, five, and six, where geography and history are taught as subjects. This request is a clear revelation of support for organized subject matter in the early as well as in the middle grades.

Curriculum materials in art and music were also on the teachers' want list after a year at the Amidon. For indefiniteness as to content, these two important subject fields rival the primary grade social studies for first honors. The teachers asked for substance and order in art and music so they can teach the subjects intelligently.

Finally, the Amidon faculty pleaded for a curtailment of visiting. The school has attracted national interest, and hence the number of visitors has exceeded the capacity of the school to absorb them. Clear-cut schedules for setting up visiting days are needed.

SUMMARY

The following summary presented by a second grade teacher is exceptionally comprehensive and succinct. She described the following as some of the strengths of the Amidon plan:

1. The plan has won the approval and respect of parents.
2. It places emphasis on the teacher as a source of information, explanation and adult guidance, thus giving her increased confidence and status.
3. The necessary careful planning and scheduling make fullest use of the school day. It eliminates many time-consuming, educationally-questionable activities, such as elaborate assembly programs and displays, films chiefly for entertainment, and certain types of trips and parties.
4. It brings the school program and responsibility into focus after a long period of hazy generalities and contradictory purposes.
5. The emphasis on the teaching of letters and sounds is not only an aid to reading and spelling, but stimulates interest in the words themselves and curiosity about their meanings.
6. Children are proud of their achievements in the skills. They have enjoyed learning "full time."

Another strong summary story is included in the principal's report of a year-end conversation with one of the Amidon teachers. She told the principal that she had taught school for many years but that this was the first time she was closing school with a sense of accomplishment and fulfillment of her teaching objectives. She added that she derived such feelings because she had a sense of knowing what she should teach in each skill and knowledge area and the opportunity to evaluate the progress of her group toward these charted teaching goals.

And for sheer enthusiasm, this direct statement from an Amidon teacher is a masterpiece and a good note on which to end this chapter:

"Using the Phonovisual approach as a technique in reading has been the most exciting, challenging and rewarding experience in my entire teaching career. I have thoroughly enjoyed working with the Amidon plan in its entirety. Success of any plan can be seen in reactions for those involved and certainly both children and parents have demonstrated in various ways their pleasure throughout the year. As one of my pupils stated, 'Time really flies and we have learned so many things and had fun learning them.' I too must agree—this year did fly and I learned many things!"

chapter ten

ACHIEVEMENT TEST RESULTS

THE TEST RESULTS TO BE REPORTED HERE WILL HAVE GREATER meaning if they are studied in relation to the characteristics of the pupils. The person most qualified to describe the Amidon pupils is the principal, Dr. Dorothy Johnson. Here is her report on the subject dated August 31, 1961. It was prepared for me because of a persistent misconception that the school was primarily for pupils "hand picked" to respond to academic instruction.

DR. JOHNSON'S REPORT

It is my understanding that there is an oft-expressed opinion that the "Amidon School is a school for gifted children." I would like to state that the Amidon School is a school for children who vary rather widely in growth patterns, possible intellectual potential, and academic achievement levels. Our 1960–61 school enrollment was accrued from three distinct sources, namely: (1) residents of the area, (2) children living on nearby military bases, and (3) applicants from citywide areas.

A. *Residents of the Area.* Approximately 150 children were transferred to Amidon from the S. J. Bowen School in September, 1960. These children were placed in every grade level of our school as well as in kindergarten and basic education classes. A study of cumulative records revealed that about one-fourth of the children had been given the standard city-wide group achievement tests. These test results revealed I.Q.'s ranging from 44 to 105. A majority of the children made scores between 85 and 98. Readiness scores were usually average and below. A class of Junior-Primary was organized for fifteen children who scored as "poor risks" and "low normal."

All children in our two basic classes were residents of the area.

These resident children also had many problems which seem to be economically based—little or no home reading materials, few travel experiences outside of their home neighborhood, limited social and cultural experiences and opportunities, transient housing, low income, public assistance, and some clothing and food needs. In a few situations, there existed a feeling of little respect or appreciation for learning.

Only four children entered from the newly-built housing. We had no records from their previous schools in other states. Approximately four other children moved into the area during April and May.

In June, 1961, no child in this group was recommended for the sixth grade "Honors" program.

B. *Children from Military Bases.* Approximately 40 children were represented in this group. These children were widely traveled, seemed economically secure, had experienced numerous and widely different school situations, and had participated in varying curriculum plans. Few test results may be reported. However, some children had attended our city schools during the testing period of the previous year. Their I.Q. scores ranged from 79 to 132.

As expected, these children became transient when new military orders were received.

One child in this group entered the Junior-Primary class. In June, one child was recommended to enter the sixth grade "Honors" program.

C. *Children by Application.* In 1960–1961, about 270 children were admitted by application from 64 other D.C. Public Schools. About one-half of them had group achievement scores. The I.Q. scores ranged from 80 to 125. In November, we admitted by request a child who was experiencing great school difficulty. His individual I.Q. score was 159.

Few test records were available from area private and parochial schools, other states, and foreign countries.

No child was admitted to basic or Junior-Primary classes.

In June, 1961, two children were recommended for the sixth grade "Honors" program.

SUMMARY STATEMENTS

1. Available test results for children entering Amidon School in September, 1960, revealed an I.Q. range of 44–132 and later to 159. Therefore, Amidon served not gifted children but children of varying abilities.
2. Many children were untested. These children were judged upon their performance at Amidon and given placement accordingly.
3. Amidon pupils varied greatly in economic-social-cultural opportunities, in academic achievement, and in potential intellectual development.
4. The children residing in the school area (A and B of this report) offer evidences of extreme differences. Children admitted by the process of application did not seem to vary to the same degree.
5. The willingness of parents to transport children to Amidon does not correlate with I.Q. scores of children. Parents of children who evidenced slower learning rate and academic retardation were particularly anxious for the opportunity to participate in the Amidon program. To illustrate, this is quoted from a mother's letter to her child's new teacher at the Amidon: "My daughter had a very devastating first grade experience. It left her emotionally upset and with what seems to me to be an actual loss of the desire to learn. When I was made fully aware of the depths of the experience, the damage had been done. This was one of the reasons which led us to have her enrolled in Amidon."

6. Amidon children were given classroom placement in accordance with the established policy of the track program for the elementary schools.

   a. Two classes were established for children in the basic track.

   b. One class was organized for Junior-Primary children.

   c. In September, 1960, no "Honors" class was established.

   d. Other classes were designated as "general" track. Additional grouping was accomplished within the level—(i.e., there were two classes on each grade level—average and above—low average and below).

7. In June, 1961, only four from approximately 60 fifth grade children were recommended for sixth grade "Honors" program.

I would like to make a few comments about the interview process held during the summers of 1960 and 1961. Only children who applied for admission were interviewed. All children living within the area were automatically enrolled. The purpose of the interview was four-fold: (1) to define transportation and lunch requirements, (2) to discuss past school performances, special abilities, and particular learning problems as a guide for classroom placement, (3) to answer questions regarding the Amidon Plan and school policies, and (4) to initiate a desirable home-school relationship.

In 1960 approximately 20 children were not admitted as a result of the interview. These decisions were reached for the following reasons: (1) distance of travel would create additional problems for brain-damaged, emotionally-disturbed, truant or attendance problem children, (2) the concept by a few parents that Amidon was a "private" school or a school for only "mentally retarded" or "remedial reading" cases, (3) public transportation for immature children could create hazards, and (4) a few who seem to use the application process as a method of "escape."

It is evident that children who entered the Amidon School in September, 1960, regardless of residential area, brought varying academic and disciplinary problems. Having attended 110 different schools the pupils were accepted by their teachers as children of varying backgrounds and abilities. It was the responsibility of the school to present a curriculum program—appropriate, planned, scheduled, and sequential—to motivate each child toward greater growth, a respect and desire for learning, and increased achievement in the learning process.

❊   ❊   ❊

THE AMIDON TEST PROGRAM

When the Amidon opened in the fall of 1960, the principal recommended against an initial achievement test program. Her reason was that the results might be adversely influenced by the newness of the situation to the children who came from all parts of the city and, in fact, from foreign countries as well. I concurred, so no first-of-the-year test was given.

We were aware, therefore, that an accurate measure of growth while under tutelage at the Amidon could not be taken. Nevertheless, we arranged to give achievement and intelligence tests to all pupils in grades one to six inclusive, in June just before the close of school to find out what the achievement levels were at this particular stage of the growth and development of these pupils.

What do the test results show? What do they mean? The first question is easy to answer, as the data will indicate. The second, having to do with the meaning of the test results, will be much more difficult to answer. Interpretations of the data will vary from person to person, depending upon the point of view. Although the test results confirm my enthusiasm for the Amidon concept, others may be unwilling to accept them as evidence of the success of the project. This is a matter of choice. I can only add that I hope when the Amidon concept is in operation on a complete scale in our school system all the pupils will do comparatively as well.

During the period June 5–9, 1961, the 353 Amidon pupils in grades one to six were given the Metropolitan Achievement Test battery and the Otis Quick-Scoring Test of Mental Ability. It will be remembered that these pupils entered the school the

September before from within the school zone and from schools outside the area. They were heterogeneous in backgrounds and abilities.

The tests were given by the teachers. The answer sheets were sent to the publisher for scoring and making certain statistical computations. The District of Columbia Department of Pupil Appraisal analyzed and interpreted the test results.

Grade 1. This group (2 classes, 65 pupils) was given the Metropolitan Achievement Test, Primary Battery, Form A, and the Otis Quick-Scoring Test of Mental Ability, Alpha. The Achievement Test consisted of four sections: Word Knowledge, Word Discrimination, Reading, and Arithmetic. The pupils made median scores in the four parts of the test that ranged from .3 grade to 1.5 grades above the national medians.

Chart 1 shows the Amidon median scores in relation to the national medians for the test. The Amidon group scored above the national group at the first, median, and third quartile points in all sections of the test. Chart 2 shows graphically that at three comparison points the Amidon pupils scored well above national standards.

Three-fourths of the Amidon group scored at or above the national norm in arithmetic and reading, and at or above the national third quartile in World Knowledge and Word Discrimination. All but two members of the class scored above the national norm in Word Discrimination, and in Word Knowledge only three pupils scored below the national norm.

In Word Discrimination 21 first grade pupils scored at 4.2 grade level and 8 first grade pupils made grade equivalents of 5.2 in Reading.

In the Mental Ability Test, the range of I.Q.'s for the group was 100 to 150 plus, with a median of 128.

The production of such unusual I.Q.'s by 65 unselected first grade pupils raises a question as to the contribution made to the ability scoring by the emphasis on phonics and direct and whole class teaching. The first grade teachers reported that their pupils were more attentive, more able to respond to directions, and more discriminating in their choices than first graders usually are. In the opinion of the teachers, this was the result of emphasis

CHART 1

GRADE 1. MEDIAN ACHIEVEMENT OF AMIDON SCHOOL COMPARED WITH NATIONAL NORM GROUP

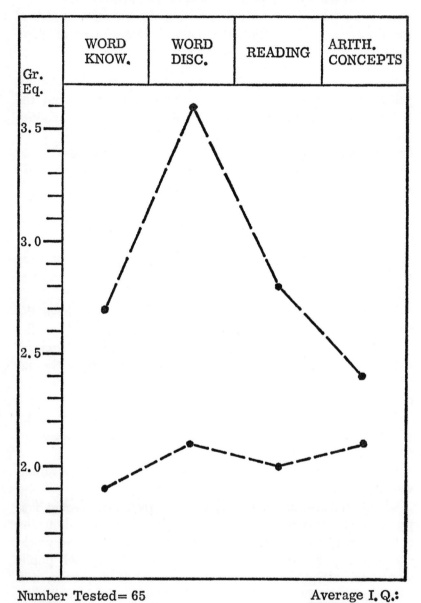

Number Tested = 65
Amidon _____ ___ ___ ___ ___ ___
Norm Group _ _ _ _ _ _ _ _ _

Average I. Q.:
Amidon = 128
Norm Group = 100+

CHART 2

GRADE 1. DIFFERENCES BETWEEN THE AMIDON AND THE NATIONAL
QUARTILES AT THE TIME OF TESTING

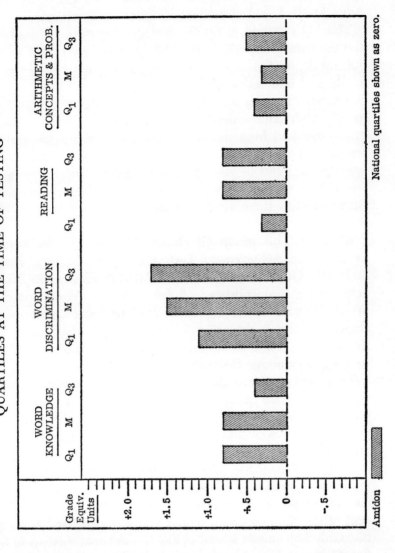

National quartiles shown as zero.

upon language improvement, particularly the use of the Phono-visual Method, and direct and systematic instruction.

The I.Q.'s turned in by the first graders must be realistically and cautiously appraised. It is likely that they reflect to a significant degree the effects of teaching and do not wholly represent innate and immutable ability.

Although there is no scientific basis for claiming that the unusually high achievement and ability scores in the Amidon first grades resulted from the employment of the Amidon system of teaching, the achievements are most unusual and promising, and confirm the point of view that first graders can achieve at high levels. It can reasonably be assumed that the Amidon method contributed to these achievements.

Grade 2. This group (2 classes, 56 pupils) was given the Metropolitan Achievement Test, Primary II, Battery, Form B, and Otis Quick-Scoring Test of Mental Ability, Alpha. The achievement test consisted of five sections: Word Knowledge, Word Discrimination, Reading, Spelling, and Arithmetic. As shown in Chart 3, the Amidon pupils made median scores in the five sections of the achievement test that ranged from .5 grade to 1.6 grades above the national norms.

They scored above the national group at the first quartile, median, and third quartile points in all sections of the test. Chart 4 shows graphically that at every comparison point the Amidon pupils scored above the national norms. In comparison with city-wide local tests, the Amidon scores were significantly higher.

In Word Knowledge, Word Discrimination, Spelling, and Arithmetic, the Amidon first quartile exceeded the national group median. In Word Discrimination and Spelling more than 75 percent of the Amidon group scored above the national third quartile. Only four pupils scored below the national median in Spelling. Six second grade pupils made Spelling scores at 5.4 grade level. Four second grade pupils scored in Reading at 6.0 grade. Eleven made scores of 5.2 grades in Word Discrimination.

In this grade the I.Q. range was from 78 to 150 with a median of 112.

As in the first grade, expectancies of achievement cannot be derived from intelligence scores because of the unreliability of

CHART 3

GRADE 2. MEDIAN ACHIEVEMENT OF AMIDON SCHOOL COMPARED WITH NATIONAL NORM GROUP

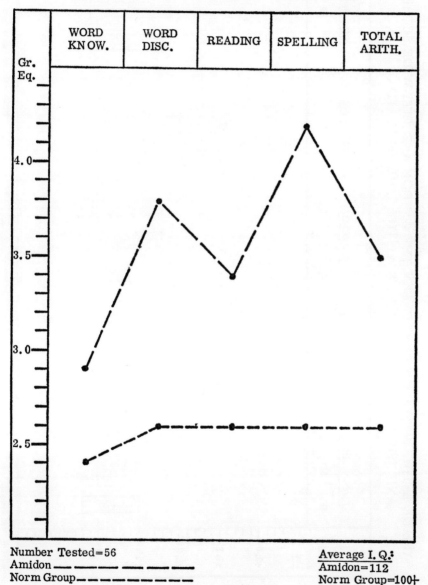

| WORD KNOW. | WORD DISC. | READING | SPELLING | TOTAL ARITH. |

Number Tested=56
Amidon ___ ___ ___ ___ ___
Norm Group ___ ___ ___ ___ ___ ___

Average I. Q.:
Amidon=112
Norm Group=100+

CHART 4

GRADE 2. THE DIFFERENCES BETWEEN THE AMIDON AND CITY-WIDE SCORES
AND THE NATIONAL QUARTILES AT THE TIME OF TESTING

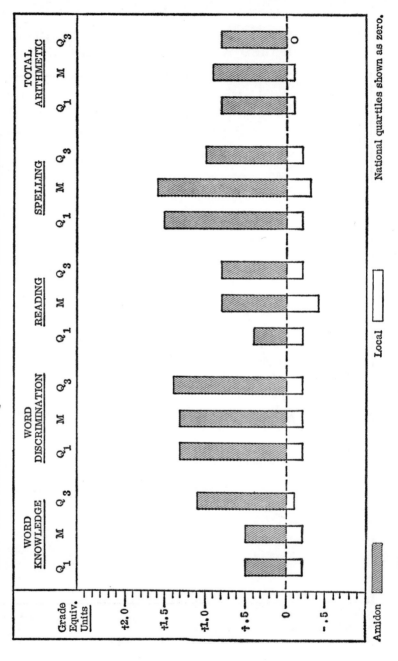

such computations at this level. The effect of Amidon teaching, upon these scores, cannot be measured but is nevertheless likely to have been significant. The superior achievement of the Amidon Grade 2 pupils suggests the value of maintaining the Amidon methodology and continuing to improve its effectiveness.

Grade 3. Different forms of the test were given to the two third grades for the reason that the pupils in one class entered the Amidon severely retarded in reading and another class was grouped as normal in achievement level at the opening of school. Given the primary test form the slow class fell below the national medians from .2 grade to .8 grades, as is shown in Chart 5.

When the median achievement is compared with expected achievement based on intelligence scores, the slow third grade is above expected achievement level by from .1 to .3 grades in Word Discrimination, Reading, and Spelling and below expected level by −.2 grade in Word Knowledge and Arithmetic. It seems doubtful that with the data at hand the differences one way or the other are significant. Setting up expectancy tables involves the statistical treatment of data which in themselves are not fully reliable as to the measures they produce. However, achievement expectancies can be cautiously used as indicators of achievement in relation to ability. They tend to say something about the quality of teaching in relation to the pupil's ability to learn, although the pupil's ability in turn may be influenced by his experiences as a pupil.

Chart 6 shows the differences between the Amidon slow third grade and the national quartiles.

In Word Discrimination at the first and third quartiles this third grade class equalled the national norms. This suggests that with the use of the phonovisual charts this group was beginning to increase its word attack power and the retardation which caused the special grouping was being reduced.

The regular third grade class, using the Elementary Battery specified for this grade level, was tested in Word Knowledge, Word Discrimination, Reading, Spelling, Total Language, Arithmetic Computation, and Arithmetic Problem Solving. Median achievements exceeded the national scores from .7 to 2.0 grades.

Achievement expectancies derived from intelligence tests given

CHART 5

GRADE 3B. MEDIAN ACHIEVEMENT OF AMIDON SCHOOL AS COMPARED WITH NATIONAL NORM GROUP AND WITH EXPECTED LEVEL OF ACHIEVEMENT BASED ON I.Q.

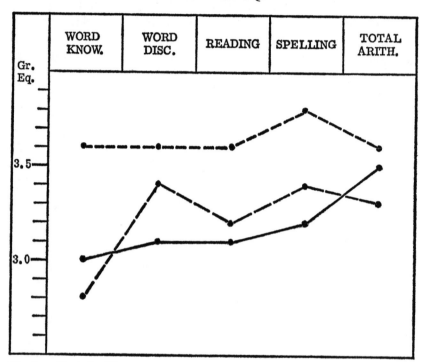

Number Tested = 27
Amidon .__ .___ .___ .___ .___ .___
Expected Achievement ._____
Norm Group .__ .__ .__ .__ .__ .__

Average I. Q.:
Amidon = 95
Norm Group = 100+

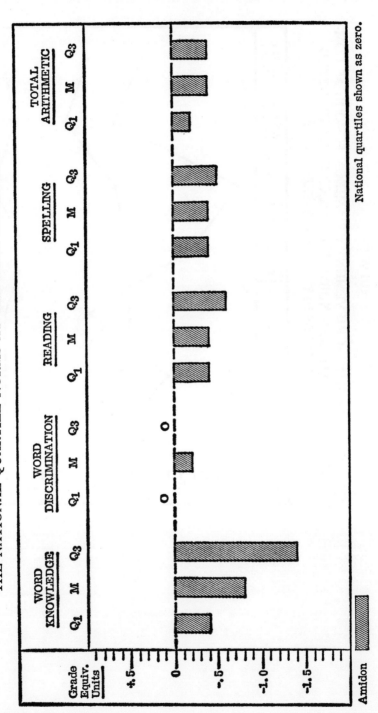

CHART 6

GRADE 3B. DIFFERENCES BETWEEN THE AMIDON AND
THE NATIONAL QUARTILE NORMS AT THE TIME OF TESTING

National quartiles shown as zero.

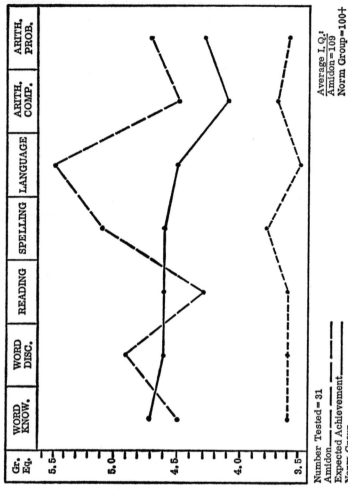

CHART 7

GRADE 3A. MEDIAN ACHIEVEMENT OF AMIDON SCHOOL AS COMPARED WITH NATIONAL NORM GROUP AND WITH EXPECTED LEVEL OF ACHIEVEMENT BASED ON I.Q.

Number Tested = 31
Amidon _____
Expected Achievement _____
Norm Group ― ― ― ―

Average I. Q.:
Amidon = 109
Norm Group = 100+

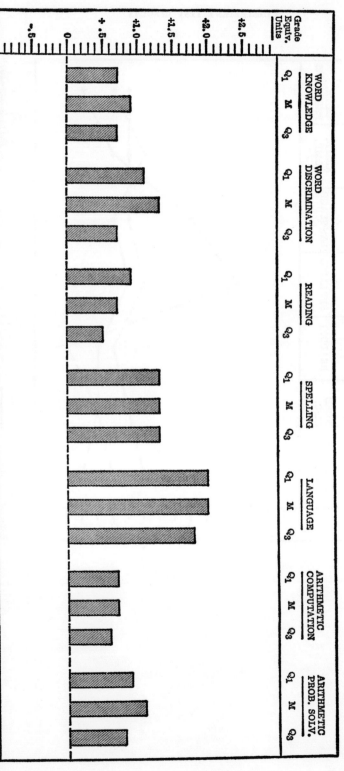

CHART 8

GRADE 3A. DIFFERENCES BETWEEN THE AMIDON AND THE NATIONAL QUARTILES
AT THE TIME OF TESTING

Amidon

National quartiles shown as zero

CHART 9

GRADE 4. MEDIAN ACHIEVEMENT OF AMIDON SCHOOL AS COM-
PARED WITH NATIONAL NORM GROUP AND WITH EXPECTED
LEVEL OF ACHIEVEMENT BASED ON I.Q.

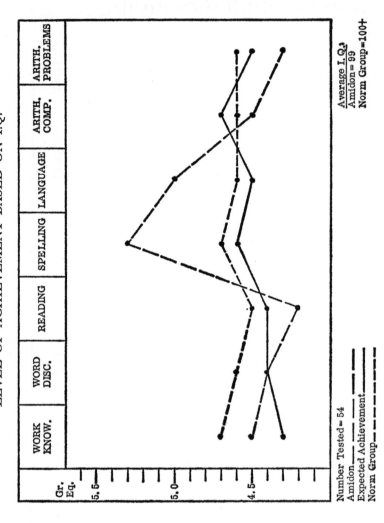

Number Tested = 54
Amidon _____
Expected Achievement _____
Norm Group _____

Average I.Q.¹
Amidon = 99
Norm Group = 100+

at the same period show that this class exceeded expectancy by from .3 to 1.0 grade in five subjects tested and fell below expectancy by −.2 and −.3 grades in Word Knowledge and Reading.

The 31 pupils in this class exceeded the national norms at all points of comparison. Chart 8 shows how the Amidon group scored above the first and third quartiles and the median. A measure of the unusual achievement is that the Amidon first quartile is at the median of the national group in one test and above in the six other sections of the test. Most unusual is the fact that in Total Language the Amidon first quartile at 4.8 grades was higher than the national third quartile of 4.4. In this same test, the Amidon third quartile was 6.2. Six third grade Amidon pupils made grade equivalents ranging from 6.4 to 7.9 grades, in Total Language.

Although superior in relation to the national standards for grade three, the Amidon scores do not supply scientific proof of the value of the Amidon system of teaching. On the other hand, they offer substantial reason for continuing to use and improve the Amidon concept.

Grade 4. In this grade (two classes, 54 pupils) the Metropolitan Elementary Battery, Form B and the Otis Mental Ability Test, Beta, E M, were given. The median achievement scores as shown in Chart 9 exceeded the national medians by .6 grade in spelling and .4 grade in language. They fell below the national norms from −.1 to −.4 grade in the five other subjects tested.

In the fourth grade, the median I.Q. was 99 and the range was 73 to 122. Expected achievements based on intelligence scores were compared with actual achievements. In four test subjects the actual achievement equalled or exceeded expected achievement up to .7 grade and fell below by .2 grades in three of the subjects.

Chart 10 shows the differences between the Amidon and the national quartiles. The city-wide local differences are also shown.

While the achievement scores in this grade were (except for the "slow" third) below those in the preceding grades, it is notable that in Spelling and Language the Amidon scores exceeded the national norms at the first and third quartiles as well as at the median point. In these two subjects only a small number

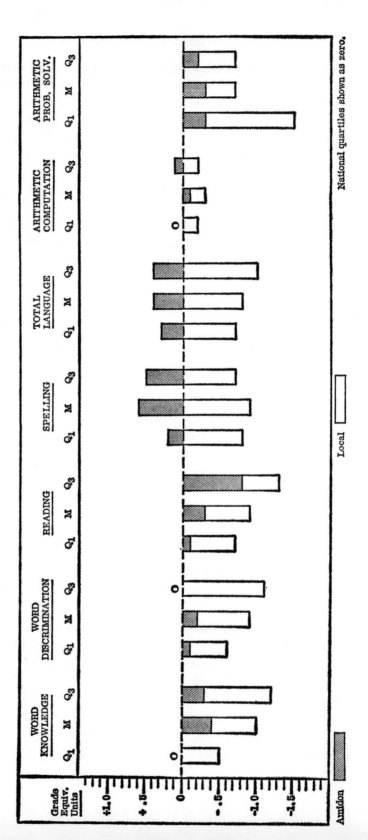

CHART 10

GRADE 4. DIFFERENCES BETWEEN THE AMIDON AND THE LOCAL QUARTILES
AND NATIONAL QUARTILES AT THE TIME OF TESTING

National quartiles shown as zero.

Amidon   Local

of scores fell within the lower 25 percent score range of the national group (8 scores, 15 percent, in Spelling and 9 scores, 17 percent in Language). At the upper end of the scale then 4 scores in Spelling, 4 in Language, 2 in Reading, and one in Word Knowledge were at the 7.8 grade level.

Grade 5. In this grade 2 classes (61 pupils) took the Metropolitan Intermediate Battery, Form A M, and the Otis Quick-Scoring Test of Mental Ability, Beta, E M. Their scores exceeded the national medians in Word Knowledge, Reading, Spelling, Total Language, Language Study Skills, Arithmetic Computation, and Arithmetic Problem Solving, and equalled the national median in Social Study Skills. As shown in Chart 11, the Amidon median scores ranged up to 1.4 grades above the national medians.

The median I.Q. for these two fifth grade classes was 103, with a range of 76 to 128. Calculations show that this group made from .4 to 1.3 grades above expected achievement based on I.Q.'s in seven of the test areas and equalled it in Social Studies Skills.

At all points of comparison, as Chart 12 shows, the Amidon scores equalled or exceeded the national scores.

In Arithmetic Computation the Amidon first quartile exceeded the national norm and in Arithmetic Problem Solving it equalled the national median.

The Amidon scores at the first and third quartiles and the median were superior to the national norms at all points except in the Social Studies Skills where the Amidon third quartile and median equalled the national scores.

While the scores ranged from as low as 2.9 grades in Word Knowledge and Spelling to 11.9 grades in Language Study Skills, a relatively small number of the Amidon scores fell below the first quartile point of the national scores. In Reading, for example, only 12 scores (20 percent) fell below grade 4.5, and none were lower than 3.5. In Total Language, only four scores fell below the national first quartile, in Arithmetic Computation only five, and in Arithmetic Problem Solving only two scores fell below the national first quartile.

The number and range of scores above the national third quartile appear to be significant. In Reading, for example, 18 scores exceeded the national third quartile, ranging from 7.3 to 11.5

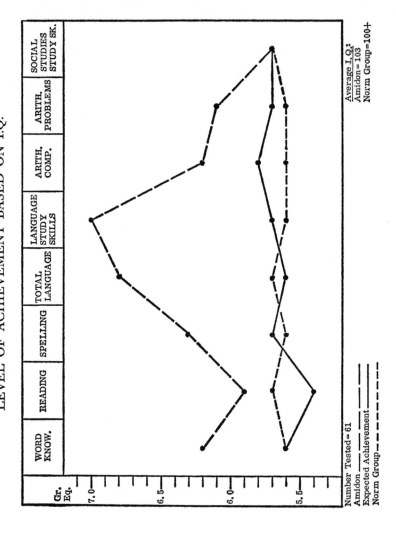

CHART 11

GRADE 5. MEDIAN ACHIEVEMENT OF AMIDON SCHOOL AS COM-
PARED WITH NATIONAL NORM GROUP AND WITH EXPECTED
LEVEL OF ACHIEVEMENT BASED ON I.Q.

CHART 12

GRADE 5. DIFFERENCES BETWEEN THE AMIDON AND THE NATIONAL QUARTILES AT THE TIME OF TESTING

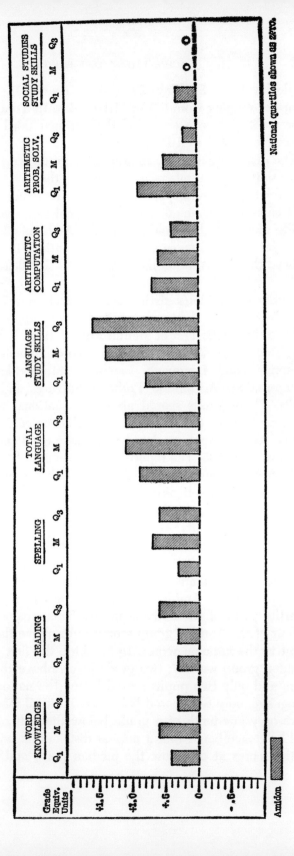

grade levels. In Spelling, 20 scores exceeded the national third quartile, ranging from 6.9 to 11.1 grades. In Total Language, 32 scores (52 percent) exceeded the national third quartile. They ranged from 6.7 to 10.9 grade.

The distribution of the Amidon fifth grade scores shows, therefore, that large numbers are found in the very superior levels and relatively few are clustered at the extremely low levels.

It cannot be claimed that the unusual superiority of the fifth grade scores resulted solely from the Amidon system of instruction, yet in the absence of other explanations it is reasonable to believe that the Amidon method made a significant contribution.

Grade 6. Amidon's sixth graders (2 classes, 59 pupils) took the Metropolitan Achievement Test Intermediate Battery, Form B M, and the Otis Test of Mental Ability, Beta, E M. The Battery consisted of eight test sections: Word Knowledge, Reading, Spelling. Total Language, Language Study Skills, Arithmetic Computation, Arithmetic Problem Solving, and Social Study Skills. These pupils scored above the national medians in the eight sections of the Metropolitan Achievement Test.

The Amidon sixth graders had an average I.Q. of 109, with a range of 78 to 135. The reported achievement of this group in the eight test sections was .6 to 2.6 grades above expected achievement based on intelligence test scores.

As Chart 14 shows the Amidon scores exceeded the national quartiles at all points. Also shown is the relationship of city-wide scores to the national norms at the quartile points.

The Amidon median scores ranged from 1.2 to 3.5 grades above the national medians. In Spelling, Language, and Arithmetic Computation the Amidon first quartile point exceeded the third quartile point of the national norms. This means that three out of four of the Amidon group scored at or above the 75 percentile point in the national scores. In Spelling, the first quartile of the Amidon group was 8.7, two grade levels above the national median, and only two pupils scored below the national median. In Language, only two scored below the national median and these were only one-tenth of a grade below the national median. (It will be remembered that a normal distribution will put one-half of the scores at or below the median point and one-half at or

CHART 13

GRADE 6. MEDIAN ACHIEVEMENT OF AMIDON SCHOOL AS COM-
PARED WITH NATIONAL NORM GROUP AND WITH EXPECTED
LEVEL OF ACHIEVEMENT BASED ON I.Q.

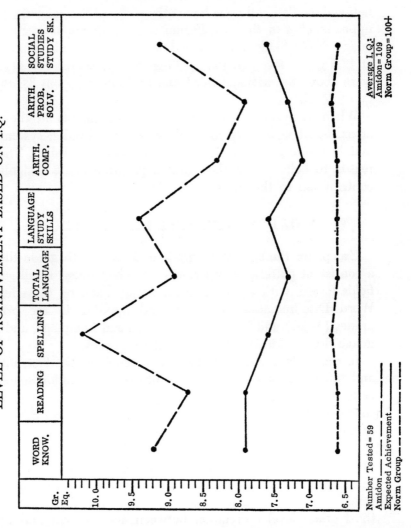

above the median.) In Reading, only five scores fell below the national median and none below the national first quartile. In the upper reaches of the distribution table, four Spelling, two Language Study Skills, one Social Studies Study Skills scores were at 12.5 grade level. In the Spelling test, 47 scores (79 percent) were above the national third quartile, ranging from 8.3 to 12.5 grade level.

When analyzed from any point, achievements in the eight areas tested were very high. Whether the Amidon system was mainly responsible cannot be *scientifically* established. There is reason to believe that the Amidon program made a significant contribution to the results.

WHAT DO THE TEST RESULTS SHOW?

Except for the slow third grade and the fourth grade there is a consistent pattern of superiority of achievement in all subject fields tested, with the best scores being made on the whole in Word Discrimination, Reading, and Spelling in the primary grades (1–3B) and Reading, Spelling, Total Language, and Language Study Skills in the intermediate grades.

In comparison with national group scores at the first, middle, and third quartiles 101 (76 percent) of the Amidon scores excelled the national scores, seven (6 percent) equalled the national scores, and 24 (18 percent) fell below. *In summary 82 percent of the Amidon scores equalled or excelled the national scores.*

The Otis Quick-Scoring Mental Ability Test was given to grades 1–6 in June, 1961, at the same time that the Achievement Tests were given. Predictions of achievement based on intelligence scores were made for grades three through six. Below the third grade level correlation between achievement and intelligence scores is undependable.

A comparison of median achievement scores expected from the intelligence scores produced by the Amidon pupils with actual median achievement scores shows that 26 (74 percent) Amidon medians in 35 were above, two (6 percent) were equal to expectancy levels, making a total of 80 percent at or above predictable levels. This fact adds further support to the judgment that the Amidon concept helps students on the average to achieve

CHART 14

GRADE 6. DIFFERENCES BETWEEN THE AMIDON AND CITY-WIDE QUARTILES AND NATIONAL QUARTILES AT THE TIME OF TESTING

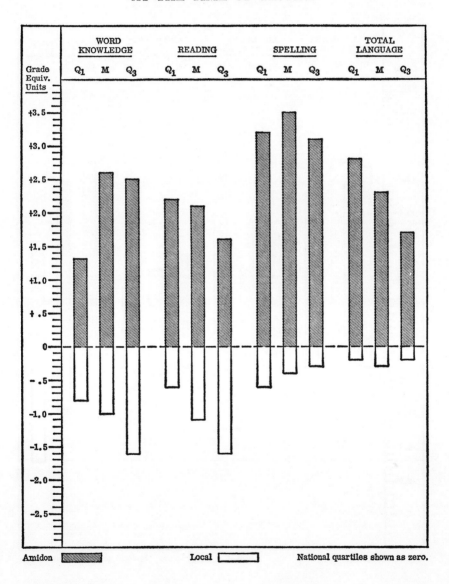

Amidon ▨▨▨   Local ☐   National quartiles shown as zero.

CHART 15

GRADE 6. DIFFERENCES BETWEEN THE AMIDON AND CITY-WIDE QUARTILES AND NATIONAL QUARTILES AT THE TIME OF TESTING

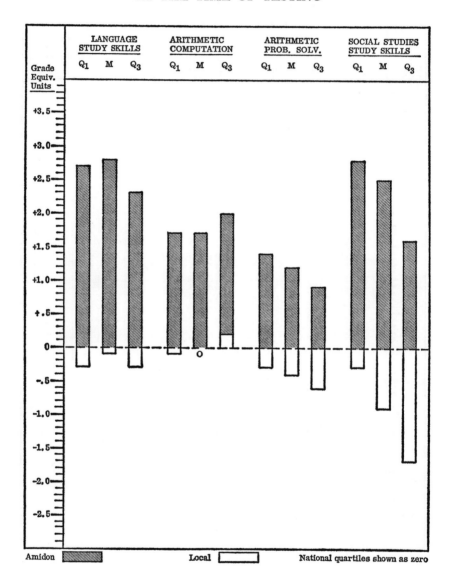

above national norms as well as above expected scores based on intelligence.

WHAT DO THE TESTS MEAN?

Though not a scientific proof of superiority of the Amidon system, the tests justify a conclusion that the instruction given the Amidon pupils last term was, in the main, markedly superior. Based on my own observation and the testimony of parents and of the principal and teachers themselves, it seems clear that the Amidon concept contributed to the superiority of instruction. After the first year of try-out, admittedly only a beginning of the new program that leaves much yet to be learned and done to improve it, I am more convinced than before that the Amidon concept of basic education is sound and workable, and, more than that, is indispensable in this period of our national life. *Continued failure to put substance into teaching short-changes American youth.* Even worse, it weakens our capacity to survive as a nation and to develop and strengthen our national objectives as a democratic society.

DIRECTION FINDERS FOR THE MECHANICS OF WRITING

COMPOSITION . . . . CREATIVE WRITING

Composition	Kindergarten	Junior Primary	Grade 1	Grade 2	Grade 3	Grade 4	Grade 5	Grade 6
LETTER WRITING	Explain the correct form for children to observe in writing dictated notes or letters with greeting, body, date, and signature as needed	Begin to teach the correct form for writing simple informal notes with greeting, body, date, and signature as needed	Teach	Reteach	Reteach to establish accuracy	Achieve habitual accuracy	Secure mastery	Maintain mastery
			Begin to teach the correct form for a friendly letter	Teach	Reteach	Reteach to establish accuracy	Achieve habitual accuracy	Secure mastery
				Begin to teach the correct form for a business letter	Teach the correct form for a business letter and also the various types of business letters	Reteach	Reteach to establish accuracy	Achieve habitual accuracy
			Begin to teach other types of correspondence such as greetings, invitations, thank-you and acceptance notes as needed	Teach	Reteach	Reteach to establish accuracy	Achieve habitual accuracy	Secure mastery
	Explain the correct form for addressing envelopes for mailing as needed	Begin to teach the correct form for addressing envelopes for mailing as needed	Teach	Reteach	Teach also the correct form for writing return address	Reteach to establish accuracy	Achieve habitual accuracy	Secure mastery
PROOF READING				Begin to teach proof reading	Teach	Reteach	Reteach to establish accuracy	Achieve habitual accuracy
BOOK REPORTS		Introduce oral reporting (as basis for written reporting)	Record children's oral book reports	Begin to teach writing short one paragraph book reports	Teach	Teach also writing more lengthy and detailed book reports and reviews with accuracy in facts and exactness in meaning	Reteach	Reteach to establish accuracy
REPORTS AND SUMMARIES				Begin to teach reporting on and summarizing various types of materials as needed	Teach	Reteach	Reteach to establish accuracy	Achieve habitual accuracy
OUTLINES				Begin to teach the simple outline	Teach	Teach topical outlines with one level subordination	Reteach	Teach also topical outlines with two level subordination
NOTE TAKING					Begin to teach notetaking as an aid to study and/or reporting from reading, observing, and listening as needed	Teach	Reteach	Reteach to establish accuracy
COPYING	Provide child with the correct form for his name when requested	Teach accuracy in copying child's own name and other appropriate materials as needed	Teach accuracy in copying all types of appropriate materials	Reteach	Reteach to establish accuracy	Achieve habitual accuracy	Secure mastery	Maintain mastery
BIBLIOGRAPHIES						Begin to teach the correct form for writing bibliographies as needed	Teach	Reteach
ARTICLES AND EDITORIALS						Begin to teach writing original articles and editorials as needed	Teach	Reteach
CREDIT LINES FOR EDITORIALS, ARTICLES AND BOOKS							Teach the use of the credit line when using quoted material from articles, books, and editorials	Reteach
BLANKS AND FORMS			Explain filling in simple blanks and forms as needed	Begin to teach filling in blanks and forms as needed (name, age, grade, and date, name of school, teacher's name)	Teach	Teach filling in more detailed blanks and forms regarding personal history and other data as needed	Reteach	Reteach to establish accuracy
					Begin to teach filling in other type blanks and forms (money...		Teach	Reteach

Creative Writing

POETRY	Record children's original poems as they observe the form and pattern	Record children's original poems as they observe the form and pattern	Begin to teach the ability to write short original poems	Teach		Teach poetry writing with attention to good form, meaning, thought, expression, and originality	Reteach		Reteach
STORIES	Record children's short dictated stories with attention to good standards	Record children's short dictated stories with attention to good standards	Begin to teach the ability to write short original stories	Teach	Teach writing short imaginative stories with attention to good standards in opening, plot development, climax, and ending	Teach writing short imaginative stories with attention to good standards in opening, plot development, climax, and ending	Reteach	Teach writing longer imaginative stories with attention to good standards in opening, plot development, climax, and ending	Reteach

SENTENCE . . . . . PARAGRAPH

Sentence and Paragraph

SENTENCE SENSE	Develop sentence sense through usage	Begin to teach the concept of the sentence	Teach	Reteach	Reteach	Reteach to establish accuracy	Achieve habitual accuracy	Secure mastery
		Begin to teach the concept of telling and asking sentences	Teach	Reteach	Reteach	Teach the concept of declarative and interrogative sentences	Reteach	Reteach to establish accuracy
				Begin to teach the concept of sentences that command or request and also the concept of exclamatory sentences	Teach	Teach the concept of imperative sentences	Reteach	Reteach to establish accuracy
		Begin to teach the concept that all sentences begin with a capital letter and end with a punctuation mark	Reteach	Reteach	Reteach to establish accuracy	Achieve habitual accuracy	Secure mastery	Maintain mastery
				Begin to teach the concept that sentences begin in different ways	Teach	Teach also good arrangement of ideas and separating ideas into sentence wholes	Reteach	Reteach to establish accuracy
SENTENCE STRUCTURE		Begin to teach the concept that every sentence has two important parts and that these parts are related	Teach	Teach	Teach also the concept that every sentence has a subject and a predicate, and the subject-predicate relationship	Reteach	Reteach to establish accuracy
				Begin to teach simple diagramming to show sentence structure. Begin to teach also agreement and reference: verb to subject; pronoun to antecedent	Teach	Reteach
				Begin to teach phrases and clauses in sentence structure	Teach also the use of complex and compound sentences for variety and emphasis in writing	Teach the kinds of phrases and clauses	Reteach
					Begin to teach the use of conjunctions (when, while, if, for, until, since, as, if, because, unless) to avoid the loose use of and and choppy run-on sentences	Teach	Reteach
PARAGRAPH				Teach the writing of short paragraphs	Begin to teach the concept of the paragraph and paragraph form	Teach also the meaning and use of topic sentences in paragraph writing	Teach also the use of transitional words in clarifying the order and relationship of ideas	Reteach
				Begin to teach the concept of the paragraph and paragraph form	Begin to teach paragraph form in writing conversation	Teach	Reteach

Chart I of the three charts on **"MECHANICS OF WRITING"**

PUBLIC SCHOOLS OF THE DISTRICT OF COLUMBIA

WASHINGTON, D.C., 1961

Chart II . . . . DIRECTION FINDERS FOR THE MECHANICS OF WRITING

FORMAL GRAMMAR . . . . CAPITALIZATION

Formal Grammar

	Kindergarten	Junior Primary	Grade 1	Grade 2	Grade 3	Grade 4	Grade 5	Grade 6
NOUNS			Explain the meaning and correct use of name words	Begin to teach the meaning and correct use of name words (nouns)	Teach	Teach the meaning and correct use of nouns and also the kinds of nouns	Reteach	Reteach to establish accuracy
VERBS			Explain the meaning and correct use of action words	Begin to teach the meaning and correct use of action words (verbs)	Teach	Teach the meaning and correct use of verbs	Reteach	Reteach to establish accuracy
ADJECTIVES				Begin to teach the meaning and correct use of descriptive words (adjectives)	Teach	Teach the meaning and correct use of adjectives	Reteach	Reteach to establish accuracy
ADVERBS					Begin to teach the meaning and correct use of when, where, why, how (adverbs)	Teach also the meaning and correct use of adverbs	Reteach	Reteach to establish accuracy
PRONOUNS		Begin to teach the meaning and correct use of the pronouns "I" and "me"	Teach correct use of all personal pronouns	Reteach	Reteach to establish accuracy	Achieve habitual accuracy	Begin to teach the use of pronouns with correctness as to case and reference	Teach
CONJUNCTIONS			Begin to teach the meaning and correct use of the conjunctions and, but, or	Teach	Reteach	Reteach to establish accuracy	Teach the meaning and correct use of a variety of connectives	Reteach
PREPOSITIONS					Begin to teach the meaning and correct use of prepositions in sentence structure	Teach	Reteach	Reteach to establish accuracy
INTERJECTIONS			Explain the use of interjections in sentences as needed	Begin to teach the use of interjections in sentences as needed	Teach	Reteach	Reteach to establish accuracy	Achieve habitual accuracy
ARTICLES			Explain the use of the articles a, an, the	Begin to teach the use of the articles a, an, the	Teach	Reteach	Reteach to establish accuracy	Achieve habitual accuracy
PARTS OF SPEECH IN SENTENCE STRUCTURE						Teach the meaning and correct use of all parts of speech (nouns, verbs, adverbs, adjectives, pronouns, prepositions, conjunctions, articles, interjections) in sentence structure	Reteach	Reteach

Capitalization

	Kindergarten	Junior Primary	Grade 1	Grade 2	Grade 3	Grade 4	Grade 5	Grade 6
PERSONS	Explain the use of capital letters when writing child's own first name	Teach the use of capital letters when writing child's first and last name	Reteach	Reteach to establish accuracy	Achieve habitual accuracy	Secure mastery	Maintain mastery	Maintain mastery
		Teach the use of capital letters when writing Mother and Father (as names) and other proper names as needed	Reteach	Reteach	Teach the use of capital letters in beginning all proper names	Reteach	Reteach to establish accuracy	Achieve habitual accuracy
		Begin to teach the use of the capital letter for the pronoun "I"	Teach	Reteach to establish accuracy	Achieve habitual accuracy	Secure mastery	Maintain mastery	Maintain mastery
ABBREVIATIONS	Explain the use of capital letters when beginning titles as a part of names (Mrs., Mr.) in dictated sentences	Begin to teach the use of capital letters when beginning titles as a part of names (Mrs., Mr.)	Teach	Reteach	Teach also the use of capital letters in writing initials, days of the week, certain months and holidays	Teach also the use of capital letters in writing generally ca...	Reteach	Reteach to establish accuracy

This page is a rotated scope-and-sequence chart on the use of capital letters. The leftmost column is truncated at the top; its visible header fragment reads "…dictated by children to the teacher." Columns run from earliest instruction (left) to mastery (right).

Category	(1)	(2)	(3)	(4)	(5)	(6)	(7)	(8)
QUOTATIONS		Explain the use of capital letters when beginning the first word of a quotation as needed	Begin to teach the use of capital letters when beginning the first word of a quotation as needed	Teach	Reteach	Begin to teach the use of capital letters when beginning the first word of a quotation within a sentence	Reteach to establish accuracy	Achieve habitual accuracy
CALENDAR	Explain the use of capital letters when beginning the names of days and months whenever the child inquires about them	Begin to teach the use of capital letters when beginning the names of days and months	Teach the use of capital letters when beginning the names of days, months, and holidays as needed	Reteach	Reteach to establish accuracy	Achieve habitual accuracy	Teach	Reteach
TITLES			Teach the use of capital letters when writing titles of stories, poems, books, and songs	Reteach	Teach also the use of capital letters in beginning important words of titles of outlines and reports	Reteach	Reteach	Secure mastery
ADDRESSES	Begin to teach the use of capital letters in writing child's own address and school address as needed		Teach	Reteach	Teach the use of capital letters in writing any address	Teach the use of capital letters in writing names of monuments and buildings	Reteach	Reteach
GEOGRAPHICAL AND HISTORICAL NAMES AND ITEMS		Begin to teach the use of the capital letter when beginning the name of own city	Teach the use of capital letters when beginning the name of own city and country and other cities, states, and countries as needed	Reteach		Reteach to establish accuracy	Achieve habitual accuracy	Achieve habitual accuracy
			Begin to teach the use of capital letters when beginning other geographical items such as: names of rivers and mountains as needed	Reteach		Teach the use of capital letters when beginning names of geographical areas, historical events, and races	Teach also the use of capital letters in writing adjectives derived from proper nouns	Secure mastery
						Teach also the use of capital letters in writing names of historical documents	Teach also the use of capital letters in writing names of historical documents	Reteach
ORGANIZATIONS			Begin to teach the use of capital letters when beginning names of organizations (Red Cross)	Teach	Teach also the use of capital letters when beginning commercial trade names	Reteach	Reteach	Reteach
BIBLICAL NAMES			Begin to teach the use of the capital letter for the Deity and the Bible	Teach	Teach also the use of capital letters in writing Biblical names as needed	Reteach	Reteach	Reteach to establish
LETTER WRITING	Explain the use of capital letters when beginning the greeting and closing of a note or letter dictated to the teacher		Begin to teach the use of capital letters when beginning the greeting and closing of a note or letter	Teach	Reteach	Reteach to establish accuracy	Achieve habitual accuracy	Secure mastery
OUTLINES				Begin to teach the use of capital letters when beginning each topic of an outline	Teach	Reteach	Reteach to establish accuracy	Achieve habitual accuracy
SCHOOL SUBJECTS					Begin to teach the use of capital letters when beginning the names of certain school subjects such as: French, Spanish, and English	Teach	Teach the distinction between school subjects which begin with capital letters and those which do not	Reteach

Chart III . . . . DIRECTION FINDERS FOR THE MECHANICS OF WRITING

PUNCTUATION

Punctuation

	Kindergarten	Junior Primary	Grade 1	Grade 2	Grade 3	Grade 4	Grade 5	Grade 6
PERIOD	Explain the use of the period at the end of a statement	Begin to teach the use of the period at the end of a statement	Teach	Reteach and begin to teach the use of the period after a sentence that commands or requests	Teach	Teach the use of the period after an imperative sentence	Reteach	Reteach to establish accuracy
			Begin to teach the use of the period after abbreviated titles such as: Mr., Mrs., Dr., as needed and after own initial	Teach	Teach also the use of the period after any abbreviation (name of days, months, streets, avenues and states, and after initials)	Reteach	Teach the use of the period after an abbreviated name	Reteach
			Begin to teach the use of the period in writing numbered lists as needed	Teach		Reteach to establish accuracy	Achieve habitual accuracy	Secure mastery
						Teach the use of the period after numbers and letters in an outline	Reteach	Reteach to establish accuracy
QUESTION MARK	Explain the use of the question mark at the end of a question	Begin to teach the use of the question mark at the end of a question	Teach		Reteach to establish accuracy	Achieve habitual accuracy	Secure mastery	Maintain mastery
				Reteach		Begin to teach the use of the question mark after a quoted question	Teach	Reteach
EXCLAMATION POINT			Explain the use of the exclamation point at the end of a sentence showing strong feeling and after an interjection	Begin to teach the use of the exclamation point at the end of a sentence showing strong feeling and after an interjection	Teach	Reteach	Reteach to establish accuracy	Achieve habitual accuracy
COMMA			Teach the use of the comma to separate the day from the year in a date	Reteach	Reteach	Reteach to establish accuracy	Achieve habitual accuracy	Secure mastery
	Explain the use of a comma after the greeting in an informal note or letter	Begin to teach the use of the comma after the greeting in an informal note or letter	Teach	Teach the use of the comma after the greeting and closing of a friendly note or letter	Reteach	Reteach to establish accuracy	Secure mastery	Maintain mastery
			Begin to teach the use of the comma to separate city from state	Teach	Reteach to establish accuracy	Achieve habitual accuracy	Secure mastery	Secure mastery
			Begin to teach the use of the comma after such introductory words as: yes, no, O	Teach	Reteach	Reteach	Reteach to establish accuracy	Achieve habitual accuracy
			Begin to teach the use of the comma to separate the name of a person addressed from the rest of the sentence	Teach	Reteach	Reteach	Reteach to establish accuracy	Achieve habitual accuracy
				Begin to teach the use of the comma between words in a series	Teach	Reteach	Reteach to establish accuracy	Achieve habitual accuracy

PUBLIC SCHOOLS OF THE DISTRICT OF COLUMBIA

	Begin to teach the use of the comma to separate sentences joined by and, or, but	Teach		Reteach	Reteach to establish accuracy	Achieve habitual accuracy
Explain the use of the comma to separate a quotation from the rest of the sentence	Begin to teach the use of the comma to separate a quotation from the rest of the sentence	Teach		Reteach	Reteach to establish accuracy	Achieve habitual accuracy
			Begin to teach the use of the comma to separate an interjection from the rest of a sentence	Teach	Reteach	Reteach to establish accuracy
QUOTATION MARKS	Explain the use of quotation marks in writing conversation	Begin to teach the use of quotation marks in writing conversation	Teach	Teach	Reteach	Teach the use of quotation marks in writing titles of stories, poems, songs, and titles of books and magazines if underlining is not used	Reteach
APOSTROPHE		Teach the use of the apostrophe to show missing letters in the contractions: can't, don't, didn't	Teach also the use of the apostrophe to show missing letters in contraction such as: I'm, aren't, won't, weren't, doesn't, don't	Teach	Teach the use of the apostrophe to show omitted letters in any contraction	Reteach	Reteach to establish accuracy
		Teach the use of the apostrophe to show the possessive form of a singular noun and a plural noun not ending in s	Reteach	Reteach	Reteach	Reteach to establish accuracy	Achieve habitual accuracy
				Begin to teach the use of the apostrophe to show the possessive form of plural nouns ending in s	Teach	Reteach	Reteach
COLON AND SEMICOLON		Begin to teach the use of the colon after the greeting in a business letter	Teach also the use of the colon to separate hours from minutes when expressing time in numbers	Reteach and begin to teach the use of the colon in writing bibliographies as needed	Teach	Teach also the use of the semicolon as needed in other writing situations
HYPHEN			Begin to teach the use of the hyphen to separate parts of some compound words, to separate syllables in words, and to divide a word between syllables at the end of a line	Teach	Teach	Reteach	Reteach to establish accuracy

WASHINGTON, D.C. 1961

CURRICULUM CHART:

Direction Finders for Mechanics of Writing

This chart, based on Dr. Hansen's Behavioral Goals, is made available to schools on a trial basis to guide study of the Amidon Plan in the Elementary Schools of the District of Columbia in 1961-62. Suggestions from the field are welcomed.

INDEX